Denise can read Phoenician/Hebrew ⟶ biblical Hebrew

p. 4 Phoenicians, the only immi... throughout the Med.

Phoenician gods: p. 43 (and see p. 75 for sea travel)
Baal & Astarte (deity of mariners)
(temples in Athens)

Athena Lindia (goddess)
⟶ city state of Lindos and Rhodes

- Phoenician priests living in Greek communities p. 43 ⟶ worship of divinities

Melqart & Baal (patron deities of Tyre & Berytos p. 53 (Phoenician coast)

patron of navigation p. 75

p. 63 Baal in Greek, Poseidon / Astarte Palestinian translated in Greek, into Aphrodite p. 59 (sexuality, fertility, navigation & warfare)

Phoenicians among Others

Phoenicians among Others

Why Migrants Mattered in the Ancient Mediterranean

DENISE DEMETRIOU

OXFORD
UNIVERSITY PRESS

OXFORD
UNIVERSITY PRESS

Oxford University Press is a department of the University of Oxford. It furthers the University's objective of excellence in research, scholarship, and education by publishing worldwide. Oxford is a registered trade mark of Oxford University Press in the UK and certain other countries.

Published in the United States of America by Oxford University Press
198 Madison Avenue, New York, NY 10016, United States of America.

© Oxford University Press 2023

All rights reserved. No part of this publication may be reproduced, stored in a retrieval system, or transmitted, in any form or by any means, without the prior permission in writing of Oxford University Press, or as expressly permitted by law, by license, or under terms agreed with the appropriate reproduction rights organization. Inquiries concerning reproduction outside the scope of the above should be sent to the Rights Department, Oxford University Press, at the address above.

You must not circulate this work in any other form
and you must impose this same condition on any acquirer.

Library of Congress Control Number: 2022947948

ISBN 978–0–19–763485–1

DOI: 10.1093/oso/9780197634851.001.0001

Printed by Sheridan Books, Inc., United States of America

*For Alexis and Alexandra,
Myrto and Melina*

Contents

List of Illustrations   ix
Acknowledgments   xi
List of Abbreviations   xvii

Introduction: Why Phoenician Migrants Matter   1

1. The Adaptive Repertoires of Immigrants   15

2. Phoenician Trade Associations   50

3. Managing Migration   70

4. Honors, Privileges, and Greek Migration Regimes   92

5. Phoenicians beyond Greek Communities   120

Conclusion   157

Bibliography   161
Index   193

Illustrations

Maps

1.	The Mediterranean	xxi
2.	The Levant	xxii
3.	The Aegean	xxiii
4.	The central Mediterranean	xxiv

Figures

1.1.	Grave Stele of Shem——/Antipatros from Ashkelon, c. 300 BCE (*IG* II² 8388)	16
1.2.	Tombstone of Benhodesh/Noumenios the Kitian, 350–300 BCE	26
1.3.	Tombstone of Abtanit/Artemidoros from Sidon, c. 400 BCE	32
1.4.	Close-up of the relief and epigram of Shem——/Antipatros' tombstone with the relief and epigram (*IG* II² 8388)	35
1.5.	Marble stele of Abdeshmoun, early fourth century BCE	39
1.6.	Tombstone of Eirene from Byzantion, early fourth century BCE	40
1.7.	Painted funerary stele of Mettounmikim of Ashkelon from Demetrias, third century BCE	41
2.1.	Stele with the Kitian traders' request for the right to own property, 333/332 BCE (*IG* II³ 1 337)	51
2.2.	Plan of the building of the Berytian association of traders, shippers, and warehouse workers (the Poseidoniastai) on Delos	64
3.1.	Bilingual dedication by the Sidonian royal family on Kos, late fourth century BCE (*IG* XII.4 2 546 = *KAI* 292)	74
3.2.	Bilingual dedication in the Sanctuary of Apollo on Delos by the Tyrian *hieronautai*, 340s–330s BCE (*I.Délos* 50 = *CIS* I 114)	78

3.3.	A Sidonian koinon honoring one of its members in Athens, late fourth / early third century BCE (*IG* II² 2946 = *KAI* 60)	84
4.1.	Stele recording the honors and privileges granted to Herakleides over the period of 330–325 BCE (*IG* II³ 1 367)	93
4.2.	Attic stele honoring King Abdashtart of Sidon, c. 360s BCE (*IG* II² 141)	109
5.1.	Dedicatory stele by Paalashtart with a Phoenician and hieroglyphic inscription, second or first century BCE	121
5.2.	Dedication to Tanit and Baal Hammon by a descendant of a Tyrian immigrant in Carthage, fourth–second centuries BCE	131
5.3a–b.	Bronze statuette of Harpokrates with a Phoenician inscription (*KAI* 52)	138
5.4a–b.	Bronze statuette of Harpokrates with a Phoenician inscription and hieroglyphic inscription	139
5.5a–b.	One of the twin monuments from Malta dedicated by two Tyrian brothers, second century BCE (*IG* XIV 600 = *KAI* 47 = *CIS* I 122bis)	149
5.6.	The second of the twin monuments from Malta dedicated by two Tyrian brothers, second century BCE (*IG* XIV 600 = *KAI* 47 = *CIS* I 122bis)	150
5.7.	Bronze altar base with a trilingual inscription in Latin, Greek, and Punic, from Sardinia, first century BCE (*CIL* 10 7856 = *IG* XIV 608 = *KAI* 66)	152
5.8a–b.	Ivory hospitality token between a Phoenician and a Greek from Lilybaion, second or first century BCE (*IG* XIV 279)	154

Acknowledgments

LIKE MOST OF you, I am an immigrant. My extended family has experienced migration for many generations. My maternal grandfather was sent as an eleven-year-old from his village to my hometown, the city of Larnaca on Cyprus, to attend school, and his siblings later all became refugees. My maternal grandmother, one of nine children, saw one sister emigrate to South Africa to marry and a nineteen-year-old brother leave for the United States. My paternal grandmother was French, but her father was born on Cyprus to French and Maltese immigrants. Both my parents have lived abroad, as has my brother, and my sister-in-law is an immigrant from Greece. My family is bilingual or trilingual—including my nieces, who perceive the Cypriot dialect as a language different from their mother's Greek. I came to the United States for college with no intention to migrate. But I became a US citizen a few days after my birthday in January 2017, having applied for citizenship after Donald Trump became president and xenophobia threatened the abilities of even documented immigrants to remain in the United States.

Aside from personal history, this book began as I was finishing my first book. While revising *Negotiating Identity in the Ancient Mediterranean*, I noticed two dedications made by Phoenician kings on the islands of Delos and Kos. Both were bilingual, both had a religious aspect, and both left me wondering why Phoenician kings made dedications in Greek sanctuaries in the fourth century BCE. For several years, while I collected and studied bilingual inscriptions and other epigraphic sources that involved Phoenicians present in Greek communities, I thought I was writing a book about ancient diplomacy. As I read and began to interpret the sources, I eventually realized I was really writing a book about migration and its consequences in antiquity.

I completed most of this book and revised it during the lockdowns and social isolation of the pandemic that began in the United States in March 2020. During the journey of writing this book, many people and institutions have supported me. People provided me with intellectual conversations that helped improve it, institutions supported me financially, and together with these, my family and friends made my life happier and easier. Although here I single out some of them, I am grateful to them all.

My first task was to learn to read Phoenician. When I told Carolina López-Ruiz that I wanted to learn Phoenician, she casually replied: "No problem; first learn biblical Hebrew." Her confidence reassured me that I could learn a new language as an adult. In 2015, the summer before moving to the University of California, San Diego (UCSD), I attended Union Theological Seminary in New York, where Amy Meverden—a skilled and talented instructor—taught me elementary biblical Hebrew. Subsequently, at UCSD, my colleague in biblical and Judaic Studies, William Propp, met with me weekly for a year to provide tutorials in biblical Hebrew and help me transition to reading Phoenician.

When I thought that this book would be about fourth-century BCE diplomacy in the eastern Mediterranean, my high-school friend Antonis Ellinas, now professor of political science at the University of Cyprus, organized a bibliography on international relations and anarchic systems. As my book began to focus on migrants in the ancient world, several of my former colleagues and friends at Michigan State University provided inspiration. Leslie Moch, an authority in migration studies, was one of the first scholars to shift the attention from the perspective of the state to that of the lives and experiences of migrants in France. Her coauthored book with Lewis Siegelbaum on internal migration in the Soviet Union was influential in my conceptualizing migrants' adaptive strategies as they navigated life in a foreign land. Finally, Kirsten Fermaglich's study on name changing among twentieth-century Jews in New York illuminated my understanding of this practice.

I have been fortunate to have had so many supportive colleagues. Denver Graninger (UC Riverside), Jeremy LaBuff (Northern Arizona University), John W. I. Lee (UC Santa Barbara), and Matt Simonton (Arizona State University) are a cohort of ancient historians with whom I continue to meet twice a year to workshop research projects. They have read and commented on several chapters of this book. Josephine Quinn read the first draft of the first chapter and provided me with insightful suggestions. Carolina López-Ruiz read an early version of the introduction and helped me make it concise and clear. Sara Saba has my immense gratitude for reading all the chapters, some more than once, and listening and encouraging me throughout. Her gentle push for me to look at Phoenician communities led me to realize this book was about immigrants and their influences. Despite all their help, any errors in this book are my own.

Audiences at Bryn Mawr College, Columbia University, Oxford University, Wake Forest University, and the members of the group Migrants and Membership Regimes in the Ancient Greek World, at the University of Copenhagen, provided helpful feedback on various parts of this book that pushed me to think about the evidence from different angles. My colleagues who contribute to UCSD's Classical Studies Program and the Center for Hellenic Studies—Mira Balberg, Page duBois, Monte Johnson, Jacobo Myerston, and Ed Watts—were always happy to answer my random questions about Phoenician philosophers in Athens, Zeno's stoicism, Ezekiel's prophecies regarding Tyre, or ideas of inclusion and exclusion in the Demosthenic corpus. Our graduate students in ancient history inspire me daily. Kevin Westerfeld, Miguel Sanchez Morquecho, Jamie Marvin, Nile de Jonge, and Matthew Crum have all contributed to this book by sending me references, asking probing questions, and even sharing their own migration stories.

The final stages of putting a book together are always hectic and difficult, especially during a pandemic that limited access to libraries. At the last minute, my friends Jeremy Ott, Gil Renberg, and Celia Schultz helped me with citations. Miguel Sanchez Morquecho collated the data for what became the index of this book and the maps skillfully created by Ian Mladjov. I also owe thanks to various colleagues who helped me acquire the permissions to reproduce images from museums around the Mediterranean basin: Amelia Brown, Hédi Dridi, Maria Grazia Griffo, Lorenzo Nigro, Maria Stamatopoulou, Monika Trümper, and Samir Aounallah (Institut National du Patrimoine—Tunisie), Sharon Sultana, Marcia D. Grima, and Nancy Mizzi (Heritage Malta), Marianthe Raftopoulou (Ephorate of Magnesia), Alexandra Sirogianni (Ephorate of Antiquities of Piraeus & the Islands), Eleni Zavvou and Maria Englezou (Epigraphical Museum, Athens), Despina Ignatiadou (National Archaeological Museum, Athens), Maria Michaelidou (Ephorate of the Dodecannese), Núria Benavent and Felipa Díaz (Museo Arqueológico Nacional, Madrid), Annamaria Bava, Rosario Maria Anzalone, and Simona Contardi (Musei Reali Torino—Museo di Antichità), Anna Maria Parrinello (Parco Archeologico di Lilibeo-Marsala). Susan Winchester, Ryan Moore, and Jennifer Hollis at UCSD provided invaluable administrative assistance.

When I started revising the book, I worked with the professional editor Jeanne Barker-Nunn, the most astute reader I have met. Her talents have improved the arguments, logic, and readability of the book and, I hope, taught me to be a better writer. The peer reviewers for Oxford University Press (OUP) also provided invaluable suggestions, criticisms, and bibliographic suggestions. At OUP, my thanks go to my editor, Stefan Vranka, for his interest in this project and his insightful comments on the manuscript and to Zara Cannon-Mohammed for overseeing production.

Two fellowships that I held during the 2020–2021 academic year enabled me to complete this book. The Center for Hellenic Studies in Washington, DC

(CHS) and the Getty Research Institute (GRI) allowed me to conduct these fellowships remotely. The staff members at both, especially Lanah Koelle at the CHS and Alexa Sekyra at the GRI, made the difficult pandemic situation navigable. Gerry and Jeannie Ranglas in San Diego, with their philanthropic vision and support of the study of ancient Greek history, including endowing my chair, have transformed UC San Diego's commitment to Hellenic studies. Alexia and Paul Anas, Jeanette Rigopoulos, Carol Tohsaku, and the other members of the Hellenic Cultural Society in San Diego continue to inspire me with their friendship and support of Greek studies.

H. Alan Shapiro, my doctoral adviser, remains an inspiration to me. I am grateful to him for his gentle guidance and unwavering faith in me over the years. He and Irad Malkin, my other adviser, have been staunch supporters of my projects and career and have influenced me with their own innovative thinking about the ancient Mediterranean world.

In my travels westward from Larnaca to San Diego, I have made many lasting friendships that have sustained me during the otherwise isolating time of writing a book. At Michigan State University, Sean Forner, Karrin Hanshew, Leslie Moch, Ani Sarkissian, Lewis Siegelbaum, Mickey Stamm, Steve Stowe, and Naoko Wake have remained friends even after I moved to San Diego in 2015. Elias Strangas and Jane Turner, also friends from Michigan State, continue to be a second family and models of generosity and balanced life. Iva Naffziger and Fumiko Fukushi, whom I first met in college as fellow international students, have been steadfast friends. My monthly exchanges with Jessica Lamont, whose own terrific book will come out with OUP, have pushed me to keep deadlines, meet my goals, and laugh. Amalia Avramidou, a friend and collaborator since graduate school, believed in me even when I had my doubts. So did Lila Diapouli and Sara Saba, thanked above, who also belongs in the friend category. New friends in San Diego—Mira Balberg, Tim DeBold, Page duBois, Monte Johnson, Micah Muscolino, Sarah Schneewind, Rebecca Wolniewicz—have helped me settle into a rich and rewarding life. When I moved to San Diego, I was determined to have a balanced life that took me to the ocean. I am grateful to Chris Callaghan, Hiromi Imai-Dellario, and Joanne Stolen, who have supported my efforts to learn to row, both in San Diego and on Lake Dillon, nestled nine thousand feet high, in the Colorado Rockies.

Karl Gerth, with his love and support, has transformed all aspects of my life for the better, including this book. My parents, Myrto and Andreas Demetriou, have unconditionally supported and loved me throughout my life. They, too, have read and commented on this book, which begins with one of their fellow Kitians. My brother and sister-in-law, Alexis Demetriou and Alexandra Mastrokostopoulou, and their daughters, Myrto and Melina, are always there for me. Whatever I say will not be enough to thank them for who they are and what they mean to me. This book is dedicated to them.

Nearly every single person I have thanked here is a migrant or has been a migrant, whether from Japan to California, Nebraska to Michigan, or Cyprus to the UK and back. Like many of the Phoenician immigrants described here, my family and friends have lived most of our lives as citizens of two or more worlds and have developed our own adaptive strategies to cope with the excitement of encountering a new place, the nostalgia we feel for home, and the anxiety of not quite belonging to any of the worlds we inhabit. Among other things, writing this book revealed to me that telling stories about migration and how individuals try to make sense of their experiences can challenge the fears underlying xenophobia and confirm our shared humanity.

Abbreviations

ALL TRANSLATIONS ARE my own unless otherwise indicated. In general, I prefer to transliterate rather than anglicize Greek names and words, but I am not consistent and I often use the more familiar spellings in English.

Abbreviations of journals follow the conventions set by *L'année philologique*. References to editions of papyri follow the conventions in Oates et al. 2001. In addition, I have used the following works:

Agora XVII	Bradeen, D. W. 1974. *Inscriptions: The Funerary Monuments*. The Athenian Agora 17. Princeton: American School of Classical Studies at Athens.
Bosnakis, *Epigraphes*	Bosnakis, D. 2008. Ανέκδοτες επιγραφές της Κω. Επιτύμβια μνημεία και όροι. Athens: Ministry of Culture.
CEG	Hansen, P. A. 1983–89. *Carmina epigraphica graeca*. 2 vols. Berlin: De Gruyter.
CIA	Kirchhoff, A. et al. 1873–97. *Corpus inscriptionum atticarum*. 4 vols. Berlin: G. Reimer.
CIG	Böckh, A. et al. 1828–77. *Corpus inscriptionum graecarum*. 4 vols. Berlin: Officina Academica.
CIJud	Frey, J.-B. 1936–52. *Corpus inscriptionum iudaicarum*. Sussidi allo studio delle antichità cristiane. 2 vols. Rome: Pontificio istituto di archeologia Cristiana.
CIL	Mommsen, T. et al. 1863–. *Corpus inscriptionum latinarum*. Berlin: G. Reimer and De Gruyter.
CIS	Renan, E. et al. 1881–1951. *Corpus inscriptionum semiticarum*. Paris: Reipublicae Typographeo.
Clara Rhodos	Jacopi, G., A. Maiuri, and L. Laurenzi. 1928–41. *Clara Rhodos*. Studi e materiali pubblicati a cura dell'Istituto storico-archeologico di Rodi. 10 vols. Rhodes: Istituto storico-archeologico.

FD III	Colin, G. et al. 1909–85. *Fouilles de Delphes* III. *Épigraphie*. 6 vols. Paris: De Boccard.
FGrHist	Jacoby, F., ed. 1923–58. *Die Fragmente der griechischen Historiker*. Berlin: Weidmann.
Helly, *Gonnoi*	Helly, B. 1973. *Gonnoi*. 2 vols. Amsterdam: Hakkert.
I.Beroia	Gounaropoulou, L. and M. B. Hatzopoulos. 1998. Ἐπιγραφές Κάτω Μακεδονίας (μεταξύ του Βερμίου ὄρους καὶ του Ἀξιοῦ ποταμοῦ). Τεῦχος Α΄. Ἐπιγραφὲς Βέροιας. Athens: National Research Institute.
I.Cos Paton	Paton, W. R. and E. L. Hicks. 1891. *The Inscriptions of Cos*. Oxford: Clarendon Press.
I.Cos Segre	Segre, M. 1993–2007. *Iscrizioni di Cos*. Monografie della Scuola Archeologica di Atene e delle Missioni Italiane in Oriente 6. Rome: "L'Erma" di Bretschneider.
I.Délos	Durrbach, F. et al. 1926–2008. *Inscriptions de Délos*. 7 vols. Paris: H. Champion.
I.Ephesos	Engelmann, H. et al. 1979–84. *Die Inschriften von Ephesos*. 8 vols. IGSK 11–17. Bonn: Rudolf Habelt.
I.Estremo oriente	Canali De Rossi, D. 2004. *Iscrizioni dello estremo oriente Greco*. IGSK 65. Bonn: Rudolf Habelt.
I.Iasos	Blümel, W. 1985. *Die Inschriften von Iasos*. 2 vols. IGSK 28. Bonn: Rudolf Habelt.
I.Kaunos	Marek, C. 2006. *Die Inschriften von Kaunos*. Vestigia 55. Munich: C. H. Beck.
I.Kios	Corsten, T. 1985. *Die Inschriften von Kios*. IGSK 29. Bonn: Rudolf Habelt.
I.Kition	Yon, M. 2004. *Kition dans les textes: Testimonia littéraires et épigraphiques et corpus des inscriptions*. Kition-Bamboula 5. Paris: Recherche sur les Civilisations.
I.Knidos	Blümel, W. 1992–2019. *Die Inschriften von Knidos*. IGSK 41–42. Bonn: Rudolf Habelt.
I.Labraunda	Crampa, J. 1969–72. *Labraunda Swedish Excavations and Researches* 3: *The Greek Inscriptions*. 2 vols. Lund: Gleerup.
I.Lindos	Blinkenberg, C. 1941. *Lindos: Fouilles et recherches, 1902–1914*. Vol. 2: *Fouilles del'Acropole: Inscriptions*. 2 vols. Berlin: De Gruyter.
I.Magnesia	Kern, O. 1967. *Die Inschriften von Magnesia am Maeander*. Berlin: De Gruyter.
I.Milet	Herrmann, P., W. Günther, and N. Ehrhardt. 1997–2006. *Inschriften von Milet (Milet VI)*. 3 vols. Berlin: De Gruyter.

I.Olbia	Knipovič, T. N. and E. I. Levi. 1968. *Inscriptiones Olbiae (1917–1965)*. Leningrad: Nauka.
I.Oropos	Petrakos, V. C. 1997. *Οι Επιγραφές του Ωροπού*. BAAH 170. Athens: Greek Archaeological Society.
I.Priene B-M	Blümel, W. and R. Merkelbach. 2014. *Die Inschriften von Priene*. 2 vols. IGSK 69. Bonn: Rudolf Habelt.
I.Rhénée	Couilloud, M.-T. 1974. *Les monuments funéraires de Rhénée*. Exploration archéologique de Délos 30. Paris: De Boccard.
ICS	Masson, O. 1961. *Les inscriptions chypriotes syllabiques: Recueil critique et commenté*. Paris: De Boccard.
IG	Dittenberger, W. et al. 1873–. *Inscriptiones Graecae*. Berlin: G. Reimer.
IGBulg	Mihailov, G. 1956–97. *Inscriptiones graecae in Bulgaria repertae*. Sofia: Academiae Litterarum Bulgaricae.
IGR	Cagnat, R. et al. 1906–27. *Inscriptiones graecae ad res romanas pertinentes*. Paris: E. Leroux.
IGUR	Moretti, L. 1968–90. *Inscriptiones graecae urbis Romae*. 4 vols. Rome: Istituto italiano per la storia antica.
IScM	Pippidi, D. M. et al. 1980–. *Inscriptiones Daciae et Scythiae Minoris antiquae. Series altera: Inscriptiones Scythiae Minoris graecae et latinae*. 4 vols. Bucharest: Editura Academiei Republicii Socialiste România.
ISE	Moretti, L. 1967–76. *Iscrizioni storiche ellenistiche. Testo critico, traduzione e commento*. 3 vols. Florence: "La Nuova Italia."
KAI	Donner H. and W. Röllig. 1973–79. *Kanaanäische und aramäische Inschriften*. 3 vols. Wiesbaden: Otto Harrassowitz.
Le Rider, *Monnaies*	Le Rider, G. 1966. *Monnaies crétoises du Ve au Ier siècles av. J.-C.* Paris: Librairie orientaliste P. Geuthner.
LGPN	Fraser, P. M. et al., eds. 1987–. *A Lexicon of Greek Personal Names*. 5 vols. Oxford: Oxford University Press.
M-L	Meiggs, R. and D. Lewis. 1989. *A Selection of Greek Historical Inscriptions to the End of the Fifth Century* BC. Oxford: Clarendon.
Maiuri, *Rodi e Cos*	Maiuri, A. 1925. *Nuova silloge epigrafica di Rodi e Cos*. Florence: F. Le Monnier.
Milet I.3	Kawerau, G. and A. Rehm. 1914. *Das Delphinion in Milet*. Berlin: G. Reimer.
Suppl. Rodio nuovo	Pugliese Carratelli, G. 1955–56. "Nuovo supplemento epigrafico rodio." *ASAA* 33–34: 157–181.

RE	Pauly, A. G. Wissowa, and W. Kroll. 1894–1980. *Real-Encyclopädie der klassischen Altertumswissenschaft*. Stuttgart: Metzler.
RÉS	1900–. *Répertoire d'épigraphie sémitique*. Paris: Imprimerie nationale.
SEG	1923–. *Supplementum Epigraphicum Graecum*. Leiden: Brill.
Syll³	Dittenberger, W. et al. 1915–24. *Sylloge Inscriptionum Graecarum*. 3rd ed. 4 vols. Leipzig: S. Hirzel.
TAM I	Kalinka, E. 1901. *Tituli Asiae Minoris*. I: *Tituli Lyciae lingua Lycia conscripti*. Vienna: A. Hoelder.
Thess. Mn.	Arvanitopoulos, A. S. 1909. Θεσσαλικὰ Μνημεῖα: Ἀθανασάκειον Μουσεῖον ἐν Βόλῳ. 2 vols. Athens: Hestia.
Tit. Cam.	Segre, M. and G. Pugliese Carratelli. 1949–51. "Tituli Camirenses." *ASAtene* 27–29: 141–318.

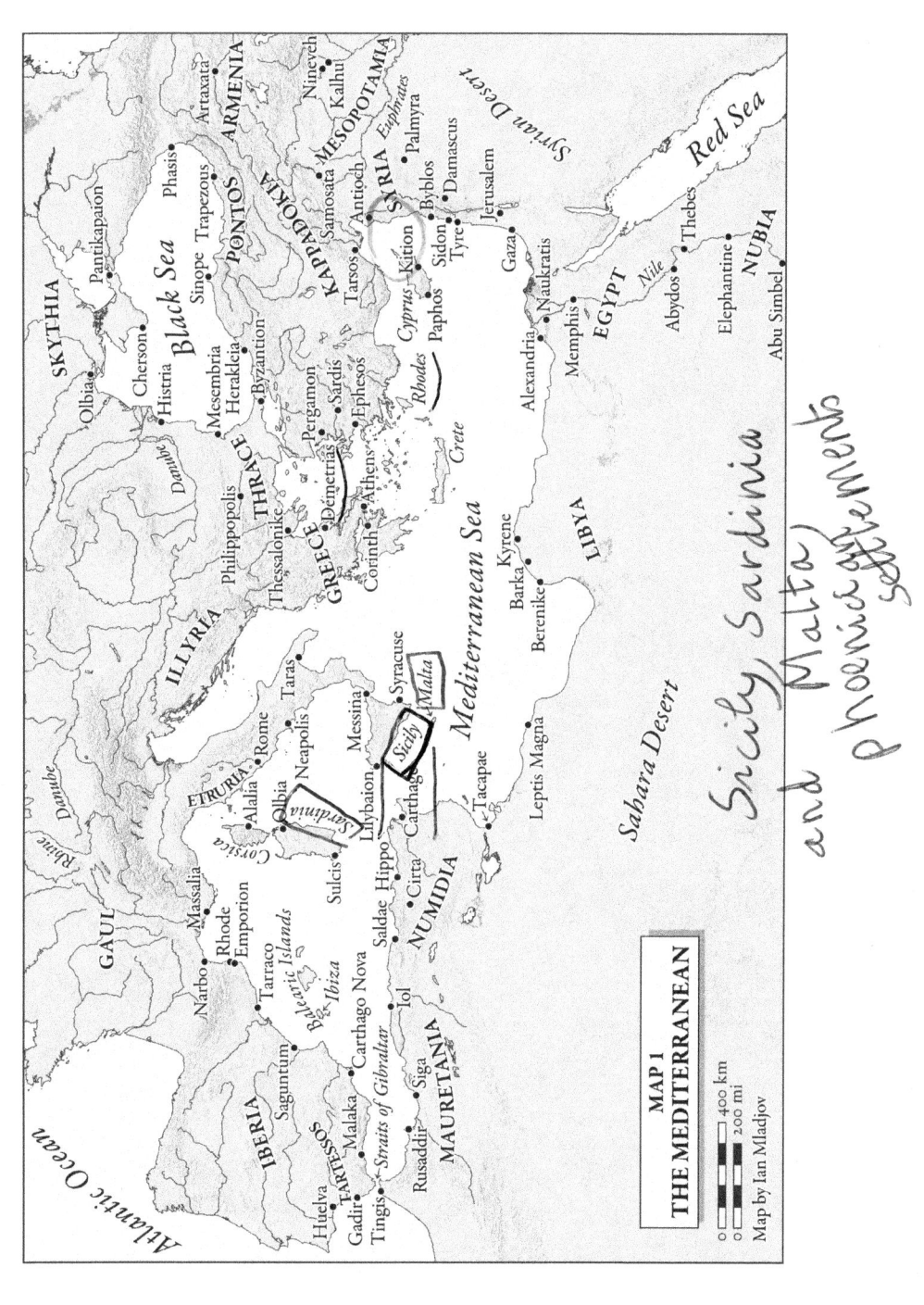

MAP 1
THE MEDITERRANEAN

Map by Ian Mladjov

Sicily, Sardinia and Malta) phoenician settlements

p. 6

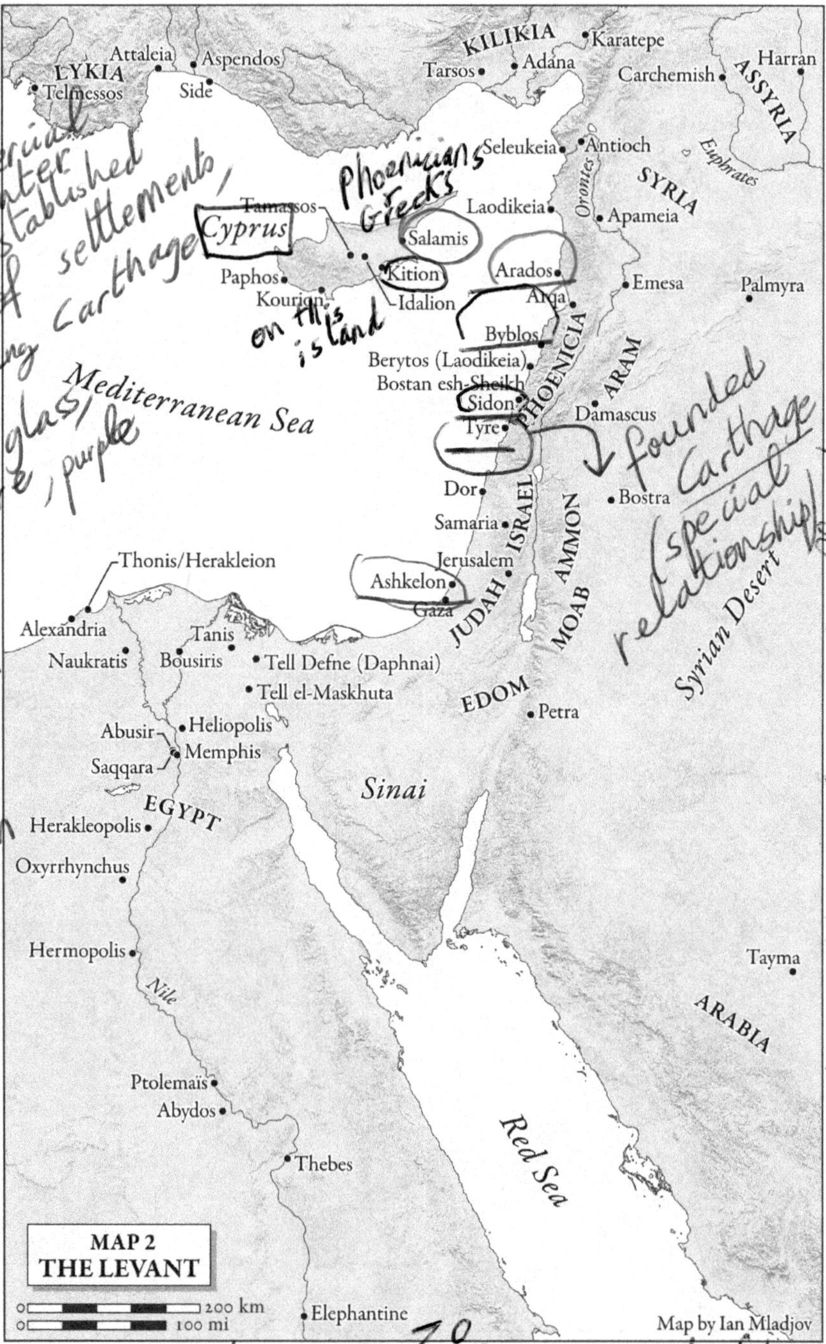

MAP 2
THE LEVANT

Map by Ian Mladjov

Annotations:

p. 7

- Tyre: a commercial center; established dozens of settlements, including Carthage
- Sidon: silverware, glass, purple dye
- Byblos: timber, earliest phoenician writing

Phoenicians / Greeks (on Cyprus — "on this island")

Tyre → founded Carthage (special relationship)

SIDON ✓ — special awards (tax exemptions) to Sidonians ONLY who had lived in and were citizens of Sidon & had emigrated to Athens, specifically because they were TRADERS!

MAP 3
THE AEGEAN

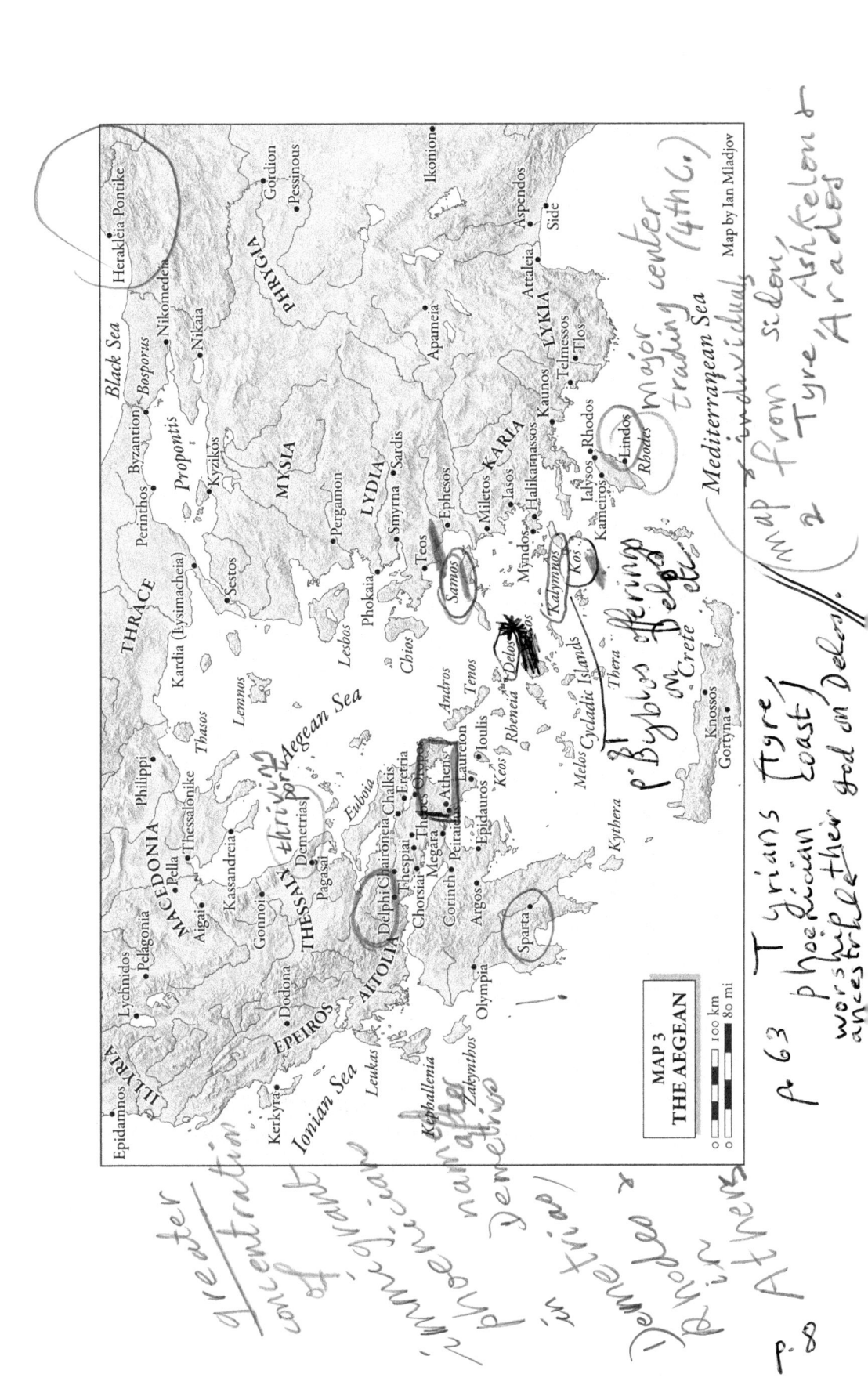

Map by Ian Mladjov

greater concentration immigrant Phoenician named Demetrios in Rhodes & Athens

p. 63 Tyrians Tyre Phoenician coast/ worship their god on Delos ancestrable individual

Byblos offering on Delos

major center trading (4th c.)

Map from Sidon & Tyre Ashkelon & Arados

p. 8

MAP 4
CENTRAL MEDITERRANEAN

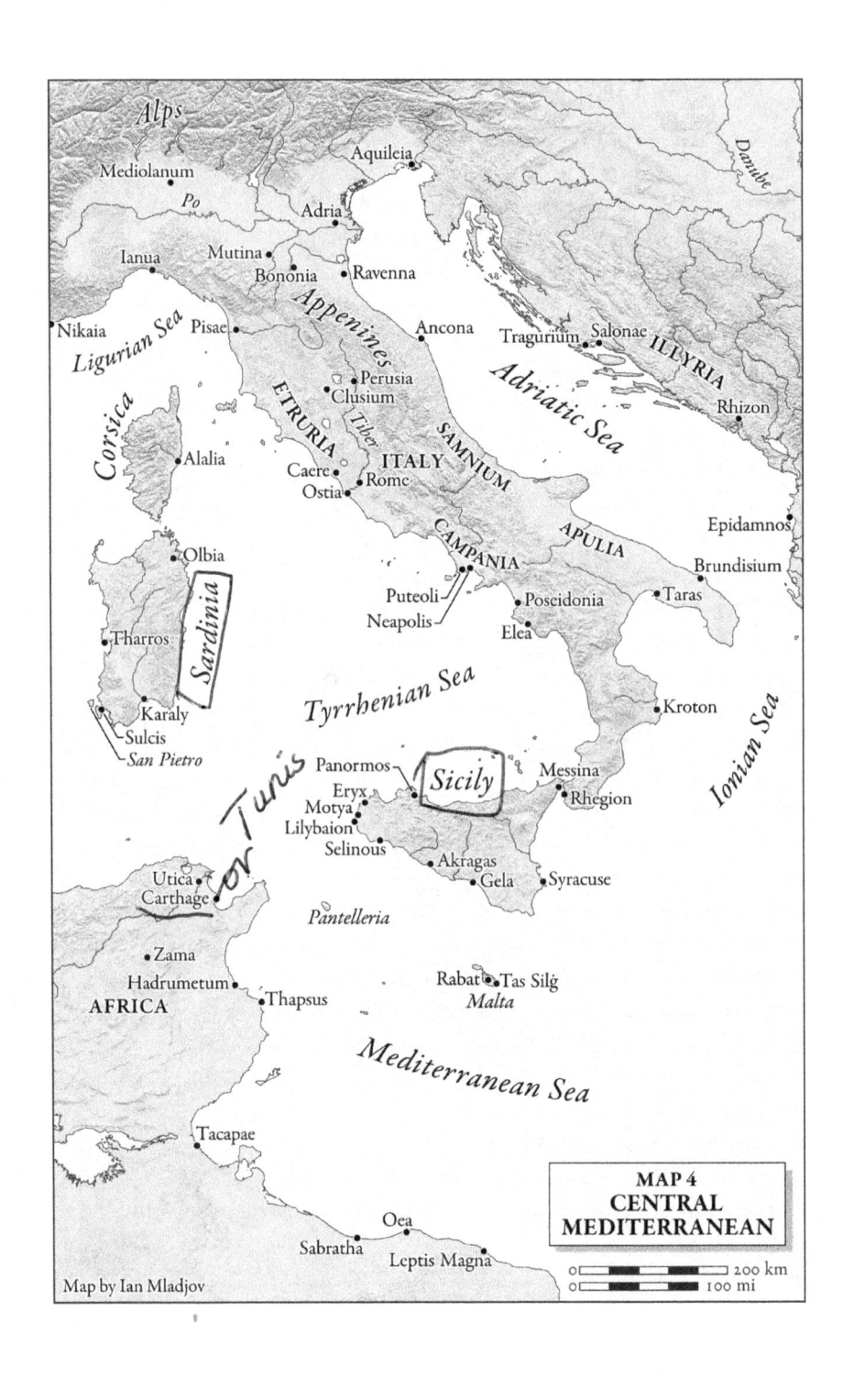

Map by Ian Mladjov

Introduction

WHY PHOENICIAN MIGRANTS MATTER

ZENO WAS THE founder of the philosophical school of Stoicism, widely recognized today as one of the major contributions of the ancient Greeks. But Zeno was not actually Greek. He was a Phoenician immigrant in Athens and originally from Kition (present-day Larnaca), a mixed Phoenician and Greek city-state on Cyprus. His arrival in Athens sometime in the fourth century BCE was inauspicious: he was shipwrecked en route to Peiraieus, the port of Athens, on a Phoenician ship carrying the quintessential Phoenician product of purple dye. After surviving the shipwreck, the first thing Zeno reportedly did was to visit a bookseller in Athens, where he picked up a book about the philosopher Socrates written by his student Xenophon, read it, and declared to the bookseller that he wanted to find a teacher like Socrates. As it so happened, the philosopher Krates—himself an immigrant from Thebes—was walking by, and the bookseller pointed him out to Zeno, who eventually studied under Krates.[1] Zeno subsequently established his own school in the heart of Athens at the Stoa Poikile (Painted Stoa), a portico where famous paintings were displayed, located in the agora, the public marketplace and civic center of the city.[2] Unlike other philosophical schools such as Plato's Academy or the Epicureans' Garden, which were situated at the outskirts of the city in private spaces or religious sanctuaries, the Stoic school, named after the building where Zeno taught, was open to the public. Stoicism later flourished among the Romans, winning over emperors such as Marcus Aurelius among its adherents, and continues to enjoy popularity even

---

1. Diogenes Laertius 7.2–3. Zeno is said to have read Xenophon's *Memorabilia*.

2. Pausanias 1.15.1–4 describes the paintings of the Stoa Poikile and other items displayed in it.

today.[3] Yet were it not for mobility and migration in the ancient Mediterranean region, especially on the part of the Phoenicians, and collaboration among different cultural groups, Stoicism may not have developed into one of the most influential philosophical schools of antiquity.[4]

Many people in motion, like Zeno, inhabited the ancient Mediterranean region. Large numbers of individuals traveled by sea and land to fight wars, sell their wares, participate in religious and athletic festivals, and conduct diplomacy. They moved across communities as refugees, settlers, enslaved persons, traders, and professionals. Ancient Mediterranean societies hosted significant numbers of foreign-born residents who, though not citizens, participated in and contributed to the civic communities they joined. These flows of migration connected individuals and states and, in the process, transformed both immigrants and the societies in which they lived. Although immigrants are rarely mentioned in the existing literature about the ancient Mediterranean, the history of the region would have been quite different without them.

To investigate the effects of migration in the ancient world, this book offers the first history of Phoenician immigrants in the ancient Mediterranean from the fourth to the first centuries BCE, primarily in Greek communities but also in

---

3. In addition to an increase in popular books on Stoicism, there are now annual weeklong events known as Stoic Week in which participants live like a Stoic. The first of these was organized at Exeter University, but they now take place online with tens of thousands of attendees. For more information, see https://modernstoicism.com/stoic-week/. Ryan Holiday has also popularized stoicism among entrepreneurs and elite athletes through both his books and consulting for companies such as Google.

4. In addition to Zeno, numerous Phoenician philosophers taught in Athens and influenced Greek thought. Besides Zeno's students Perseus and Herilos (Diogenes Laertius 7.36–37), from Kition and Carthage, respectively, and Zeno of Sidon, an Epicurean philosopher of the second to first centuries BCE (Diogenes Laertius 7.35), nine Tyrian philosophers were also residents of and practiced their craft in Athens: Diotimos the Tyrian, a fourth-century BCE philosopher and student of Demokritos; Basileides, the head of the Epicurean school at the end of the third century and first quarter of the second century BCE; Diodoros, a Peripatetic from the second century BCE; Agathokles, Mnaseas, and Zenodoros, all members of the Academy in the second century BCE; Herakleitos, also an Academician but of the first century BCE; and Antipatros and Apollonios, both Stoics of the first century BCE. Most of these philosophers (Diodoros, Agathokles, Mnaseas, Zenodoros, Herakleitos) are known from Philodemos' first-century BCE *History of the Academy* (P. Herc. 1021) or, in the case of Antipatros and Apollonios, his *History of the Stoics* (P. Herc. 1018), both preserved on papyrus scrolls from Herculaneum. Diotimos and Basileides are mentioned by multiple ancient sources: the former by (among others) Sextus Empiricus, *Against the Mathematicians* 7.140 and Clement of Alexandria, *Stromata* 2.130 (in Stählin 1906: 184) and the latter by Diogenes Laertius 10.25. Like Zeno of Kition, the founder of the Stoic school, these Phoenician intellectuals were responsible for introducing influential ideas that are normally thought of as the hallmark of Greek philosophy. See Yon 2011: 34–37 for a list of Tyrian philosophers in Athens. For Diotimos, see Warren 2002: 41–42 and 42 n. 44.

Carthage, Egypt, and the central Mediterranean islands of Sicily, Sardinia, and Malta. In addition to providing new insights into the ancient world, the examination of one group of immigrants—the Phoenicians—addresses broader issues regarding mobility and migration that continue to challenge migrants and states alike: the adaptive strategies that immigrants mobilize to mediate their experiences and encourage a sense of membership and belonging, the new identities they construct, the policies that host and home states employ to promote or manage migration, and the multiple ways migrants change both themselves and the societies they join.

Although immigrants like Zeno were often upwardly socially mobile and even honored by their host states, they also faced prejudice and discrimination. Ancient sources, for instance, describe Zeno's Phoenician ethnicity and his foreignness as undesirable traits.[5] Even his teacher Krates called him "little Phoenician," a demeaning term of endearment.[6] Diogenes Laertius, who wrote biographies of ancient philosophers, described him as a stingy foreigner.[7] And he was accused of plagiarism by a rival philosopher, Polemon, who claimed that Zeno had stolen his ideas and dressed them in a Phoenician style.[8] Even after his death, an epigram praising Zeno composed by his student Zenodotos ended with lines reflecting that his foreign origins were seen by some with suspicion: "What reproach is there, if your fatherland is Phoenicia? Did not Kadmos also come from there, from whom Hellas has writing?"[9] Despite such stereotypes, Zeno himself never denied his origins and insisted that he not be called "Zeno the philosopher" but rather "Zeno the philosopher from Kition."[10] Zeno continued to

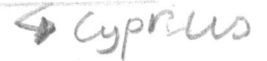

---

5. In Diogenes Laertius' biography, Zeno and his family are also characterized as stereotypically Phoenician: he is variously described as a shipowner or a moneylender (7.13) and his father Mnaseas—whose name was a Hellenized form of the Semitic name Manasseh—as a trader (7.31).

6. Diogenes Laertius 7.3: τί φεύγεις, Φοινικίδιον; οὐδὲν δεινὸν πέπονθας (Why are you running away, little Phoenician? Nothing terrible has happened to you).

7. Diogenes Laertius 7.16: ἦν εὐτελής τε σφόδρα καὶ βαρβαρικῆς ἐχόμενος μικρολογίας, προσχήματι οἰκονομίας (He was very cheap, too, having a foreigner's stinginess, on the pretense of economy).

8. Diogenes Laertius 7.25: οὐ λανθάνεις, ὦ Ζήνων, ταῖς κηπαίαις παρεισρέων θύραις καὶ τὰ δόγματα κλέπτων Φοινικικῶς μεταμφιεννύς (You do not escape my notice, Zeno, slipping through the garden gates, stealing my doctrines and giving them a Phoenician makeover).

9. *Anthologia Palatina* 7.117 = Diogenes Laertius 7.30: εἰ δὲ πάτρα Φοίνισσα, τίς ὁ φθόνος; οὐ καὶ ὁ Κάδμος κεῖνος, ἀφ' οὗ γραπτὰν Ἑλλὰς ἔχει σελίδα. Herodotus 5.58 credits the mythical hero Kadmos, who is said to have been a Phoenician, with introducing the Phoenician alphabet to the Greeks. The Greeks did indeed borrow their alphabet from the Phoenician one.

10. Diogenes Laertius 7.12: φησὶ δ' Ἀντίγονος ὁ Καρύστιος οὐκ ἀρνεῖσθαι αὐτὸν εἶναι Κιτιέα. τῶν γὰρ εἰς τὴν ἐπισκευὴν τοῦ λουτρῶνος συμβαλλομένων εἰς ὧν καὶ ἀναγραφόμενος ἐν τῇ στήλῃ

identify himself in terms of his civic identity, and his state of origin affirmed that it perceived him as one of its most famous émigrés by erecting a bronze statue of him in Kition.[11] Athens, too, honored Zeno, posthumously awarding him a gold wreath and voting to build a tomb for him in the main Athenian cemetery at public expense.[12]

Phoenicians were not the only immigrants in communities throughout the Mediterranean. But other immigrant groups did not leave behind evidence as robust and plentiful. The Phoenician case helps reveal the wider story of immigration in the ancient Mediterranean. And Zeno serves as a compelling example of this book's main argument: that immigrants, far from being excluded, and despite discrimination, profoundly shaped the political, cultural, social, economic, and religious landscape of their host societies. As the following chapters will show, Phoenician immigrants developed a number of adaptive strategies that allowed them and their families to integrate themselves into their host societies, facilitate their upward social mobility, and establish strong personal and professional networks as they continued to maintain links to their home states. Ultimately, these strategies in combination with their host states' immigration policies helped blur rigid distinctions between citizens and noncitizens and create a fluid spectrum of participatory membership in a political community. As a result, the cultural contributions of these immigrants collectively, though mostly anonymously, transformed the ancient Mediterranean.

In general, the movement of people and migration throughout the Mediterranean led to significant numbers of foreign-born residents living in polities other than their places of birth. For instance, free male resident aliens living in Athens circa 431 BCE, who were known as *metics*, constituted an estimated 16 to 20 percent of the free male population, a figure that underreports the actual number as it includes only those immigrants who registered in the city.[13]

"Ζήνωνος τοῦ φιλοσόφου," ἠξίωσε καὶ ⟨ὅ⟩τι Κιτιεὺς προστεθῆναι (Antigonos the Karystian says that Zeno did not deny he was a Kitian. For when he was among those who contributed to the restoration of the baths and his name was inscribed on the stele as "Zeno the philosopher," he demanded that "Kitian" be added).

11. Diogenes Laertius 7.6. Kitians who lived across the sea in Sidon, on the coast of present-day Lebanon, also erected a statue in his honor, according to the same passage.

12. The decree, dated to 262/261 BCE, is preserved in Diogenes Laertius 7.10–12. It has been accepted as authentic and is even listed in the third edition of the Attic volumes of *IG* as *IG* II³ 1 980. Haake 2006 questions the authenticity of the decree, noting that the specific reasons for the awards granted to Zeno are atypical and correspond to literary tropes in Hellenistic biographies of philosophers.

13. For estimates of the numbers of metics in Athens, see Duncan-Jones 1980 and Watson 2010: 268. For citizen numbers, see Gomme 1933: Table 1 (43,000); Patterson 1981: 40–81;

Yet despite their significant presence in polities throughout the Mediterranean, such immigrants have been largely overlooked in the extensive literature on the ancient Mediterranean, and Greek immigrants have received far more attention than migrants from other locales.[14] To better understand the lives and contributions of this large demographic and present a more comprehensive history of migration, this book considers a wider range of foreign residents than those who fell within the legal category of a metic, the sole known category of immigrant in ancient Athens.[15] A metic was a foreigner who was present in a state for longer than a prescribed period of time, usually at least one month; required to register as such; and subject to a tax called the *metoikion*.[16] But this legal category far from encompasses all migrants who moved either short or long distances, temporarily or permanently.[17] And it represents only one of many gradations of social status that foreign-born residents could occupy in their host state as they

---

Hansen 1988: 14–28 (60,000); and Watson 2010: 260–264 with bibliography. These demographic estimates are based on numbers of Athenian troops provided by the ancient historians Herodotus and Thucydides. For a critique of these numbers, see Akrigg 2011. By contrast, in 2022, documented permanent residents (green-card holders) in the United States were 3.9 percent of the population (https://www.dhs.gov/immigration-statistics/population-estimates/LPR), and the percentage of both documented (visa and green-card holders) and undocumented foreign-born residents in 2019, about half of whom were naturalized US citizens, was 13.6%, according to the 2020 US Census Bureau: https://data.census.gov/cedsci/profile?q=United%20States&g=0100000US.

14. For Greek migrants, see, for example, Garland 2014; De Angelis 2020. There is no systematic study that compiles all non-Greek individuals residing in Greek communities, but several ongoing efforts have moved scholars closer to identifying immigrants in Greek polities. Rebecca Futo Kennedy is currently collecting all ancient references to immigrant women, both Greek and non-Greek, in ancient Greek communities. Timothy Shea's 2018 dissertation maps Greek and non-Greek immigrant communities in Athens through an examination of their tombstones. Benedikt Boyxen's 2018 study on foreigners in Rhodes, one of the places other than Athens where evidence for immigrants abounds, has provided a corrective to the Athenocentric emphasis in scholarship.

15. Two more legal categories of immigrants are known from the island of Rhodes: the *matroxenoi* (those born to foreign mothers) and the *epidamoi* (legal residents). See Boyxen 2018. Claudia Moatti's work has illuminated the movement of people across the ancient Mediterranean. See Moatti 2004; Moatti and Kaiser 2007; Moatti, Kaiser, and Pébarthe 2009.

16. Whitehead 1977: 6–10. See also Niku 2007: 21; Fraser 2009: 111–112; and Sosin 2016. Freed persons, their children, and the children of metics automatically acquired the status of a metic. See also Meyer 2009.

17. The field of migration studies defines a migrant broadly (Manning 2020: 1–16). In Greek, there are several words that indicate migration or migrants, most of them compounds of the words *demos* and *oikos*: ἐπίδημος (sojourner), ἀπόδημος (away from one's country, abroad), μέτοικος (resident alien, denizen, metic), ἄποικος (settler), ἔποικος (settler, sojourner), and οἰκέω (dwell in, often used for metics to designate the deme of their residence). But these words do not necessarily have a legal meaning and can be used in different ways to designate different kinds of migrants. For more on the vocabulary associated with mobility and moving, see

received various awards and privileges normally reserved for citizens.[18] By adopting a broader definition of migrants, the following chapters reveal that the presence and contributions of immigrants spurred Greek states to create what was in essence a spectrum of participatory membership in a political community that over time shaped the institutions, policies, and societies of their host states.

In examining a broader range of immigrants, this book also moves beyond a narrowly legal perspective to examine the social effects of migration, shifting the focus from a contemporary understanding of migration simply as individuals crossing borders to one that views migration as a social process that has transformed the world throughout history.[19] Unlike most earlier studies of migration in the ancient Mediterranean, the body of evidence considered here is not limited to sources produced by the state or members of the host society.[20] This enables an investigation that moves beyond the state policies of exclusion and inclusion that constituted the migration and membership regimes of those societies to also illuminate migrants' repertoires, the particular practices they pursued to adapt to migration regimes.[21] Such practices commonly employed by Phoenician immigrants included name changing, the adoption of local customs and aesthetic styles, the syncretism of divinities, the production of bicultural artifacts, the creation of communities that offered a cultural locus for immigrants and helped

---

Costanzi 2020. On the modes of identification of citizens, metics, and enslaved persons, see Faraguna 2014.

18. Kamen 2013 distinguishes between only two statuses for foreign residents: metics and privileged metics.

19. Hoerder 2002: xix. For migration as a human condition, see also Manning 2006: 24 and 2020: xiii. Seminal works on migration in world history are Hoerder 2002 and 2012; McKeown 2004; Lucassen and Lucassen 2009 (see also the reactions to this influential article published in a "Discussion on Global Migration" in volume 6 of the *Journal of Global History* in 2011 by Ehmer, McKeown, Moch, and van Lottum, as well as Lucassen and Lucassen's response); Lucassen, Lucassen, and Manning 2010; Bosma, Kessler, and Lucassen 2013; Manning 2006 and 2020. The works by Manning, Hoerder 2002, and the edited volume by Bosma, Kessler, and Lucassen also include studies of migration in the premodern period.

20. This has been the case for scholarship that focuses on metics, such as Whitehead's seminal book from 1977; Bakewell 1999a, 1999b, and 2013; and recent studies on immigrants in Athens by Kennedy 2014 and Kasimis 2018.

21. On migration and membership regimes, see Bosma, Kessler, and Lucassen 2013: 1–20. On membership in particular, see Benhabib 2004. I borrow the notion of "migrants' repertoires" from Siegelbaum and Moch 2014, who introduce it in their study of internal migrants in the long twentieth century in imperial Russia, the Soviet Union, and the Russian Federation. Moch 1992 and 2012 were both instrumental works in shifting the focus in migration studies from the perspective of the state to that of the immigrants.

them maintain their traditions, and the establishment of new institutions that mediated between them and their host state.

The Phoenicians originated on the Levantine coast of Syria-Palestine and are often considered to be the Iron Age descendants of the Canaanites, the Bronze Age civilization mentioned in the Bible. They were a Semitic-speaking people who, at the dawn of the first millennium, were organized into powerful and wealthy independent city-states located primarily on the coast: Tyre, a thriving metropolis and commercial center that later established dozens of settlements throughout the Mediterranean region, including Carthage, the famed rival of the Romans; Sidon, praised in antiquity as a production center of intricate and highly desired glass and silverware, purple dye, and embroidery; Byblos, famous for its timber and for having produced the earliest Phoenician writing; and Arados, one of the northernmost Phoenician cities on an island off the coast of present-day Syria. In addition to these four main centers, Ashkelon was a famous seaport that at different points in its history was inhabited by Phoenicians, and Berytos was a major urban hub in the second and first centuries BCE with a mixed Phoenician, Macedonian, Greek, and later Roman population. It was originally a Phoenician city called Biruta, rebuilt as Laodikeia in 140 BCE, and renamed Berytos in 64 BCE when it was conquered by Pompey. Today, most of the territory home to these ancient city-states belongs to Lebanon, though some parts are in Syria in the north and Israel in the south. From these sites, Phoenician merchants, craftsmen, and settlers migrated in the ninth century BCE, first north into Samaria, Kilikia, and Syria and then across the Mediterranean Sea to Cyprus, where they established several urban centers, the most famous of which was Kition, Zeno's hometown. The migration west continued in the eighth century BCE as Phoenicians, mostly from Tyre, founded settlements in Sicily, Sardinia, Malta, the western coast of North Africa, Iberia, and the Balearic Islands, and in this same period started to settle in Egypt and in Greek communities.[22] As a consequence of their maritime prowess and migratory patterns, the Phoenician diaspora expanded widely from Assyria to Iberia and, by the seventh century BCE,

---

22. Aubet 2001 is still the authoritative text on the Phoenician presence in the western Mediterranean. Celestino and López-Ruiz 2016 focus on Phoenicians in Iberia. For recent overviews of the Phoenicians in each of these regions, as well as others that were home to Phoenicians (e.g., Anatolia, Cyprus, North Syria) see López-Ruiz and Doak 2019. A selection of the most recent literature on the presence of Phoenicians in the Greek Aegean includes Stampolidis and Kotsonas 2006; Bourogiannis 2012, 2013, 2018, and 2020; Ioannou 2017; Stampolidis 2003 and 2019; Ilieva 2019. See also López-Ruiz 2021, especially chapters 6 and 7 on the Phoenician presence in the Aegean.

Phoenicians had established an extensive network of settlements and trading posts throughout this vast region.²³

Each of the Phoenician city-states had its own history, politics, dialect, and local religious practices. The citizens of each identified primarily in terms of their civic identity as Tyrians, Sidonians, Byblians, and the like rather than in terms of their ethnicity as Phoenicians. Because there are few references by Phoenicians to their own ethnicity, several scholars have suggested that no such self-defined ethnic group as "the Phoenicians" existed in antiquity, arguing instead that such a definition has been imposed by outsiders and mobilized by both ancient and modern states in the construction of national or hegemonic identities.²⁴ Yet, other scholars have argued that, despite local dialectal variations, differences in religious practices and gods, and warfare and tension among Phoenician city-states, by the Early Iron Age (1200–600 BCE) an identifiable Phoenician culture had developed that was recognized as such by both Phoenicians and outsiders.²⁵ Indeed, the evidence presented in this book reveals that Phoenician immigrants throughout the Mediterranean region, regardless of their specific city-state of origin, exhibited remarkably similar burial and religious practices and linguistic and epigraphic habits. By examining local immigrant communities of Phoenicians who came from different city-states and identified primarily in terms of their city-state of origin, certain patterns emerge from the largely epigraphic evidence examined here that expose ethnicity as a salient mode of identification among diasporic communities.²⁶ By the fourth century BCE, this evidence suggests,

---

23. Schmitz 2012 demonstrates the geographic range of the Phoenician presence through a philological analysis of Phoenician texts from different areas in the Mediterranean. López-Ruiz 2021 studies the presence of Phoenicians in the whole Mediterranean in the Early Iron Age (1200–600 BCE).

24. The argument is most clearly articulated in Quinn 2018. See also Martin 2017 for an art-historical perspective.

25. Edrey 2016 and 2019; López-Ruiz 2017, 2021: 11–19 and forthcoming.

26. The notions of ethnic identity and ethnicity are modern: they are rooted in the modern nation-state and first became popular as terms both in the academy and in public media in the middle of the twentieth century. The term "ethnicity" first appeared in 1941 in Warner and Lunt and was included in the *Oxford English Dictionary* in 1972. The categories of identity and ethnicity are so fluid and flexible that some have questioned whether they are valid for analysis in a modern or ancient context: Brubaker and Cooper 2000. Nonetheless, most scholars agree that self-perceived ethnic groups did exist in the ancient Mediterranean, even though ethnicity is not always the most relevant category of analysis. LaBuff 2023 for instance, shows how decentering ethnicity from the study of indigeneity in antiquity reveals dynamics that have gone unnoticed and which further our understanding of ancient history. Recent work on other groups that lived in the Mediterranean—Jews (S. J. D. Cohen 1999), Nubians (Smith 2003), Egyptians (Matić 2020), among others—has demonstrated that they self-identified as ethnic groups. The Greeks rarely called themselves Hellenes, an indicator of Greek ethnicity, and even

Phoenician immigrants who lived as minorities in Greek communities and in Egypt had also begun to develop and express a broader Phoenician identity. In Greek polities, for instance, some of these immigrants referred to the larger region from which they came as Phoenicia, and others in Egypt identified themselves as Phoenico-Egyptians; other evidence indicates the presence of cooperative structures through which various Phoenician city-states or individuals from them provided services to Phoenician immigrants from elsewhere. The evidence does not address whether the notion of a Phoenician ethnicity circled back to those who lived in Phoenician city-states.

At the same time, the following chapters recognize the internal diversity and modes of self-identification among Phoenician immigrants and, in so doing, uncover the histories, identities, and agency of various individual immigrants and immigrant communities. The individual subjects of this history include Phoenician immigrants from Tyre, Sidon, Byblos, Ashkelon, Kition, and Berytos who opted to move to a new state within the ancient Mediterranean world for an extended period. Most of the economic migrants who appear in the following pages moved long term or permanently to practice their profession; they include traders and shipowners, bankers, sculptors, philosophers, and priests. Others were compelled to move: refugees driven from their homes, enslaved or formerly enslaved persons transported against their will, and mercenary soldiers who ended up in foreign lands for long periods. Besides these, individuals moved semi-permanently or permanently for a wide range of reasons, including asylum seekers, political exiles, fugitives, settlers, and laborers, among many others. The surviving evidence suggests that a greater number of Phoenicians lived in Greek communities and in Egypt, Carthage, and the central Mediterranean than did other non-Greek immigrants, such as Thracians, Skythians, Jews, and Persians. Their significant presence as immigrants across the Mediterranean region is reason alone to attempt to better integrate Phoenicians into histories of the ancient Mediterranean.

Although the origins of the Phoenician diaspora are rooted in the movements of the early first millennium that resulted in the establishment of settlements throughout the Mediterranean, in a process that predated the foundation of new Greek city-states and dispersal of Greeks in the same period, these Phoenician settler communities were different from the immigrant communities of the fourth to the first centuries BCE studied here. The latter were minorities in states

---

when they did, that word included different people at different times (Hall 1997 and 2002). The term "Hellenes" came to designate an inclusive group of Greeks only in the beginning of the sixth century BCE (Hall 2003: 27–30). See also Ruby 2006; Demetriou 2012: 8–14; and Gruen 2020.

that were predominantly Greek, Egyptian, or Carthaginian rather than settlers in states they themselves had founded. Such communities are difficult to detect in the record. But during the fourth to the first centuries BCE, Phoenician immigrants left behind written evidence of their presence and activities and did so more than any other contemporaneous immigrant group, including Greeks who lived in non-Greek states. This material includes dozens of texts inscribed on stone in the Phoenician script and language and a surprising number of bilingual texts (in Phoenician and in Greek or Egyptian), the majority of which date to the fourth century BCE.[27] Phoenicians are the only immigrant group in the ancient Mediterranean from whom a large number of bilingual texts survives. Such bilingual inscriptions have rarely been published together, and the texts in each language have been studied separately and mostly from a philological perspective.[28] The Phoenician texts have been collected in *Corpus Inscriptionum Semiticarum*, which contains most Phoenician texts known by the 1880s, when the series was published; in *Kanaanäische und Aramäische Inschriften* and *Répertoire d'Épigraphie Sémitique*, both of which provide only a selection of Phoenician texts; and in Gibson's *Textbook of Syrian Semitic Inscriptions* III: *Phoenician*

---

27. A few bilingual (and trilingual) inscriptions in Phoenician and other languages date to much earlier periods, such as the eighth-century BCE Karatepe (*KAI* 26) and Çineköy (Tekoğlu and Lemaire 2000) bilingual inscriptions in Phoenician and Luwian; an eighth-century BCE trilingual text from Incirli in Akkadian, Luwian, and Phoenician (S. A. Kaufman 2007); and the sixth-century BCE Pyrgi tablets in Phoenician and Etruscan from Etruria (*KAI* 227). For more information and literature on these texts, see Lanfranchi 2007; Belleli and Xella 2015–2016; and Yakubovich 2015. Eight bilingual texts in Phoenician and Greek written in the Cypriot syllabic script also exist from Cyprus, many from the fourth century BCE. For more literature on these, see Steele 2013: 202–211.

28. Amadasi Guzzo, one of the doyennes of Phoenician and Punic epigraphy whose publications on Phoenician and Punic inscriptions in the western Mediterranean have single-handedly elucidated the study of Phoenicians in the West (e.g., 1967, 1979, 1986, and 1990), has contributed to the study of the philology of the Phoenician language in Greek-speaking communities (e.g., Amadasi Guzzo 2013; Amadasi Guzzo and Bonnet 1991). Masson 1969 offers one of the seminal works on Phoenician inscriptions found in Greek polities. Similarly, Baslez, whose work has focused on the interactions between Phoenicians and Greeks, together with Briquel-Chatonnet, has discussed bilingualism among Phoenicians living in Greek communities (e.g., Baslez and Briquel-Chatonnet 1991a and 1991b; Briquel-Chatonnet 2012). Most of these scholars have focused on the philology of Phoenician texts and names and how the language influenced and was influenced by other languages. Corinne Bonnet's wide-ranging scholarship on the Phoenicians has dealt with philological as well as religious, social, and cultural issues presented by bilingual texts. See Bonnet 2015 and Bonnet and Bianco 2018. The Septuagint, the Greek translation of the Hebrew Bible and other apocryphal and deuterocanonical books, is another contemporary source for linguistic adaptations that result from translations, especially as it contains many Semiticisms in Greek.

Inscriptions.²⁹ In the case of bilingual Phoenician and Greek inscriptions, the Greek text is usually published in the appropriate volume of *Inscriptiones Graecae* and its supplement, the *Supplementum Epigraphicum Graecum*, which often note that the monument also bore a Phoenician inscription but seldom provide its text. But separating the texts that appear on the same monument yields only a fragmented picture. As the following chapters will show, these bilingual texts—which were never direct translations of each other—were also bicultural documents, reflecting the immigrant experiences of the people who produced them. These sources include private tombstones of individual immigrants that showcase some of the adaptive strategies that Phoenician immigrants established, administrative texts that regulated the internal affairs of Phoenician immigrant communities in foreign lands, and religious dedications that represent Phoenician immigrants' attempts to both maintain ties with their cultural traditions and integrate themselves into their host societies. Studied together for the first time, these bilingual texts from throughout the Mediterranean reveal how migrants navigated their lives as individuals who belonged to two different worlds.

This abundance of texts that record the voices of the Phoenician immigrants from the fourth to the first centuries BCE, most of which were found in Athens, Demetrias, Rhodes, Delos, Kos, Sardinia, Malta, Carthage, and Egypt, defines both the chronological and geographical parameters of this book and reveals a different Mediterranean than most popular and scholarly accounts, which typically focus on the Greeks or the Romans.³⁰ The existence of epigraphic sources produced by immigrants themselves provides an opportunity to study immigration in this period more comprehensively. Examining the perspectives of immigrants along with sources from host states or their members reveals those societies' immigration policies and attitudes toward immigrants. Such an investigation becomes possible only in the period covered by this book, as textual evidence

---

29. Gibson 1982. Richey 2019 provides a survey of Phoenician and Punic inscriptions from across the Mediterranean. These have never been published in a single collection. Xella and Zamora 2007 announced a project to provide a more comprehensive collection, but the official website, http://cip.cchs.csic.es/home, appears not to have been substantially updated since the late 2000s.

30. Though Phoenicians were also present in this period in other areas of the Levant, Iberia, and North Africa (outside Carthage), the rarity of written sources from these areas has led me to exclude them from full consideration, although references to some of the existing material from these areas may be found in footnotes, especially in chapter 5. I have also chosen not to extend the discussion to Cyprus, where Phoenician communities coexisted with Greek and indigenous Cypriot ones for centuries, in part because Phoenician Kitians are included among the Phoenician immigrants considered here and in part because the historical context of long-term coexistence between Phoenicians and Greeks on Cyprus is very different from that of the other locales studied here.

produced by immigrants from earlier periods is scarce, requiring scholars to rely on material culture to determine the presence of different groups in a specific area. The latter is a difficult task in and of itself, as an artifact that can be identified as produced by a certain group does not necessarily indicate that group's presence, and without contemporary written sources, it is nearly impossible to determine the status of that group, attitudes toward it, or its level of integration and inclusion in local societies.

The chronological parameters of this book also challenge the conventional assumption that Phoenician history ended when Alexander the Great conquered the region in 332 BCE. Whereas many studies have been published on Phoenicians in the Early Iron Age (1200–600 BCE) and Persian period (600–332 BCE), most histories of Phoenicians leave the period that follows Alexander's conquest unexamined.[31] Scholarship on the Phoenicians has also focused on those who settled in the western Mediterranean during the Early Iron Age, when Phoenicians established settlements in the West, and after the third century BCE, when the Punic Mediterranean came into contact with the Romans—an imaginary East/West divide that few works have transcended.[32] With notable exceptions, what little scholarship exists on Phoenicians after 332 BCE has concentrated on the problematic notion of "Hellenization," namely how this area became increasingly culturally Greek.[33] Such scholarship has largely overlooked that, despite the political transformation that came with Alexander the Great's conquest, changes in the religious, artistic, economic, and other social and cultural domains in the

---

31. Despite the proliferation of books on the Phoenicians since 1988, few have paid attention to the period following Alexander's conquest. Most recently, Sader 2019 uses 332 BCE as the end point of her book on the history of this region, and Bonnet, Guillon, and Porzia 2021 dedicate only a few pages to this period. Jigoulov 2010 and the many publications by Elayi (2005, 2009, 2013, and 2018) and Elayi and Elayi (2004, 2009, 2014, and 2015) concentrate on the Achaemenid period. The journal *Transeuphratène*, which often publishes articles on Phoenicians and is named after the Persian satrapy that included Phoenician city-states, focuses only on the Achaemenid period. Baurain and Bonnet 1992; Markoe 2000; Sommer 2008; Morstadt 2015; and Woolmer 2017 dedicate only a few pages in their books to the Hellenistic period and beyond.

32. For the Early Iron Age, see Aubet 2001; Celestino and López-Ruiz 2016; and the essays by Aubet Semmler, Hayne, Roppa, De Vincenzo, Vella and Anastasi, Costa, López Castro, Arruda, Martí-Aguilar, and Mederos Martín in López-Ruiz and Doak 2019 (including each of their bibliographies). For the Punic Mediterranean, see Quinn and Vella 2014; Machuca Prieto 2019; and the essays by Aliquot, de Lisle, and Hobson, in López-Ruiz and Doak 2019. For the persistence of Phoenician identities in later Roman traditions of the eastern Mediterranean, see Kaldellis 2019. Exceptions to this divide include Krings 1994; Schmitz 2012; Peckham 2014; López-Ruiz and Doak 2019; López-Ruiz 2021.

33. Grainger 1992. Elayi 1998 discusses the question of Hellenization of Phoenician city-states in the Persian period.

region were slow, complex, and indebted to a centuries-long history of interactions between Greeks and Phoenicians.[34] Moreover, these changes did not lead to the immediate abandonment of the Phoenician language, gods, or identity, even if those became hybridized in the new historical context. As this study of Phoenician immigrants demonstrates, the Phoenicians neither ceased to exist nor became fully "Hellenized" in 332 BCE; rather, they continued to contribute to and shape the societies in which they lived.

By centering this study of migration on Phoenicians, this book not only reveals their many and foundational contributions to ancient Mediterranean history but also connects the histories of groups living around the Mediterranean Sea that typically have been studied separately by different academic disciplines. In this way, it contributes to ongoing efforts to view the Mediterranean region as highly interconnected and to study Phoenicians, Greeks, and other groups together.[35] This shift has brought new attention to Mediterranean populations other than the Greeks and Romans and to cross-cultural interactions and their consequences. Yet even those works have still tended to place the Greeks at the center of their investigation, albeit showing how Greeks were shaped by their encounters with non-Greeks.[36] In contrast, this book, by capturing the Phoenicians' histories, strives to model a more comprehensive history of the ancient Mediterranean.

Phoenicians among Others contributes to efforts by scholars to restore the agency of the Phoenicians in transforming the Mediterranean region. Earlier scholarship, influenced by ancient Greek and biblical sources that characterized the Phoenicians as seafarers, traders, human traffickers, makers of silver bowls,

---

34. Notable exceptions are Millar 1983; Bonnet 2015; Aliquot and Bonnet 2015; López-Ruiz 2017; and Bonnet 2019.

35. For examples of works that adopt a Mediterranean perspective, see Horden and Purcell 2000; Abulafia 2011; Broodbank 2013. Of these, only Nicholas Purcell and Cyprian Broodbank specialize on the ancient Mediterranean. For the history of the privileging of Greco-Roman civilizations over all others of the ancient Mediterranean, see Dietler 2010: 27–54. Exceptions that have studied Phoenicians and other groups together are Dietler and López-Ruiz 2009; Bonnet 2015; Celestino and López-Ruiz 2016; Martin 2017; Hodos 2020; López-Ruiz 2021.

36. Such works have focused mostly on colonial contexts by investigating interactions between Greeks and the populations they encountered when they established settlements throughout the Mediterranean and Black Sea regions. The literature I provide here is extremely select and focuses only on recent works: Dougherty 1993 and 2001; Hodos 2006; Tsetskhladze 1999, 2006, and 2008; Donnellan, Nizzo, and Burgers 2016a and 2016b. See also Malkin, Constantakopoulou, and Panagopoulou 2009; Malkin 2011; Capdetrey and Zurbach 2012; Demetriou 2012; Garland 2014; De Angelis 2016 and 2020. The latter, an edited volume on Greeks across the ancient world, does contain an essay by Brien Garnand that compares the Greeks and Phoenicians as migrants.

and as full of guile and deceit, viewed them as conduits of the transfer of ideas from East to West and as passive recipients of Hellenic culture.[37] Such representations of the Phoenicians began to change after Sabatino Moscati, the founder of modern Phoenician studies, put on his 1988 Venice exhibition *I Fenici* (The Phoenicians) and The New York Metropolitan Museum of Art's 2014–2015 exhibition *Assyria to Iberia at the Dawn of the Classical Age*, both of which presented the Phoenicians as a vital link between East and West, especially through their trading and colonizing ventures in the Early Iron Age.[38] Even more recent works have demonstrated the fundamental contributions of the Phoenicians to the culture and history of the region.[39] Moving beyond the reductive view of Phoenicians as mere intermediaries, this book examines their participation in shaping the societies they lived in.

This investigation of the social process of migration that transformed the societies of the ancient Mediterranean during antiquity examines not only the system of laws and regulations, state policies, and values that fostered and limited human movement, but also the agency and contributions of migrants as they sought inclusion in their new societies and attempted to mediate their interactions with their host states. By integrating the voices and histories of immigrants into those of the states and regions to which they traveled, the following chapters demonstrate the diverse and complex ways migrants influenced the development of societies, introduced new institutions, shaped the policies of their home and host states, and, in the process, changed the course of local, regional, and Mediterranean histories.

---

37. These portrayals are especially prominent in Homer and in Ezekiel's prophecy on Tyre. Winter 1995 is a seminal article on the complex representation of Phoenicians in Homer. Van Dijk 1968 and Greenberg 1997 comment on Ezekiel's prophecy on Tyre (26:1–28:26). Herodotus, for whom the Phoenicians were important enough that they appear in the very first passage of his *Histories*, portrays them as cunning merchants, excellent sailors, and inventors of religious ideas inherited by the Greeks. On Phoenicians in Herodotus, see Hütwohl 2020 and Demetriou 2021 and forthcoming a.

38. Moscati 1988b. That year marks the beginning of publications and exhibits on the Phoenicians. See, for example, Gras, Rouillard, and Teixidor 1989; Baurain and Bonnet 1992; Markoe 2000; Sommer 2008; Morstadt 2015; Woolmer 2017; and Bonnet, Guillon, and Porzia 2021, all of whom have published books on the Phoenicians. The journal *Transeuphratène*, which publishes articles and supplements focused on Phoenicians, was founded in 1989. The series Studia Phoenicia began in 1983, and an earlier exhibit on Phoenicians was held in Brussels and Luxembourg (Gubel 1986). The main exhibits after Moscati's 1988 show have been Stampolidis and Karagheorgis 2003 (Museum of Cycladic Art in Athens); Fontan, Gillmann, and Le Meaux 2007 (Institut du monde arabe in Paris); and Aruz, Graff, and Rakic 2014 (The Metropolitan Museum of Art in New York).

39. Bonnet 2015 and López-Ruiz 2021.

I

The Adaptive Repertoires of Immigrants

AMONG THE THOUSANDS of tombstones in the main cemetery of ancient Athens, known today as the Kerameikos, visitors would have found the grave monument of one Antipatros, the son of Aphrodisios. When Antipatros died and was buried in Athens at the turn of the third century BCE, his burial plot was marked with a funerary stele that at first glance looks typical of other Athenian funerary monuments from the same period (Fig. 1.1). Made from marble, it is about 1.42 meters high and 0.48 meters wide and shaped like the facade of a Greek temple with a triangular pediment on top. Below the pediment is inscribed a funerary epitaph, beneath which appears an image carved in low relief that is followed by a longer poem inscribed on the stone.[1] Upon a closer look, each of these features raises questions about the identity of the deceased. The epitaph is written twice, once in Greek and once in Phoenician, and the names of the deceased and his father are different in each language. The image, which has intrigued scholars for decades, depicts a combination of elements that is unusual in Athenian or Greek art, containing some motifs drawn from Phoenician traditions and others that are familiar images on Athenian tombstones. Although the poem is in Greek and follows Greek metrical forms appropriate for a funerary epigram, it is unidiomatic, containing many grammatical mistakes and words that have been found only in this text. Ancient passersby visiting tombs of their ancestors or attending burials in this central Athenian cemetery might have been as mystified by this monument as modern scholars have been.

---

1. See Stager 2005 and Tribulato 2013 for recent analyses of the tombstone. The Greek text can be found in *IG* II² 8388 and the Phoenician in *KAI* 54 (= *CIS* I 115).

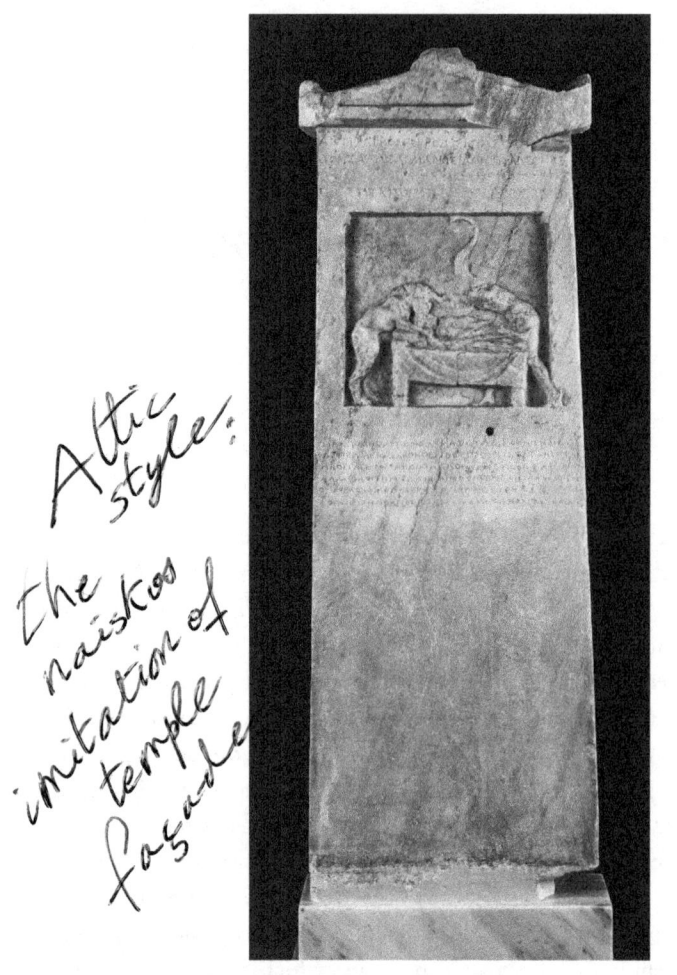

FIGURE 1.1 Grave Stele of Shem——/Antipatros from Ashkelon, c. 300 BCE (*IG* II² 8388) Athens, National Archaeological Museum, Inv. No. Γ 1488. © Hellenic Ministry of Culture and Sports / Hellenic Organization of Cultural Resources Development. Photographer: M. Zorias.

Yet the peculiarities of Antipatros' tombstone and even his use of two different names become less mysterious when understood as products of migration. Antipatros, the epitaph announces to the viewer, was from Ashkelon, a coastal city now located in southern Israel that, while outside the main corridor of Phoenician city-states concentrated in modern Lebanon, is considered to have been a Phoenician city-state at different points in its history, including the rough date of Antipatros' death. His remarkable tombstone was a hybrid product of two different cultures, as was he. As this monument suggests, Antipatros was a

Phoenician immigrant living in Athens who belonged to both the Phoenician and the Greek worlds.

The existence of Phoenician immigrant communities within Greek polities is today visible mostly through bilingual funerary inscriptions on monuments such as Antipatros' tombstone. Despite its baffling look and puzzling imagery, Antipatros' tombstone was not one of a kind but resembles many other grave monuments from cemeteries throughout the polis or city-state of Athens, especially those from Peiraieus, one of Athens' demes or administrative subdivisions and the city's harbor area, where many immigrants resided.[2] Indeed, the stone also resembles funerary monuments from other Greek communities that similarly bear bilingual texts in Greek and Phoenician and unusual iconography that drew from foreign artistic traditions as well as Greek ones. Nor are gravestones the only objects that exhibit such mixed iconography or bear bilingual texts; numerous other dedicated objects in religious sanctuaries and public spaces in various Greek polities also bear witness to a strong Phoenician presence within Greek communities.

As such monuments demonstrate, Phoenician immigrants who lived among Greeks retained and used their native language not only privately but also in public settings. The extant evidence suggests that before the Roman period (146 BCE–330 CE), the Phoenicians were the only group of non-Greeks living in predominantly Greek polities who inscribed their tombstones and dedications in their own language or with bilingual texts, although they sometimes exclusively used Greek.[3] Collectively, monuments such as Antipatros' funerary stele offer a rare glimpse into the lives and experiences of immigrants, recorded in their own voices. Through an examination of primarily bilingual inscriptions on tombstones from fourth-century BCE Athens, third-century BCE Demetrias in Thessaly, and second-century BCE Rhodes, the respective periods in each state that have yielded most of those inscriptions, this chapter explores the lives of individual Phoenician immigrants in three Greek city-states over three centuries.

All three sites were multiethnic polities in those centuries. And while, as attested to throughout this book, there is evidence that Phoenician immigrants lived in various other Greek communities, nowhere were they found in greater

---

2. Whitehead 1986: 83–84. Of the 366 metics whose deme affiliation is known, 69 were registered in Peiraieus.

3. The only exception from Athens is a bilingual inscription in Greek and demotic on a fourth-century BCE tombstone of an individual from Naukratis, in Egypt: *IG* II² 9987 (Ginestí Rosell 2012: 346 no. 493).

concentration than in Athens, Demetrias, and Rhodes.[4] In Athens, as mentioned earlier, right before the beginning of the Peloponnesian War, an estimated 16 to 20 percent of the free male population consisted of male resident aliens, known as metics. By the next century, that percentage was most likely higher, as suggested by the greater number of funerary epitaphs of foreigners from that period and implied by other demographic studies.[5] The immigrants living in Athens at this time had come both from other Greek communities and from non-Greek polities, including Skythians, Thracians, Phrygians, Egyptians, and many Phoenicians from the city-states of Kition, Sidon, Ashkelon, Arados, and Tyre.[6] Based on the

---

4. Several lived on Delos and the nearby island of Rheneia. I discuss the ones from Delos in chapters 3 and 4. Funerary stelae from Rheneia record eight Ashkelonites (*I.Rhénée* 21, 87, 228, 229, 241, 284, 468), three Sidonians (*I.Rhénée* 6, 386, 476) and three Tyrians (*I.Rhénée* 325, 421, 457). Phoenicians also lived in other Greek communities throughout the Mediterranean. Kitians: *IG* XII.9 1128; *I.Milet* VI.2 414. For the presence of other Cypriots (including non-Phoenician speakers) in Greek city-states, see Nicolaou 1986; Pouilloux 1973, 1975, 1976, and 1988; and Raptou 2000. Askhelonites: *IGR* I 550. Aradians: *IG* XII.5 85; *SEG* 18 450; *I.Knidos* I, 23; *SEG* 16 693; *SEG* 28 1037; *I.Kition* 2077. Byblians: *IG* XII.7 305. Tyrians: *AD* 26 A (1971): 34–40 and 36 VI; *I.Oropos* 525 = *IG* VII 417 + 415; *SEG* 44 420; *SEG* 47 1359; *I.Cos Paton* 165a and 341; Bosnakis, *Epigraphes* 87; *IG* XII.6 2.618; *I.Beroia* 160 and 308; *I.Ephesos* 1608b; Cook 1973: 407 no. 41; *I.Kios* 71 (on the name Sillis recorded on this inscription, see Masson 1969: 679–687); *IGUR* II 304; *IG* XII.5 712 7; *IG* XIV 2405 3; *IG* XIV 2554; *KAI* 47 = *IG* XIV 600 = *CIS* I 122bis (I discuss these last two bilingual texts from Malta in chapter 5). Sidonians: *IG* IV 171; *CIJud.* II 1430; *SEG* 31 1577; *SEG* 23 620 and 626; *IG* VII 1760; *IG* VII 3226; *IG* IX.1² 1 24; *IG* XII.5 525; *IG* XII.5 439; *IG* XII.6 2 754; *IG* XIV 2410 2a; *SEG* 32 875; *SEG* 24 1200; *IGUR* I 111; *SEG* 46 910; Maiuri, *Rodi e Cos* 526; *I.Cos Paton* 194a; *I.Cos Segre* (Fun.) EF 644; Bosnakis, *Epigraphes* 40 and 108; *SEG* 18 450; *I.Kaunos* 38 and 152; *Milet* I.3 67, 79, 180 B and *I.Milet* VI.3 1060.

5. For funerary epitaphs, see Vestergaard 2000: 81–89. The census figures reported by Demetrios of Phaleron during his governorship of Athens (317–307 BCE) and recorded in Athenaios 272c that suggest that one of every three residents of Athens was a metic have been challenged by van Wees (2011), who has shown that this figure is inflated as it includes former citizens who had lost their citizenship because they could not meet the property qualification imposed by Demetrios of Phaleron. Instead, van Wees estimates the ratio of citizen to metic as six to one. A recent discussion of Athenian demography (Akrigg 2019, especially chapters 4 and 5), suggests that the population of Athens was stable throughout the fourth century BCE, but that the fifth century BCE saw both a population explosion between the Persian and the Peloponnesian Wars (479–431 BCE) and a contraction during the Peloponnesian War due to the war and a plague that devasted Athens. During the fourth century BCE, Athenians emigrated to other Greek communities and non-Athenians emigrated to Athens, making the metic population relatively higher in the fourth century BCE. See also Hansen 1985 and 1988 and Németh 2001.

6. Bäbler 1998 offers a survey of the archaeological material relating to the presence of foreigners in Athens, including Phoenicians on pp. 115–155. Ginestí Rosell 2012 provides a catalog of all tombstones of foreigners buried in Athens, including Phoenicians on pp. 336–343. Shea 2018 studies tombstones of non-Athenians in Athens mostly from the fifth century BCE. Known tombstones of Sidonian and Kitian immigrants in Athens date mostly to the fourth and third centuries BCE, and those of Aradian, Tyrian, and Ashkelonite immigrants mostly afterward. These include six Kitian tombstones: *IG* II² 9031–9036. Of these, *IG* II² 9031 (= *I.Kition* 162),

number of tombstones and other evidence they left behind, Phoenicians made up the largest percentage of non-Greek foreigners living in Athens in this period.

The population of Demetrias, founded by and named after Demetrios Poliorketes upon his accession to the throne of Macedon (294–288 BCE), was even more diverse. The earliest citizens of the city's approximately twenty-five thousand residents were all internal migrants displaced from urban centers, villages, and towns in the coastal area of central Thessaly, near the modern-day city of Volos, who together constituted this new polity in a process called *synoikism* (a coming together of households).[7] The new city was specifically designed to be one of the capitals of the Macedonian kingdom and situated strategically in a location commanding Thessaly and with access to the sea.[8] These first citizens of Demetrias were soon joined by numerous individuals from other Greek and non-Greek states, who moved here because of Demetrias' thriving port and political importance, including Phoenicians, Syrians, Egyptians, and Greeks from across the western and eastern Mediterranean, whose presence is known from several painted funerary stelae from the third and second centuries BCE.[9] These

---

IG II² 9033 (= *I.Kition* 164), *IG* II² 9034 (= *KAI* 55 = *CIS* I 117), and *IG* II² 9035 (=*KAI* 57) are bilingual. Thirty of the stelae of men and women are from Sidon: *IG* II² 10265a–10286; *Agora* XVII 661; *SEG* 16 182; *SEG* 19 292; *SEG* 29 238; *SEG* 32 309; *SEG* 37 173; *SEG* 51 284; and *CIS* I 121. The bilingual inscriptions are *IG* II² 10270 (= *KAI* 53 = *CIS* I 116), 10271 (= *KAI* 59 = *CIS* I 119); *SEG* 51 284; and *CIS* I 121. Epigraphic evidence for the presence of Tyrians, both funerary and dedicatory, dates from the second and first centuries BCE: *IG* II² 4540, 4698, and 10468–10473. Ashkelonites appear on five tombstones (*IG* II² 8388–8390; *MDAI(A)* 67 (1942) 105, 199 and 187, 405a) and Aradians on four (*IG* II² 8357–8358a, 9205). None of the Tyrians, Ashkelonites, or Aradians inscribed bilingual texts. By the first century BCE, Greek was the most common language even in Phoenician city-states.

7. For the history, archaeology, and epigraphy of Demetrias, see Stählin, Meyer, and Heidner 1934; Milojčić and Theocharis 1976–87; Mili 2015, esp. 197–212; and Stamatopoulou 2018. Population estimates are notoriously difficult, but Marzolff's scale of a population under 100,000 (and c. 25,000) is probably correct (1994: 61).

8. Strabo 9.5.15. On the *synoikism* of Demetrias and its implications for old and new cults, see Kravaritou 2011.

9. The funerary stelae record twelve Sidonians, six Ashkelonites, five Aradians, three Tyrians, and one Kitian. See Vattioni 1982. Three of the twenty-seven securely identified epitaphs of Phoenicians are bilingual, showing the continued use of this language even after it disappears in Athens (*Thess. Mn.* 206–207 no. 31, 290–291 no. 76; Masson 1969: 694–697 [*SEG* 25 681]). For the Phoenician texts, see also Röllig 1972: 1–5. Vattioni 1982 includes in his list of Phoenician residents in Demetrias two men who identify themselves as being from Gaza (*Thess. Mn.* 331–332 no. 109 and 461–462 no. 215), one who identifies as a Phoenician (*Thess. Mn.* 412–413 no. 162), four individuals whose Greek names are likely to be translations of Phoenician names (*Thess. Mn.* 122–127 no. 9—Stratonikos, son of Straton; *Thess. Mn.* 348–350 no. 120—Phila, daughter of Straton; Arvanitopoulos 1929: 28–31 no. 419—Gerostratos and Philostratos, sons of Histiaios), and two others whose patronymics suggest a Phoenician origin (*Thess. Mn.* 281–282 no. 68—Dionytas son of Sathon; Arvanitopoulos 1947–1948: 11

tombstones had been removed from the local cemetery and reused as building material for fortification walls hastily constructed to protect the city from an impending attack in 88 BCE by Mithridates, the king of Pontos.[10] About 40 percent of the individuals commemorated on Demetrias' repurposed tombstones identified as having come from other polities.[11] Most of the Phoenicians appear on epitaphs from the first century of the city's existence, in the third century BCE.

The island of Rhodes, a major trading center from the fourth century BCE onward, was similarly multiethnic and attracted numerous foreigners both as resident aliens and as visitors to its harbors.[12] From the third to the end of the first centuries BCE, texts inscribed on tombstones, dedications in religious sanctuaries, administrative texts related to private associations, and lists of citizens and foreign residents indicate that more than 1,560 foreigners from 214 states lived on Rhodes.[13] Among these were several dozen individuals from Sidon, Kition, Tyre, Ashkelon, and Arados, recorded on Greek and bilingual texts especially in the second century BCE.[14]

---

no. 229—Artemisia Azaratou). Masson 1969 also discusses some of the Phoenicians on the painted stelae from Demetrias. In addition to Phoenicians, funerary inscriptions record the presence of individuals from Egypt, Thrace, Illyria, Boiotia, Epidauros, Kalymnos, Crete, Epeiros, Syracuse, and Naxos, among others. Arvanitopoulos published the epigraphic corpus from Demetrias, including the funerary inscriptions, in a monograph on Thessalian monuments (Arvanitopoulos 1909), a catalog of the painted stelae from Demetrias and Pagasai (Arvanitopoulos 1928), and a series of articles in the journal *Polemon*. For a general overview of the funerary stelae of Demetrias, see Wolters 1979. For a study of how the stelae contribute to the understanding of the history, demographics, and funerary practices of Demetrias, see Stamatopoulou 2016 and 2018.

10. See Helly 1992 for more on the reuse of these stelae and the fortification walls.

11. Stamatopoulou 2018: 363 n. 152, citing Bruno Helly as the source of this information.

12. Already in the 330s, the Athenian orator Lykourgos, who ushered the silver age in Athens, mentions that Rhodes attracted merchants from many places (*Against Leokrates* 14–15). For a history of Hellenistic Rhodes, see Gabrielsen 1997. For the relationship between Rhodes and Rome in this period, see Gruen 1975. For the possible presence of Phoenicians on the island in the Early Iron Age, see Coldstream 1969.

13. See Appendix II in Boyxen 2018: 349–391 and previously Morelli 1956 and Sacco 1980. Most of the foreigners on Rhodes are recorded on inscriptions pertaining to associations (*koina*). Maillot 2015: 143, esp. n. 37, includes comparisons with Athens, where 1,259 foreigners from 340 different places have been identified from among 3,300 sepulchral inscriptions (c. 55% of these date from the fourth to the first centuries BCE: Vestergaard 2000: 81–82) and Delos, where 1,626 foreigners from 254 places are known (Tréheux 1992). In Athens, 8,029 foreigners who came from 380 different territories are known from a variety of sources from the archaic to the Roman period. See Németh 2001: 333.

14. For the presence of Phoenicians on Rhodes, in general, see Ribichini 1995; Kourou 2003; and Lipiński 2004: 145–149. For the presence of Phoenicians mostly in the second century

Despite the multiethnic composition of these and other states, evidence suggests that Phoenician immigrants, as well as immigrants from other polities, had to contend with stereotyping, prejudice, and legal limitations imposed on them by the host states in which they lived. These states' policies, laws, and values regarding immigration and immigrants—known as migration and membership regimes—included prescriptions of pathways to citizenship, definitions of the legal status of a citizen, various legal categories of immigrants, policies to limit or foster migration, and cultural attitudes toward immigrants. Unsurprisingly, given the abundance of extant sources from Athens and Rhodes and their multiethnic composition, most of the evidence regarding the migration and membership regimes of Greek polities comes from these two cities. For example, Perikles' citizenship law of 451 BCE, which famously restricted citizenship to children born to parents who were both Athenians, must have excluded a great number of children born in mixed marriages who would have previously been considered citizens. Although the law was suspended during the Peloponnesian War (431–405 BCE), it was reinstated in 403 BCE after the end of the war and the restoration of Athenian democracy. Intermarriage was allowed until the 380s, when Athens banned it, only to reverse the ban in the second century BCE. These switches back and forth are indicative of attempts to define the civic body in response to different social pressures.

For its part, Athens had one legal category of immigrants—the metic, usually translated as "foreign resident"—which was introduced sometime in the 460s or 450s BCE, perhaps because of a significant increase in the number of immigrants and a desire to define the legal status of citizens in the light of Athens' hegemony in the Aegean in this period.[15] Metics were foreign residents who were present in the city for longer than a prescribed period of time (about a month), subject to a tax called the *metoikion*, and by the fourth century BCE had to register in the city and have a patron (*prostates*) who would represent them before a court of law. Freed persons, their children, and the children of metics automatically acquired the status of a metic.[16] Other limitations were also imposed on metics: they could

BCE, see Fraser 1970 and Amadasi Guzzo 2013: 163–167, who also discuss the Phoenician texts discovered on the island.

15. See Patterson 1981: 134–135. Watson 2010: 271–272 dates the origins of metic status to 451 BCE and relates it to Perikles' citizenship law. See also Kennedy 2014: 12–16.

16. Whitehead 1977: 6–10. See also Niku 2007: 21 and Fraser 2009: 111–112. For the lack of legal distinction between freeborn and freed metics, see Sosin 2016. For discussions of enslaved persons and their manumission in Attica, see Meyer 2009. For the presence of enslaved persons from the Near East, see D. M. Lewis 2011 (none of those mentioned on inscriptions from Athens whose ethnicity is given was securely a Phoenician: 111–113). In an inscribed text of 405 BCE, two individuals are listed as enslaved to Alexippos and Eucheiros, both of whom bear

not own property, vote, hold office, or serve in governing bodies and had limited access to the judicial system. In other respects, they shared some of the obligations of citizens, such as serving in the army and, depending on one's wealth, being liable for the annual religious and military financial contributions to the state known as liturgies—sponsoring a chorus, managing a gymnasium, and maintaining a naval ship (a trireme) and its crew, among others. Metics and other types of immigrants rarely became citizens, which could only happen by decree of the state when they performed an extraordinary service for the state. The migration and membership regime on Rhodes was more complicated in that it included several other formal categories of foreign residents in addition to metics, such as the *epidamoi* (legal residents) and the *matroxenoi* (residents born from a foreign mother).[17] Although neither the specific restrictions on and obligations of each of these immigrant statuses nor the exact distinctions among them are known, they must have affected the lives of people who fell into these legal categories, including their children, since these statuses were inheritable. Even if immigrant groups or families lived in their host state over generations, such legal distinctions and the limitations or obligations that came with them typically demarcated them as immigrants for decades.

Migration and membership regimes and polities' relationships with migrants at both the state and individual level were also shaped by cultural attitudes toward migration, which were popular among both politically influential elite circles and the common people. Such attitudes are more difficult to detect not only because they changed over time and could be conflicting, but also because of the fragmentary state of the surviving evidence. Only from Athens do texts survive that provide detailed accounts of such community opinions on immigration. A number of Athenian fifth- and fourth-century BCE literary texts include statements about the supposed dangers posed by foreigners and immigrants in Athens, the fear that noncitizens were acting or passing as citizens, the precarity of being an immigrant, and even the vulnerability of foreigners who had been granted citizenship.[18] In contrast, other authors saw immigrants and foreigners

---

the personal name Phoinix (*IG* I³ 1032 107 and 274), which could be indicative of their ethnic origin.

17. Boyxen 2018.

18. Select examples of such texts are Euripides, *Ion* and *Medea*; Lysias 12 and 31 (*Against Eratosthenes* and *Against Philon*); ps.-Xenophon, *Constitution of the Athenians* (also known as The Old Oligarch); Demosthenes' *Against Euboulides*, *Against Neaira*, and the many speeches involving Apollodoros, the son of Pasion (possibly a Phoenician), a manumitted person who was granted citizenship by Athens because of his many benefactions to the city. See Trevett 1992 and Fisher 2006.

as potential revenue sources for Athens and wrote in favor of the creation of a system of rewards that would attract immigrants to the city.[19] These differing perceptions of immigrants were publicly acted out in theatrical performances, debated in court cases, and advocated in political treatises, ultimately pervading all levels of Athens' population, including the immigrants themselves.

While laws, policies, and literary sources produced by members of the host state can help uncover the perspectives of these host states and their citizens, they reveal less about the experiences of the immigrants, which can only be discovered through texts produced by the immigrants themselves. Particularly informative in the case of the Phoenicians are the many bilingual inscriptions they commissioned on gravestones and to accompany their dedications in sanctuaries, especially because the Phoenician text, though brief, is often longer and more detailed than the Greek text. Consequently, a comparison of the two texts within the context of the monument on which they were inscribed reveals many details about the lives of Phoenician immigrants that have gone largely unnoticed or unexplored. By focusing on texts and artifacts that were commissioned or produced by Phoenician immigrants, this chapter moves beyond the usual analyses of state-produced sources or texts written by members of the host state to incorporate the voices of the Phoenicians themselves in a new history of migration.[20]

The numerous source materials from Athens, Demetrias, and Rhodes produced by and regarding Phoenician immigrants make these three polities particularly useful sites for studying how those immigrants coped with migration and how their experiences may have varied in different Greek locales. In addition, the chronological range of these source materials—from the fourth to the early first centuries BCE—reveals the similarities across time and space in the adaptive strategies or repertoires that Phoenician immigrants adopted to facilitate their lives as immigrants and encourage a sense of belonging in their new homes. As this chapter will show, three main strategies—name changing, the adoption and incorporation of local customs into immigrants' cultural practices, and immigrants' eventual participation in the civic life of their host city—allowed Phoenician immigrants to become better integrated into their new societies, despite their persistent use of the Phoenician language and script on both private and public monuments. Such integration was a two-way process that involved both the migrants' adaptive repertoires discussed here and the migration and membership regimes of the host states, and eventually led to the acceptance, inclusion, and incorporation of migrants into the civic bodies of their host states.

---

19. Xenophon, *Poroi*.

20. For a similar approach that studies foreign immigrants in Rome, see Abrecht 2020.

Changing Names

Name changing has long been a familiar practice among immigrants, as evidenced by the many stories of immigrants arriving at Ellis Island and either declaring English-sounding names or officials giving them ones.[21] In most instances, such name changes followed later, even in the next generation, and were voluntary. Between the 1910s and the 1960s, for instance, thousands of Jewish New Yorkers facing antisemitism and racism filed petitions to change their names, in most cases retaining the roots or initials of their immigrant names in their adopted American ones: Rosenberg became Rose, Golding became Gould, and Kantrowitz became Kaye. Even as their petitions claimed that their foreign- or Jewish-sounding names were an impediment to finding employment, the Jews of New York who changed their names did not intend to abandon or erase their Jewish heritage and were, in many cases, active members in Jewish communities.[22] Changing their names, as they themselves suggest in their petitions, was a strategy intended to facilitate their social mobility and integration into US society.

This custom appears to have been one of the most common adaptive strategies used by ancient Phoenician immigrants. Many Phoenician immigrants in ancient Greek communities seem to have voluntarily changed their names in one of three ways: translating their Phoenician name into a Greek one, adopting a Greek name unrelated to their Phoenician one, or modifying their Phoenician name by Hellenizing it in spelling or grammar.[23] These permutations of name changing among Phoenician immigrants are illustrated by the Greek and the Phoenician epitaphs on the previously discussed tombstone of Antipatros (Fig. 1.1). Antipatros' Phoenician name was Shem—— (part of his name is missing from the stone); his father's name was Aphrodisios in Greek and Abdashtart in Phoenician; the Greek name of the person who commissioned and set up the inscription was Domsalos, the son of Domano from Sidon, and his Phoenician

---

21. Despite the popularity of stories of immigrants changing their names, the phenomenon has only recently received treatment: Fermaglich 2018 offers the first history of name changing in the United States by focusing on twentieth-century Jewish communities in New York. For name changing, broadly construed, in antiquity, see Parker 2019. Besides Parker's introduction see also Corsten 2019: 147–152, who studies name changes of individuals; Dana 2019, who discusses name changing resulting from interactions between Greeks and Thracians; and Schuler 2019, who does the same for the region of Lykia.

22. The specific examples offered in this paragraph are drawn from Fermaglich 2018.

23. For different types of name changing in southern Gaul, which parallel those practiced by the Phoenicians, see Mullen 2013: 134–135.

name was Domseleh, the son of Domhano.[24] In the first of these differences, Shem—— adopted the Greek name Antipatros to use in Athens, a name that does not correspond to his Phoenician name, which derives from the word meaning "name."[25] In the second, Antipatros' father's Greek name, Aphrodisios, is a close translation of his Phoenician one, as Abdashart means "servant of Astarte," a goddess traditionally identified by both Greeks and Phoenicians with Aphrodite. And in the third, Domseleh Hellenized his name into Domsalos by adding a Greek masculine ending, thereby making his name more easily comprehensible to the Greeks and perhaps himself more easily accepted in Greek society. All three examples reveal ways in which Phoenician immigrants voluntarily changed the way they identified themselves, most likely in an attempt to fit in their new homes.

The common translation of Phoenician theophoric names—names derived from a deity's name, such as Abdashtart—into their Greek equivalents suggests that, through the processes of mobility and migration, Greeks and Phoenicians had become intimately familiar with each other's divinities as well as each other's languages. Indeed, such translations are evident in most of the extant bilingual tombstones from Athens, Demetrias, and Rhodes.[26] For instance, the Greek name Noumenios appears in bilingual inscriptions on two fourth-century BCE tombstones of Kitian immigrants living in Athens as the translation of two different Phoenician names: Benhodesh (*bnḥdš*), meaning son of the new moon, and Mahdash (*mḥdš*), meaning from the new moon (Fig. 1.2).[27] Although these Phoenician names are notably different from each other, Noumenios, which means "child of the new moon," serves as a good translation for both and conveniently happens to be a preexisting Greek name.[28] Similarly, Herakleides, another Greek name, was extremely common among

---

24. *IG* II² 8388: Ἀντίπατρος Ἀφροδισίου Ἀσκα[λωνίτης] | Δομσαλὼς Δομανῶ Σιδώνιος ἀνέθηκε (Antipatros, son of Aphrodisios, the Ashkelonite | Domsalos, son of Domano, the Sidonian dedicated [this]). *KAI* 54: (1) 'nk šm[–] bn 'bd'štrt 'šqlny (2) 'š ytn't 'nk d'mṣlḥ bn d'mḥn' ṣdny (I am Shem[–], son of Abdashtart, the Ashkelonite, [this is what] I have erected, Domseleh, son of Domhano, the Sidonian).

25. Bonnet 2015: 468 suggests that "Shem" evokes some element of patrimony inherited from father to son. But this is a stretch.

26. For translations of theophoric names, see Parker 2017, especially 33–76 and 181–183 (Appendix B).

27. *IG* II² 9034 and 9035. The full texts of these two inscriptions appear in the next section.

28. Masson and Sznycer 1972: 32–33 n. 2; Bentz 1972 s.v. ḥdš; Masson 1994: 167–173. The same translation of Benhodesh into Noumenios appears on a third bilingual inscription in Phoenician and Cypriot-syllabic Greek from Tamassos on Cyprus (*ICS* 215 [=Nicolaou 1971: 15–16 pl. 13]; fourth century BCE).

FIGURE 1.2 Tombstone of Benhodesh/Noumenios the Kitian, 350–300 BCE Paris, Musée du Louvre, AO 4834. © Musée du Louvre / Thierry Ollivier.

both Phoenicians in Kition and Phoenician immigrants in Greek communities and was an apt translation of the Phoenician theophoric name Abdmelqart, meaning "servant of Melqart," a Phoenician god who was identified with the Greek hero Herakles.[29] The name appears on a funerary stele from Rhodes dated to c. 200 BCE of a Kitian whose Phoenician name was Abdmelqart[30] and on two fourth-century BCE tombstones from Athens, again of Kitians, one

---

29. Bentz 1972 s.v. *'bd* and its compounds. Herodotus equated the two divinities (2.44), and other bilingual texts translate one into the other (*KAI* 47). See also Bonnet 1988 and Bonnet and Bricault 2016: 35–43. The identification of the two divinities with each other is discussed in more detail in chapter 5. Based on this onomastic evidence, Herakleides of Salamis on Cyprus, whom Athens honored with multiple awards and who is discussed in chapter 4, was probably a Phoenician (*IG* II³ 1 367).

30. *I.Kition* 172; Fraser 1970: 31 and pl. 12. The Greek reads Ἡρακλείδης | Κιτιεύς (Herakleides, the Kitian). The Phoenician text is *l'bdmlqrt bn 'bdssm bn tgnṣ* (for Abdmelqart son of Abdsasom, son of *tgnṣ*).

with a bilingual epitaph in which the Phoenician text is unfortunately illegible and one inscribed only in Greek.[31] The name of the Phoenician god Eshmoun, who was especially prominent in Sidon, was often translated into that of the Greek god of medicine, Asklepios, and a third-century BCE bilingual inscription from Demetrias suggests that theophoric names deriving from Eshmoun's name, especially common among Sidonians, were translated into Asklepiades.[32] The ease with which the names of gods were translated from one language to the other indicates not only that long-term contacts and interactions among populations rendered them familiar with each other's customs but also made the meaning of their names comprehensible to the Greeks and conveyed shared religious connotations.

Many of the adopted Greek names mentioned thus far, such as Herakleides and Asklepiades, seem to have comprised a corpus of names that were commonly used by Phoenicians who lived in Greek communities and appear often in the pages of this book. On funerary or other types of inscriptions of Phoenicians written only in Greek, names such as Antipatros, Apollodoros, Apollonios, Demetria/Demetrios, Diodoros, Dionysia/Dionysios, Heliodoros, Straton, Theodoros, and Zenon occur frequently.[33] Although these names may

---

31. *IG* II² 9032 and 9033. Both read: Ἡρακλείδης Κιτιεύς (Herakleides, the Kitian). The bilingual one is *IG* II² 9033. See *I.Kition* 164.

32. *SEG* 25 681. The Greek text is Ἀσ]κληπιάδας | [Φιλ]οκλέους | [Σιδ]ώνιος ἱερεύς (Asklepiades, son of Philokles, the Sidonian, a priest). The Phoenician reads ʾšmn[-] ṣdn (Esmnoun — — the Sidonian). Another Sidonian with the same name appears on *Thess. Mn.* 164–166 no. 21. The identification of Asklepios with Eshmoun also appears on a trilingual inscription from Sardinia discussed in chapter 5 (*CIL* 10 7856 = *IG* XIV 608 = *KAI* 66 = *CIS* I 143). See also Ribichini 2009.

33. I include here only names appearing on tombstones from Athens, Demetrias, and Rhodes; the existence of a Herakleides from Kition on Rhodes, as well as two Kitians in Athens, has already been mentioned. Other epigraphic and literary evidence provides many more examples of these same names used for Phoenicians living in Greek communities. Antipatros: *IG* II² 8388 (Ashkelonite); *IG* II² 9484 (Berytian); *Agora* XVII 521 (Kitian); *MDAI(A)* 67 (1942) 220 no. 12 (Kitian); *IG* IX.2 373 (father of a man who identified himself as a Phoenician). Apollodoros: *IG* II² 10265a, 10272, 10280, 10281 (Sidonians); *Thess. Mn.* 208–209 no. 34 (Tyrian). Apollonia: *IG* II² 10267/8 (Sidonian). Apollonios: *IG* II² 10266, 10267/8, 10269, 10284 (Sidonian). Diodoros: *IG* II² 10274 (Sidonian); *Thess. Mn.* 290–291 no. 76 (Kitian). Dionysia: *IG* II² 10275/6 (Sidonian); *Thess. Mn.* 278–280 no. 66 (Sidonian). Dionysios: *IG* II² 10273 (Sidonian); *IG* IX.2 402 (Sidonian); Arvanitopoulos 1949–1951: 160–161 no. 294 (Aradian); *IG* XII.1 104c (Aradian). Demetrios: *Thess. Mn.* 206–207 no. 31 (Aradian). Demetria: *IG* IX.2 373 (wife of a man who identified himself as a Phoenician). Heliodoros: *IG* II² 10270 (Sidonian); *IG* II² 10469 (Tyrian); Arvanitopoulos 1952–53: 9–10 no. 323 (Sidonian). Straton: *IG* II² 141 (Sidonian); *Thess. Mn.* 435–436 no. 185 (Sidonian). Theodoros: *IG* II² 10282 (Sidonian); *IG* II² 10283 (Sidonian). Zenon: *IG* II² 8389 (Ashkelonite); *IG* II² 10285a (Sidonian); Arvanitopoulos 1952–53: 17 no. 347 (Ashkelonite); *SEG* 39 788e (Kitian); *IG* XII.1 32 and 104c and *I.Lindos* 120 (Aradians). Based on typical

have been translations of or sounded like the immigrants' Phoenician names, they were also easily recognizable Greek names that might have allowed Phoenician immigrants to fit in Athenian society and perhaps avoid certain forms of prejudice.

In comparison, the Hellenization of names of Phoenician immigrants, as by the addition of the common *-os* nominative masculine noun ending, would have made their name more Greek-sounding while remaining unmistakably foreign. Similarly, the few Phoenicians who did not change their name but rather transliterated it remained obviously foreigners.[34] The Hellenized name Domsalos, for instance, follows Greek morphology but is identifiable as a non-Greek name. Another example is the common name Abdaios, found on a fifth- or fourth-century BCE bilingual tombstone from Athens of a Phoenician immigrant from Kition.[35] Both the Greek and the Phoenician inscriptions are fragmentary.[36] The name derives from the root *'bd*, meaning "servant," and is often combined with the name of a divinity, such as Abdashtart or Abdmelqart. A different Hellenized form of this name, Abdes is also encountered among the third-century BCE Phoenician community in Demetrias, as is the Hellenized name Sillis (Shillem), one of the most common names within this community.[37] Although such Hellenized names were probably more accessible to the Greeks among whom the Phoenicians lived, their adoption did not erase the Phoenicians' foreign ethnicity and identity.

---

onomastics of Phoenicians among Greek communities, Arvanitopoulos identified several individuals in Demetrias as Phoenicians despite the lack of mention of their civic origin.

34. One such example is Mettounmikim, son of Abdeleb, the Ashkelonite, an immigrant in third-century BCE Demetrias: Arvanitopoulos 1952–53: 18 no. 349. On this name and the name of his father, both unique, see Masson 1969: 693–694. His tombstone is illustrated in Figure 1.7.

35. Masson 1969: 689–690 lists all the instances of Abdaios or Abdes in the Greco-Roman world and suggests that the name on this text should be reconstructed as Abdaios and not Abdes. A baker with a similar name, Abdes, is recorded on a list dating to 401 BCE, also from Athens: *SEG* 12 84. Abdaios was probably a nickname.

36. *IG* II² 9031. The Greek text reads Ἀβδ[-] | Κιτι[εύς] (Abdaios the Kitian). Only the last three letters survive from the Phoenician text (*I.Kition* 162), which is placed underneath the Greek text, and they read *kty*, the toponym of Kition.

37. Abdes: *Thess. Mn.* 327–328 no. 107 (Tyrian). Sillis or Sylllis: *Thess. Mn.* 280–281 no. 67 (Sidonian); *IG* IX.2 1190 (Sidonian) and *SEG* 25 684d (Sidonian); *Thess. Mn.* 294 no. 80 (Ashkelonite). For the names Sillis and Abdes, see Masson 1969: 679–687 and 689–690, respectively. Masson proposes that the Hellenized form Sillis derives from the Phoenician -shillem and is a nickname. Sillis occurs also among Phoenicians (Kitians, Tyrians, Sidonians, and Aradians) who lived in Kition, Kios, and Delos.

Indeed, it seems that Phoenician immigrants did not aim to hide their foreign origins by changing their names because on their monuments they almost always identified themselves by including their home state of origin and continued to use the Phoenician language and script. Rather, as the study of modern name changing has shown, this practice might have made immigrants seem more familiar to their host society and might also have been mobilized at specific moments when immigrants faced antiforeign or anti-Phoenician sentiments to avoid or lessen these feelings. And as suggested by the disparaging comments that Zeno, the founder of Stoicism, was subjected to for being a foreigner and by numerous other sources, Phoenicians did face prejudice. Similarly, speeches written by professional speechwriters and delivered in Athenian courts that mention Phoenician immigrants consistently identified them by their ethnicity as Phoenicians rather than by referring to their city-state of origin, the latter being the overwhelmingly predominant mode of self-identification among Phoenicians.[38] By identifying free non-Athenian Greeks by their state of origin but free non-Greeks by their ethnicity, especially in moments of tension such as court cases, such speeches publicly constructed these Phoenicians as foreign others. Even on Cyprus, where Phoenician city-states had existed for hundreds of years and large Phoenician communities lived within predominantly Greek cities, Phoenicians faced discrimination. For example, Arkeophon from the Cypriot city-state of Salamis, despite his extraordinary wealth, was denied the opportunity to marry the daughter of the king of Salamis in the late fourth century BCE because he was born of Phoenician parents.[39] But regardless of such discrimination, the strategy of voluntarily adopting Greek names might have allowed ancient Phoenicians to acquire more social mobility, job opportunities, prosperity, and stronger professional networks and may have engendered a stronger sense of belonging in their host societies.

---

38. Demosthenes, *Against Phormio* 6 describes the moneylender Theodoros (one of the common Greek names Phoenicians adopted) as a Phoenician, and Isokrates, *Trapezitikos* 4 identifies the banker Pythodoros as a Phoenician. Both cases involve the banker Phormio and his former owner Pasion. Originally enslaved, Pasion worked as banker in Peiraieus. By 394 BCE he had been manumitted and become a metic and was later granted the award of citizenship. When he was too old to work, Pasion handed his bank over to his slave Phormio, and in his will made Phormio the guardian of his youngest son. Phormio even married Pasion's wife to keep the property within the family. Although no source specifies Pasion's or Phormio's origin, scholars have speculated that both came to Athens from the Near East and were perhaps Phoenician. This assumption is based on the stereotype of banking being a common profession among Phoenicians. See Trevett 1992: 1; R. Osborne 2012: 331. For more on Phormio and his family, see chapter 4.

39. Hermesianax fr. 2 in Lightfoot 2009.

Changing Customs

As earlier scholars have shown, when individuals migrate to join host communities composed predominantly of one cultural group, their interactions with the host society and its culture often leads to the creation of new, transcultural goods, customs, and modes of identification.[40] In the case of the Phoenician immigrants who lived in Athens, Demetrias, and Rhodes, the available evidence indicates that such novel, hybrid products and identities both transformed the immigrants themselves and helped integrate them into their host society by creating a cultural space in which they could comfortably operate and interact with their Greek hosts. Texts on tombstones, whether bilingual or not, indicate several such cultural changes among Phoenician immigrants that appeared across Greek communities, indicating that regardless of which city-state they came from and which polity they lived in, migration tended to impact immigrants in similar ways. But once again, the evidence suggests that these modifications did not mean that these immigrants were abandoning their own cultural traditions, any more than adopting Greek names signified jettisoning their Phoenician ones or denying their foreign origins.

One such admixture of cultural practices that can be found on bilingual texts inscribed on tombstones of Phoenician immigrants was the adoption of the Greek custom of identifying oneself with only a patronymic instead of a series of ancestors. Antipatros/Shem——, for example, provided only his father's name when identifying himself, in the Phoenician epitaph as well as the Greek one.[41] So did Mahdash from Kition, mentioned above, who translated his name into Noumenios and provided only his father's name, Pene-Similt, in the Phoenician text.[42] Indeed, most Phoenician immigrants living in Greek polities switched their mode of identification to this Greek habit, whereas in their home states, Carthage, and Egypt they usually included multiple generations of

---

40. Bhabha 1994 discusses the concept of cultural hybridity in colonial contexts. Only more recently has this concept found an audience among migration historians, literary scholars, and sociologists. See, for example, Liu 2015 and Nyongesa 2018 for studies on cultural hybridity among Chinese immigrants and in East African migration literatures, respectively.

41. *KAI* 57 = *IG* II² 9035. Greek: Νουμήνιος Κιτιεύς (Noumenios, the Kitian). Phoenician: *'nk mḥdš bn pnsmlt 'š kty* (I am Mahdash the son of Pene-Similt, a man from Kition).

42. *KAI* 55 = *IG* II² 9034 = *CIS* I 117. Greek: Νουμήνιος Κιτιεύ[ς] (Noumenios, the Kitian). Phoenician: (1) *lbnḥdš bn 'bdmlqrt* (2) *bn 'bdšmš bn tgnṣ 'š kty* (For Benhodesh, son of Abdmelqart, son of Abdshamash, son of *tgnṣ*, a man from Kition).

their ancestors in their self-identifications.⁴³ Notwithstanding switching to this Greek custom even in their Phoenician epitaphs, they still retained several traditional Phoenician habits. For example, in a bilingual funerary inscription from Demetrias, c. 200 BCE, both the Greek and Phoenician text provide the names of the deceased and his father (Demetrios/Abdy, a name similar to Hellenized Abdes, and Hieronymos/Abdalonym) and the state of origin of the deceased. But the Phoenician text begins with a statement identifying that this is the deceased's grave stele (*mṣbt qbry*), a formula that appears on tombstones of Phoenicians both in Athens and in Phoenician city-states.⁴⁴ Although the epitaphs on a fourth-century BCE bilingual funerary epitaph excavated near the Academy in Athens (Fig. 1.3) adopted the Greek custom of providing a short genealogy and translated the name of the deceased Abtanit into the Greek Artemidoros and that of his father, Abdshamash, into the Greek Heliodoros (in the process translating the Phoenician goddess Tanit into the Greek Artemis and Shamash—the Sun—into Helios),⁴⁵ the Phoenician text again begins with a phrase common in Phoenician inscriptions specifying that the stele commemorates the deceased among the living (*mṣbt skr bḥym*).⁴⁶ These texts suggest that changes in funerary customs of Phoenicians living in Greek communities through the adoption of

---

43. See, for example, the dedications and funerary inscriptions of Phoenicians in Carthage and Egypt discussed in chapter 5, as well as *KAI* 36, a Phoenician inscription from Kition. Briquel-Chatonnet 2012: 622–623.

44. *Thess. Mn.* 206–207 no. 31. The Phoenician text reads *mṣbt qbry 'nk 'bdy | bn 'bd'lnm 'rwdy* (This is the grave stele. I am Abdy, the son of Abdalonym, the Aradian). The Greek is Δημήτριος Ἱερω|νύμου Ἀράδιος (Demetrios, the son of Hieronymus, the Aradian). See also Masson 1969: 698; Röllig 1972: 3–4; Vattioni 1979: 159. Other examples are *KAI* 34, 35, 53 (the latter is the Attic epitaph of Artemidoros, the Sidonian, discussed next [*IG* II² 10270]).

45. *IG* II² 10270 = *KAI* 53 = *CIS* I 116. In Greek: Ἀρτεμίδωρος | Ἡλιοδώρου | Σιδώνιος (Artemidoros, son of Heliodoros, the Sidonian). In Phoenician: (1) *mṣbt skr bḥym l'bdtnt bn* (2) *'bdšmš ḥṣdny* (This grave stele [is] dedicated to the memory among the living of Abtanit, son of Abdshamash, the Sidonian). For recent editions of this text, see Hildebrandt 2006: 255–256 no. 80 and Pitt 2022: 37–39. The name Abdtanit is common in Punic nomenclature. This funerary inscription is the only instance that a Sidonian bears this name. See Bentz 1972: 164. *'bd* is rendered in both names as "doros" (gift) rather than servant, the usual meaning of that word, but it nonetheless indicates that the person bearing the name was in a sense dedicated to the specific god the person was named after. Bonnet 2015: 452 records the date as c. 400 BCE. All other editions prefer 350–317 BCE because they relate this epitaph to honors granted to Sidonian traders in Athens in the middle of the fourth century BCE, recorded on *IG* II² 141 and discussed in the chapters that follow. But Sidonian immigrants could have been present in Athens before the awards were granted to the Sidonian traders.

46. For similar examples, see *KAI* 34 and 35, and even the much earlier bilingual inscription in Phoenician and Luwian from Karatepe (*KAI* 26 IV 2–3).

FIGURE 1.3 Tombstone of Abtanit/Artemidoros from Sidon, c. 400 BCE London, British Museum 1937, 1211.1. © The Trustees of the British Museum.

Greek practices coexisted with the retention of some of the religious funerary practices of their home states.

Even though most Phoenicians living in the Greek world adopted the Greek custom of providing only their patronymic, a few exceptions are indicative of the variety of circumstances and the range of choices available to individual immigrants. In contrast to most Phoenicians in Athens, Benhodesh, the Kitian immigrant living in fourth-century BCE Athens who translated his name into the Greek Noumenios, used a longer genealogy to identify himself: he was the "son of Abdmelqart, son of Abdshamash, son of *tgnṣ*, the Kitian" (Fig. 1.2).[47] Similarly, on the island of Rhodes, Abdmelqart, another Kitian who, as mentioned above, had translated his name into Herakleides, included both his father (Abdsasom) and his grandfather (*tgnṣ*) in his genealogy on his tombstone (c. 200 BCE).[48] The

---

47. *KAI* 55 = *IG* II² 9034 = *CIS* I 117.

48. Fraser 1970: 31–32 and pl. 12; *I.Kition* 172. The vocalization of the name *tgnṣ* is not known, and the name is thought not to be Phoenician but either Cypriot or Anatolian: Fraser 1970: 32 n. 5. See also Briquel-Chatonnet 2012: 622–623 and Amadasi Guzzo 2013: 163–166

persistence of this particular Phoenician custom on the tombstones of the Kitian immigrants can be explained as a consequence of the centuries-long coexistence of Phoenicians and Greeks on Cyprus. Living in such mixed communities, in which bilingualism was probably stable, may have made some Kitians more comfortable with continuing their traditions than Phoenicians who came from other city-states.

The example of those Kitians is a strong reminder that immigrants from different Phoenician city-states had different histories and customs. While there were similarities among their adaptive strategies, there were also variations that were contingent on both their state of origin and their new home. A case in point is the evidence that Sidonian immigrants in Athens reused the tombstones of other Sidonians. On an early fourth-century BCE gravestone, for example, an initial Phoenician inscription was erased and reused about fifty years later by Demetrios, a Sidonian, whose name survives on the Greek text inscribed at the top of the stele.[49] The Sidonians of Athens may have resorted to the strategy of reusing burial plots and funerary stones because, as foreigners, they did not have the right to own property (*enktesis*) unless it had been granted to them by the state, which meant they could not be buried in public cemeteries. But the practice of reusing gravestones suggests that once an individual had achieved this rare privilege, other members of his community may have also used the same plot.[50] This perhaps represents another way in which acting as a community may have allowed Sidonians to find ways around the restrictions that they faced because of Athenian legislation regarding foreigners.

Just as coming together as a community may have solved practical problems for Sidonian and other immigrants, it also allowed them to retain burial practices of their homelands that may have likewise facilitated their lives (and afterlives) as immigrants. Some of the inscriptions on tombstones that mention the name of the person who commissioned the stele indicate that it was common practice for the person who erected the tombstone to claim having done so. It might have been considered an honorable act that showed one had fulfilled a duty to their

---

(esp. 164–166) on the connections between *KAI* 55 = *IG* II² 9034 = *CIS* I 117 and the inscription from Rhodes.

49. *SEG* 51 284.

50. Shea 2018: 104–108 explains the proximity of tombstones from individuals from the same city-state as a consequence of immigrant communities (or prominent members of it) having been given the grant of ownership of property. Boyxen 2018: 150–181 makes a similar argument regarding the burial plots of foreigners in Rhodes. The find spots of Phoenicians' tombstones are not always known precisely enough to be able to draw similar conclusions, even though most were discovered in Peiraieus.

family, friends, or community more generally and thus worthy of advertising to the rest of the community. For example, Shem——'s funerary epitaph honors not only the deceased but also the man who buried him, Domseleh the Sidonian, who takes credit for commissioning the stele, even stating that he "dedicated it" (ἀνέθηκε), an unusual verb on funerary epitaphs. In another example from Athens, a third-century BCE bilingual funerary epitaph of a Sidonian woman named Asept provides only her transliterated name, father's Hellenized name, and place of origin in Greek but in Phoenician includes details about the person who erected the tombstone for her.[51] This man, Yatonbaal (who was probably also Sidonian given his father's name, Eshmnousaloh, as theophoric names deriving from the god Eshmoun are predominantly Sidonian), informs the Phoenician readers of this tombstone that he was the one who commissioned it and also identifies as a priest of the god Nergal, originally a Mesopotamian deity adopted by the Phoenicians.[52] Such inscriptions indicate that civic identity remained an important part of one's immigrant identity, worthy of expression to both one's Greek and one's Phoenician-speaking audience. So too did one's profession, as in the case of Yatonbaal, who provided his professional identity as a priest. More broadly, these texts illustrate that the wider Sidonian community seems to have played an integral role in commissioning commemorative grave monuments for members of the larger Phoenician immigrant community. In turn, such monuments brought the community together in commemorating the dead.

It may even have been the case that Phoenician individuals, perhaps invested with a religious function, traveled from Phoenician states to provide the appropriate funerary rites to immigrants who died abroad. Such a practice, which would have arisen only if migration was common enough to warrant it, is alluded to on the epigram that adorns Shem——'s tombstone (Fig. 1.4), which describes the imagery on the relief and refers to events associated with the deceased's death and funerary rites:

> *Let no one wonder at this image—*
> *that on one side of me a lion and on the other a prow are stretched out.*

---

51. *IG* II² 10271 = *KAI* 59 = *CIS* I 119. In Greek: Ἀσεπτ Ἐσυμσελήμου Σιδωνία (Asept, daughter of Esymselos, the Sidonian). In Phoenician: (1) *'nk 'spt bt 'šmnšlm ṣdnt š ytn' ly* (2) *ytnbl bn 'šmnṣlḥ rb khnm 'lm nrgl* (I am Asept, daughter of Eshmounshillem, the Sidonian. This is [what] was erected for me by Yatonbaal, son of Eshmounsaloh, the high priest of the god Nergal).

52. On the god Nergal, see Chiodi 1998. While previous scholarship has considered this inscription as evidence that Nergal was worshiped in Athens (Garland 2001: 109; Demetriou 2012: 208–209), it is also likely that he was not, and that Yatonbaal did not reside in Athens and traveled there to commission the funerary stone for Asept.

The Adaptive Repertoires of Immigrants 35

FIGURE 1.4 Close-up of Shem——/Antipatros' tombstone with the relief and epigram (*IG* II² 8388)
Athens, National Archaeological Museum, Inv. No. Γ 1488. © Hellenic Ministry of Culture and Sports / Hellenic Organization of Cultural Resources Development. Photographer: M. Zorias

> For a hateful lion came, wishing to tear my things asunder.
> But friends warded [it] off and built me a tomb here,
> those whom I desired affectionately, coming from a sacred ship.
> I left Phoenicia and I am a body hidden here in this earth.[53]

The form of the text is Greek but not the content. The spelling is peculiar, the phrasing obscure, and the grammar awkward, as is typical of a bicultural product, suggesting that it was perhaps composed by someone for whom

---

53. *IG* II² 8388: μηθεὶς ἀνθρώπων θαυμαζέτω εἰκόνα τήνδε
ὡς περὶ μέν με λέων, περὶ δὲγ πρῶιρ' ἰγκτετάνυσται·
ἦλθε γὰρ εἰχθρολέων τἀμὰ θέλων σποράσαι·
ἀλλὰ φίλοι τ' ἤμυναν καὶ μου κτέρισαν τάφον οὔτηι
οὓς ἔθελον φιλέων, ἱερᾶς ἀπὸ νηὸς ἰόντες·
Φοινίκην δ' ἔλιπον τεῖδε χθονὶ σῶμα κέκρυνμαι.

Greek was a second language who was trying to convey, in Greek, ideas and customs that were Phoenician.[54] And although the content of the poem, which begins with "Let no one wonder at this image," seeks to explain the image, it remains mysterious without an understanding of its specific cultural references. Although interpretations of the epigram have varied, scholars agree that it (and the accompanying relief) reflects Phoenician burial traditions translated into Greek.[55] The reference to the scattering of one's things, for instance, may reflect a Phoenician (and, more generally, Near Eastern) anxiety about having one's bones scattered rather than buried.[56] The assertion at the end that the deceased is now a buried body could be read as expressing relief that the body had received a proper burial. A literal reading of the epigram would suggest that the deceased's friends—Domseleh may have been one of them—came from a sacred ship with the specific purpose of commemorating him with a tombstone in Athens. Perhaps these men and the sacred ship had the official function of ferrying across the sea Phoenicians who would be able to perform the customary rites for immigrants who died while living abroad, enabling Phoenician immigrants to maintain the religious customs of their homeland.[57] Such a role would not be unusual: other examples from among immigrants in Athens suggest that non-Athenians were responsible for commemorating their fellow immigrants.[58] That Domseleh was an individual from a different Phoenician city-state (Sidon) than Shem—— (Ashkelon) suggests a similarity of burial rites across Phoenician city-states and reveals a cooperative structure that served immigrants who were Phoenicians even if from different city-states of origin.

---

54. Recent work on this inscription includes Barbanera 1992; Stager 2005; Hölscher and Möllendorff 2008; R. Osborne 2011 and 2012; Tribulato 2013; Bonnet 2015: 462–471. For the ethnicity of the composer, see R. Osborne 2012: 324–330 and Tribulato 2013: 466–470, with further bibliography.

55. Stager 2005: 442–443 argues that Shem—— died at sea because the goddess Astarte, with whom both the lion and the ship are related, did not favor Shem—— and caused his shipwreck. Tribulato 2013 points out several problems with Stager's interpretation.

56. Tribulato 2013: 478–480.

57. Instead, Tribulato 2013: 480–483 suggests that the "sacred ship" symbolized the trip to the Underworld.

58. Shea, who discusses these topics throughout his 2018 dissertation, finds that at the end of the sixth century BCE, Timomachos, probably a Naxian, commissioned the tombstone of Anaxilas from Naxos in the Kerameikos cemetery (*IG* I³ 1357; Shea 2018: 95–101). Maillot 2012: 254–255 and Ismard 2010: 354–367 also note that certain types of social associations in Athens were responsible for organizing funerals for their members.

The practice of combining Greek and Phoenician elements in funerary customs, perhaps to try to make Phoenician practices comprehensible to a Greek audience, is also visible on the enigmatic image on Shem——'s tombstone. The relief depicts a corpse lying on a bed, with the prow of a ship emerging in the background, a lion menacingly hovering over the corpse on one side, and a nude man reaching over the dead body as though to protect it from the lion on the other side (Fig. 1.4).[59] As in the epigram that follows this image, the iconography and composition of the relief exhibits both Attic and Phoenician motifs. The lion, for instance, appears in classical Attic funerary art, as does the ship, but the depiction of a corpse is an unusual element in such images. And, though encounters between lions and heroes are common in both Phoenician and Greek art, they are an uncommon funerary motif. Still, Greek viewers might have interpreted this image as representing one of the most popular myths of the twelve labors of Herakles, his fight with the Nemean lion, which was a popular representation on Attic vases and even temple decoration.[60] Athenians viewing this image would have made connections that would have helped them understand some parts of the image but not others, and Phoenician viewers might also have had difficulties fully comprehending the intended meaning of the image because the representation was carved following Greek aesthetic ideals.[61] Phoenician immigrants in Athens seem to have been comfortable operating in this hybrid space that existed between two worlds. Such images as the one on Shem——'s stele and others discussed below reflect the desire both to maintain the rites and rituals of their homeland and to be understood by and included in Athenian society.

These examples and others like them demonstrate how the form and imagery of tombstones could appeal to both Greeks and Phoenicians and allow them to retain their own traditions, adopt those of their host state, and in the process express hybrid cultural identities. All their tombstones reflect Greek funerary styles that were popular in Athens, Demetrias, and Rhodes. For instance, the funerary stelae of the two Kitians, Benhodesh (Fig. 1.2) and Mahdash, and that of Abtanit the Sidonian (Fig. 1.3) were tall, narrow, and rectangular, topped with

---

59. Because the prow of the ship seems to grow out of the man's neck, many scholars have believed that the man is an amalgam of a creature, half man, half ship: see Hansen in *CEG* 596; Bäbler 1998: 136–137; Fantuzzi in Fantuzzi and Hunter 2002: 439; Hölscher and von Möllendorff: 2008; Bruss 2010: 402; R. Osborne 2011: 126. Noting that mixed creatures were always composed of living organisms in antiquity and more closely examining the stone, Barbanera 1992 and Stager 2005: 434, followed by Tribulato 2013: 462 n. 5, have instead argued that the prow of the ship and the man are distinct.

60. Tribulato 2013: 476–478.

61. See also R. Osborne 2011 and 2012.

an elaborate acanthus finial, and with two rosettes on the shaft, a common type in fourth-century BCE Athens.[62] The shape of the grave stele of Shem—— is in a different but still typically Attic style: the *naiskos*, with a triangular pediment on top imitating the facade of a temple (Fig. 1.1). Similarly, most of the extant tombstones from Demetrias are shaft stelae with either a pedimented top (like a *naiskos*) or sometimes a horizontal top, but with a painted rather than a carved image, like most gravestones from Demetrias. Although the funerary stelae of the Phoenician immigrants in Greek communities were probably locally purchased and adhered to local styles, they would have seemed similar enough to Phoenician funerary stelae that Phoenician immigrants most likely found them easy to adopt as their own. Phoenician votive stelae from Sardinia ranging from the sixth to the third centuries BCE greatly resemble the *naiskos* shape, rendering the Greek tombstones familiar to the Phoenicians in form.[63] Moreover, by the fourth century BCE, art in their homeland exhibited Persian, Egyptian, and Greek influences, often presenting Phoenicians as dressed in Persian or Greek dress and headgear, with an Egyptian winged disk and a uraeus—a stylized cobra that symbolized sovereignty in Egypt—decorating the top of the stele and hanging down on either side.[64] The eclecticism that characterized Phoenician art and the resemblance of Greek styles to Phoenician ones may have facilitated the adoption of Greek styles by Phoenician immigrants living in Greek communities.

Other types of adoptions of Greek art can be found among the funerary stelae of Phoenician immigrants, which ultimately modified and added artistic motifs to familiar Phoenician ones without leading to their erasure. A partially preserved marble *naiskos*-style tombstone with fragmentary Greek and Phoenician inscriptions, dating from the early fourth century BCE and discovered in Peiraeius, borrows features from both Phoenician and Attic art: the deceased was probably depicted frontally, given the location of the arm and hand on the surviving fragment; is draped in Attic fashion; and holds something in his left hand, perhaps a scroll (Fig. 1.5).[65] A frontal rather than profile or three-quarter view is atypical in Attic funerary reliefs, but those found in Phoenician city-states often depict

---

62. *IG* II² 10270 = *KAI* 53 = *CIS* I 116 (Abdtanit/Artemidoros); *KAI* 55 = *IG* II² 9034 = *CIS* I 117 (Benhodesh/Noumenios); and *KAI* 57 = *IG* II² 9035 (Mahdash/Noumenios).

63. Moscati 1988a illustrates the variety of Phoenician stelae from across the Mediterranean.

64. Martin 2017: 115–117 offers some examples of these influences.

65. *CIS* I 121.The Phoenician text names the deceased as Abdeshmoun, son of Shalloum, son of . . . (*'bd'šmn bn šlm bn* ⌈ . . . ⌉); the Greek only preserves a single letter, a Ξ, which scholars have assumed was the last letter of the word Φοῖνιξ, designating the ethnicity of the deceased. See Xagorari-Gleisner 2009: 114; Bonnet 2015: 458. The name Abdeshmoun points to perhaps a Sidonian origin of the deceased. For a possible reconstruction, see Xagorari-Gleisner 2009: 115.

FIGURE 1.5 Marble stele of Abdeshmoun, early fourth century BCE
Athens, Archaeological Museum of Peiraieus MP 3580. © Hellenic Ministry of Culture and Sports / Hellenic Organization of Cultural Resources Development.

figures frontally, raising their right hand in greeting, and holding some object in their left hand.[66] The hybridity of Phoenician art may have enabled immigrant communities to maintain a sense of cultural identity within their new homes.

A final grave stele from Athens not only showcases these changes in customs but also offers a rare example of intermarriage among common people rather than political elites, another way in which individuals who moved and migrated to new places formed new networks that connected the ancient Mediterranean world. The early fourth-century BCE *naiskos* tombstone of Eirene of Byzantion, also discovered in Peiraieus, depicts a three-quarter view of a seated woman, whom scholars have traditionally identified as the deceased, lifting her veil (the gesture of *anakalypteria*) and looking at another woman who is standing and holding an infant in her arms, perhaps a daughter and grandchild who survived her (Fig. 1.6). While the dress of the seated woman is typically Attic,

---

66. See Moscati 1988a for some examples.

FIGURE 1.6 Tombstone of Eirene from Byzantion, early fourth century BCE
Athens, Archaeological Museum of Peiraieus MP 3582. © Hellenic Ministry of Culture and Sports / Hellenic Organization of Cultural Resources Development.

the short-sleeved dress of the standing woman recalls Near Eastern dress.[67] The monument bears two short inscriptions underneath the pediment of the *naiskos*.[68] The Greek text is written in the Megarian dialect, which was spoken in Byzantion, founded by the city-state of Megara in the seventh century BCE, demonstrating that non-Athenian Greeks living in Athens also retained their linguistic identities on their tombstones.[69] Although Eirene the Byzantian was probably an immigrant in Athens of Greek ethnicity, the companion text in Phoenician indicates that her husband was probably a Phoenician speaker who commissioned this Attic grave relief for his Greek wife. The glimpse into the life

---

67. Xagorari-Gleisner 2009: 117–120, and esp. 118 on the dress.

68. *IG* II² 8440 = *KAI* 56. The Greek text reads Ε[ἰ]ρήνη Βυζαντία (Eirene the Byzantian). The Phoenician text is *hrnʿbʿlt bznty*.

69. Ginestí Rosell 2012: 21–139.

of immigrants in Athens offered by this bicultural monument reflects a shared desire to retain and declare their ties to the culture of their birth even while borrowing from those of others.

The production of such hybrid artifacts by immigrants was not specific to Athens but was common in Demetrias, where the painted tombstones of Phoenician immigrants included both adoptions of local artistic forms and incorporations of themes popular in Phoenician city-states. One of the most prominent motifs on the tombstones of Phoenician immigrants found here was banqueting: several of the tombstones of Phoenician speakers represent the deceased as banqueters, such as those of Mettounmikim from Ashkelon (Fig. 1.7), Asklepiades the Sidonian, Demetria and Histiaios from Sidon, Dorotheos from Ashkelon, Dionysios from Arados, and Abdes from Tyre (who was married to the Argive Dorkas, yet another instance of intermarriage within the broader immigrant

FIGURE 1.7 Painted funerary stele of Mettounmikim of Ashkelon from Demetrias, third century BCE

Volos, "Athanasakeion" Archaeological Museum Λ 349. © Hellenic Ministry of Culture and Sports / Hellenic Organization of Cultural Resources Development. Photographer: Maria Stamatopoulou.

community).⁷⁰ Although banquet scenes were a popular iconographic motif on Demetrias' tombstones regardless of the ethnicity of the deceased, they appear to have held a special significance for Phoenician immigrants, as banqueting also appears on funerary monuments in Sidon and the ritual feast of the *marzeaḥ*, a religious festival common among Phoenicians, had been imported into Greek polities and practiced by Phoenician immigrants.⁷¹ Whereas banqueting scenes may have carried connotations of Phoenician practices for the Phoenicians who commissioned or saw these painted stelae, it also connected them to a local tradition common at Demetrias. They offer yet another example of bicultural representations that could be read and understood differently by different viewers and both reflected and facilitated the Phoenicians' civic presence in Demetrias.

The transference of religious traditions from their homeland to their host states also helped Phoenician immigrants living in Greek communities to maintain their traditions, often in modified ways, rather than abandon them. The religious flexibility that was common in the ancient Mediterranean region facilitated Phoenician immigrants' translating their theophoric names into appropriate Greek names and also frequently entailed syncretisms—the amalgamation of divinities. Yet Phoenician immigrants also introduced and maintained the worship of their own Phoenician gods within Greek societies. In addition to the worship of the god Nergal in Athens mentioned in the inscription on Asept's tombstone, the worship of other Phoenician deities is documented in Athens, Demetrias, and Rhodes, and most probably wherever there were Phoenician immigrants. A fourth to third-century BCE dedicatory inscription from Peiraieus inscribed on a marble altar exclusively in Phoenician records the dedication of the altar to the god Sakon, whose worship was common in Sidon and Carthage.⁷² This inscription follows Phoenician epigraphic conventions by providing a longer

---

70. Arvanitopoulos 1952–1953: 18 no. 349; *Thess. Mn.* 164–166 no. 21; *Thess. Mn.* 276–277 no. 64; Arvanitopoulos 1952–53: 8–9 no. 322; Arvanitopoulos 1949–51: 160–161 no. 294; *Thess. Mn.* 327–328 no. 107. Another element that appears frequently on the Phoenician tombstones was a painted knotted filament. For example: *Thess. Mn* 206–207 no. 31, 208–209 no. 34, 294 no. 80, 412–413 no. 162, 435–436 no. 185, 437 no. 187, 444–445 no. 195.

71. The festival of the *marzeaḥ* is discussed in more detail in chapter 3. Fabricius 1999: 48–49 has suggested that the banquet motif was especially popular among foreigners or individuals of low social status, but Stamatopoulou 2016: 432–433 shows that this was not the case. See also Couilloud in *I.Rhénée* pp. 161–166 and Baslez 2006.

72. *KAI* 58 = *CIS* I 118. The Phoenician text reads *mzbḥ z 'š ynt bnḥdš bn b'lytn hšpt · bn 'bd'šmn ḥḥtm · l'skn 'dr · ybrk* (This is the altar that Benhodesh built, son of Baalyaton the suffete, son of Abdeshmoun the seer, for Sakon the powerful. Blessings be to him). The mention of suffetes, one of the legal offices in Carthage, and the frequency of the worship of this god there may suggest that Benhodesh was Carthaginian, though the office is also attested in fourth-century BCE Kition and third-century BCE Tyre. For the function of this office in Phoenician city-states, see

genealogy as well as the profession of the dedicant, as on Asept's tombstone. As will be discussed in more detail later in the book, other temples in Athens were dedicated to Phoenician gods, such as Baal and Astarte. In addition, several other tombstones record Phoenician priests who were living in Greek communities. From Rhodes comes a second-century BCE dedication from a religious sanctuary by a certain Baalmilk, who was a temple official known as the "bridegroom of Astarte," an office common on Cyprus and in Carthage, suggesting that the goddess Astarte may have been worshiped on Rhodes.[73] In Demetrias, two of the third-century BCE funerary stelae of Sidonians specify that they were priests. One is the bilingual inscription commemorating Asklapiades/Eshmoun——, mentioned above, which specifies only in the Greek text that the deceased was a priest, and the other that of Dionysios son of Dionysios, which was written only in Greek.[74] Although these terse texts provide no further details, not even the name of the god(s) these men served as priests, they reflect that in multiethnic communities, preserving the religious traditions of one's culture was of paramount importance to immigrants.[75] In multiethnic communities, where a

---

Teixidor 1979. For Carthaginians among Greek communities, see Dridi 2019b. See also Bonnet 2015: 459–460.

73. The Greek text is]ς Μυλ[.]ι | [χαριστή]ριον. The Phoenician (*KAI* 44) is (1) *b'lmlk bn mlkytn* (2) *mqm 'lm mtrḥ 'štrny bn ḥ[...]* (Baalmilk, son of Milkyaton, temple official, bridegroom of Astarte, son of H——). *I.Kition* 173 includes this text in a list of possible Kitians attested on Rhodes. For the suggestion that these are Kitians, see Fraser 1970: 33–34. The Greek name (Myl—— has been reconstructed as the name of the deity (Mylite, a Greek name for Astarte, according to Herodotus 1.131), but it is just as possible that it is either the dedicant's name or his father's. On the office of the bridegroom of Astarte, see Amadasi Guzzo 2013: 167. A koinon of the Lapathiastai, named after Lapethos, a polity on Cyprus, is attested on Rhodes from the Hellenistic period: *IG* XII.1 867 and *Clara Rhodos* 2 (1932) 203 36.

74. *SEG* 25 681 and *IG* IX.2 402. Another bilingual dedication in Rhodes does not specify the god to whom it was dedicated: Fraser 1970: 35 (= *KAI* 45 = *I.Kition* 174). Only two letters survive from the Greek text (-ις). The Phoenician text reads (*KAI* 45): *'š ndr trt[' bn 'bd'š]|mn bn b'lytn bn [...]* (This is what *trt*, son of [——]mun, son of Baalyaton, son of... has vowed). The name *trt* is attested in Abydos in Egypt and might indicate an Egyptian rather than a Phoenician, or perhaps a Cypriot since Egyptian names were also common among families on Cyprus: Donner and Röllig 1973: 62 no. 45. Lipiński 2004: 148 suggests that *trt* is a transcription of the common Rhodian name Trityllos. See also *LGPN* I: 448.

75. Other non-Greek priests are also attested among the painted stelae of Demetrias. The most famous of these is Ouaphres (a Hellenized Egyptian name), son of Horus, from Bousiris in Egypt, who is identified as a priest of Isis: *Thess. Mn.* 248–252 no. 52. The figured scene on his tombstone shows a beardless male, with a shaved head—typical of an Egyptian—standing in profile view. He wears a white linen robe and holds a *phiale* in his right hand from which he pours a libation over an altar, holds another object in his left hand, and has a situla attached to his hip. He gazes upward into a figure, now worn off, probably an image of a god. These iconographic motifs have some parallels in depictions of other Isiac priests, especially in the Roman world. See Stamatopoulou 2008: 251–253. Decourt and Tziafalias 2007 discuss the Isiac cult in

multiplicity of Greek and a variety of non-Greek cults coexisted, priests were instrumental in facilitating the worship of divinities prominent in their home state and around which immigrant communities could rally. The presence of Phoenician (and other) deities in Greek polities and their temples, as well as their priests and the communities they served, ultimately also changed the physical and social landscapes of the host societies for immigrants and nonimmigrants alike.

Participating in Civic Institutions

Despite these adaptive strategies that provided Phoenician immigrants with a sense of belonging in their new homes and led to their further acceptance and incorporation in their host states, laws and policies, local attitudes toward immigrants, and the immigrants' own desire to retain elements of their civic or ethnic identities kept immigrants from being completely integrated into a polity. Although the legal constraints of bearing an immigrant status—whether as a metic or not—prevented immigrants from participating in several of the civic institutions of the polities in which they lived, such restrictions were often lessened or removed by the host states as their migration and membership regimes changed, especially as Greek city-states began to lose their own autonomy to Rome from the second century BCE onward. In Athens, for instance, starting in the last third of the second century BCE, the state allowed foreigners living there to participate in Athenian institutions once reserved exclusively for citizens, such as the *ephebeia*, a military and cultural education for young men known as the *epheboi*; athletic competitions; and intermarriage, especially between Athenian men and non-Athenian women, which had been made illegal in the 380s BCE.[76] The wide participation of immigrants in these institutions indicates the changing attitudes toward immigrants and foreigners, perhaps in the context of Rome's conquest of the Greek peninsula. Through their inclusion in civic institutions, immigrants began to be recognized as invaluable members of the polities they lived in, even though they were not citizens. Athenian records listing the names of ephebes and their officers from the first century BCE include Sidonians, Aradians,

---

Thessaly in general and on pp. 337–342 and 349 in Demetrias in particular. A unique second-century BCE inscription that records a sacred law reveals the worship of a complex of Greek and non-Greek (Levantine) divinities in other places in Thessaly. See Decourt and Tziafalias 2007 and 2015; Parker and Scullion 2016. Carbon 2016 suggests that these laws may have been issued by a Semitic association in Larisa.

76. See Niku 2007: 20 and 66–70 and Oliver 2010: 156 and his appendix of Athenian funerary inscriptions indicating intermarriage between Athenian men and non-Athenian women (162–163).

Ashkelonites, and Berytians,[77] as do lists of young men enrolled in the *ephebeia* from Delos from the late second century BCE, when the island was administered by Athens.[78] Victors' lists from athletic games held in Athens and elsewhere from the second and first centuries BCE also contain names of foreigners, including Sidonians, Tyrians, and Kitians.[79] These Phoenician immigrants' participation in the Athenian *ephebeia* and athletic contests, starting in the second century BCE, was instrumental in promoting their inclusion and a stronger sense of belonging in their host state.

Intermarriage among Greeks and Phoenician immigrants is more difficult to detect from the available sources, but several tombstones of Sidonian women from the second and first centuries BCE suggest that they were married to Athenian men, a practice that had become legal in the second century.[80] A Sidonian woman buried in the second century BCE, for example, is identified as the daughter of Theodoros and the wife of Eunikos, the son of Kallatianos; another was Dionysia the daughter of Herakleides and the wife of Dioskourides, the son of Acharnes, who died in the first century BCE.[81] Although the epitaphs do not specify where the women's husbands were from, that a state of origin is absent and that their names do not appear elsewhere as Greek names adopted by Phoenicians (whereas the women's fathers' names do) indicate that their husbands may have been Athenian. Intermarriage between immigrants and members of the host society led to the further integration of immigrants, including through their potential children, who might even have been citizens if they had a Greek father.

In Rhodes, Phoenician immigrants not only intermarried with Rhodians but also sought membership in private associations, a characteristic institution of Rhodian society. Especially in the Hellenistic period, Rhodian civic society was overlaid with private associations that created networks among their members. Membership in these associations was not restricted to citizens, and both citizens

---

77. *IG* II² 960, 1008, 1011, 1028, 1043, 1960; *SEG* 15 104; *SEG* 39 187; *SEG* 41 115.

78. *I.Délos* 1923, 1925, 1937, 2593, 2598, 2599. These lists also include Tyrians. Berytian ephebes are also attested at Delphi: *FD* III.2 24.

79. *IG* II² 2314–2316; *SEG* 16 182; and *SEG* 41 115. Tyrians and Sidonians are also included on victor lists from games held outside Athens: *I.Oropos* 525 = *IG* VII 417 + 415; *AD* 26 A (1971): 34–40; *IG* VII 1760.

80. Intermarriage among immigrant communities was not uncommon, as evidenced by the example of the Byzantian Eirene, who had married a Phoenician. Similarly, an Aradian woman was married to a Sidonian man: *IG* II² 8358.

81. *IG* II² 10282 and *IG* II² 10275/6. Other Sidonian women who were probably married to Athenian men are recorded on *IG* II² 10273 and 10284.

and different categories of immigrants could be members of the same association. Such associations acted as mediators between the state and their individual members, forming connections with the political elites and state officials through which they appear to have been able to influence state policies.[82] Several sources indicate that Phoenician immigrants living in Rhodes were members of these associations, such as two undated inscriptions that record the honors given to a certain Protimos, a benefactor (*euergetes*) of an association who is identified as a Sidonian, and subscription lists for an association that includes among its members a Tyrian woman, a Sidonian man, and Laodikeian men and women.[83] Membership in an association afforded immigrants an opportunity for inclusion and the ability to interact on an equal basis with citizens, constructing in the process stronger professional, social, and political networks and allowing them to participate even in politics.[84] Whereas these associations were private, the public benefactions that individuals performed, such as paying for the refurbishment of buildings or dedicating statues, were visible not only to members of the association but to all residents of the polity, indicating that their immigrants members were important members of their host states' civic society.

Over time, immigrant families continued to participate in the civic institutions and became increasingly involved in the civic life of their host states. Inscriptions regarding such participation by two different Phoenician families demonstrate the ways in which migration could lead to social mobility and eventual social integration. The first is the family of the Aradian Zenon (a typical Phoenician name), the son of Naoumos (a Hellenized Phoenician name), who made several offerings (what exactly is not known) in various Greek temples on Rhodes.[85] These offerings bore inscriptions so that passersby would know who had given these gifts to the gods. In two such inscriptions from c. 225 BCE, one dedicated to Zeus Soter and the other to Athena Lindia, Zenon specified that he was a *proxenos*, an honorary office that had been granted to him by the state of Rhodes for good deeds he had performed for the state and which entailed his being responsible for Rhodian citizens in his home of Arados.[86] As will be

---

82. Thomsen 2020 offers the most recent study of Rhodian associations that views them as a corporate polis existing within the state. For the participation of noncitizens in Rhodian associations, see Boyxen 2018: 96–149.

83. For Protimos, see Maiuri, *Rodi e Cos* 192 and 193. For the subscription lists, see *SEG* 43 526.

84. Boyxen 2018: 122–149.

85. Maillot 2015: 171 also discusses this family.

86. *IG* XII.1 32: Ζήνων Ναούμου | Ἀράδιος πρόξενος | Διὶ Σωτῆρι (Zenon, son of Naoumos, the Aradian, a proxenos, [dedicated this] to Zeus Soter). *I.Lindos* 120: Ζήνων Ἀράδιος πρόξενος ὑπὲρ τῶν παιδίων | Βατοῦς καὶ Ἡρακλείτου καὶ Ῥοδιάδος | Ἀθάναι Λινδίαι (Zenon the Aradian, a

The Adaptive Repertoires of Immigrants an honorary office

discussed in more detail in the following chapters, being a proxenos implied that Zenon had become part of a larger Greek institution that was intended to develop connections between states. Being given the duties of a proxenos also implied that Zenon was not a permanent resident on Rhodes, even if he visited the island frequently. His dedication to Athena Lindia, a goddess worshiped prominently in the city-state of Lindos but also on the island of Rhodes more generally, reports that it was made on behalf of his children and suggests that Zenon had such close ties to Rhodes that he had chosen to name his daughter Rhodias after the island's name.

Two other dedications made by second-generation immigrants who may have been members of the same family suggest that a family's mobility could lead to more permanent migration over time. These dedications were made by Dionysios, the son of Zenon, here described as an Aradian and a proxenos, and his Sidonian wife Astis, the daughter of Mnaseas, a Hellenized Phoenician name. Dionysios was the offspring of a mixed marriage, a practice common on Rhodes as well as in Athens and Demetrias during this period. Dionysios made his dedication c. 215 BCE to Artemis and another deity, whose name is missing, on behalf of his mother in the city of Rhodos.[87] In a second dedication, made with his sister Phila, of a statue of his mother to both Athena Lindia and Herakles, he is also called a benefactor, a title especially associated with private associations on Rhodes.[88] While his father was a proxenos and probably not a resident of Rhodes, even if his ties to the island were close and regular, Dionysios was a resident on the island, a well-to-do member of an association, and an established member of an immigrant community on Rhodes.

The inscriptions associated with a second family illustrate how over multiple generations, some immigrant families at least could gradually transition from identifying as individuals from their home state to declaring their status as full-fledged members of their host state. This family included several generations of famous Tyrian bronze sculptors whose work was commissioned throughout the Aegean, including Athens, Halikarnassos, Delphi, and the four Rhodian cities of Kameiros, Lindos, Ialysos, and Rhodos. The father, Artemidoros, son of Menodotos, founded this dynasty of sculptors in the middle of the second

---

proxenos, [dedicated this] to Athena Lindia, on the island of Rhodes, on behalf of his children, Batos, Herakleitos, and Rhodias).

87. *IG* XII.1 104c. The sculptor of this piece was Macedonian.

88. *I.Lindos* 132. The sculptor was from Halikarnassos. For benefactors and associations, see Maillot 2015: 150–152.

century BCE.[89] His sons, Menodotos and Charmolas, continued in their father's profession, as did Charmolas' son, also named Menodotos. Artemidoros always identified himself as a Tyrian, whether he signed his works alone or with his son Menodotos and whether his work was commissioned on Rhodes or elsewhere.[90] His sons Menodotos and Charmolas also self-identified as Tyrians, in their joint artists' signatures on the bases of statues found on Rhodes and in Athens.[91] Yet Charmolas also signed some of his work in Rhodes and Delphi on his own, and there he identified himself as a Rhodian, as he also did on some works that he cosigned with his son Menodotos.[92] And Charmolas' son Menodotos, a third-generation immigrant, always signed his work as a Rhodian.[93] As these signatures show, although the family's Tyrian provenance was the prominent factor in their identity during their early years on Rhodes, it had completely disappeared by the third generation and the family identified only as Rhodian. Such a shift in one's civic identity might have entailed a change in one's citizenship status, which probably occurred in the second generation.[94] In any case, this shift illustrates the effect of time on both issues of residency and identity, showing how this family's Tyrian origins were forgotten or purposefully erased and their new Rhodian residence became not only their home but also their new identity.

---

89. On this family, see Badoud 2010. Another known Phoenician sculptor on Rhodes is the Sidonian Technon, who made a statue that someone else dedicated to Athena Lindia and Zeus Polieus (*I.Lindos* 74).

90. Alone: *I.Lindos* 216; *Tit. Cam.* 95; *EA* 4, 1984, 82, no. 2. With his son Menodotos: *I.Lindos* 245.

91. *Clara Rhodos* 2 (1932) 190, 19; *I.Lindos* 281; *IG* XII.1 109; *I.Lindos* 245; *SEG* 33 643; *IG* II² 3147.

92. *I.Lindos* 285; *SEG* 39 750; *SEG* 41 647. The inscription on the statue base from Delphi is fragmentary and the name of the sculptor is missing, but the patronymic and his state of origin survive: "son of Artemidoros the Rhodian" (Marcadé 1953: no. 13). On this inscription, see Badoud 2010: 135. On *I.Lindos* 293, 702, Charmolas cosigned his work with his son Menodotos.

93. *I.Lindos* 305, *Suppl. Rodio nuovo* 159.4.

94. When a single individual used two different city-ethnics, that person had most likely exchanged one citizenship for another. See Savalli-Lestrade 2012. Besides ad hominem citizenship grants, states gave grants of potential citizenship (*isopoliteia*) to entire states. See Saba 2020. Complicating the picture painted here of the status of the individuals who used the identifier "Rhodian" is that some have argued that they were not full citizens but foreign residents who had limited citizenship. See Fraser 2009: 83.

Conclusion

As this analysis of the mechanisms of integration and inclusion visible from the material remains of Athens, Demetrias, and Rhodes has shown, the strategies migrants deployed that promoted their integration and inclusion in their host societies eventually transformed immigrants' lives and identities and changed the societies in which they lived. For their part, Phoenician immigrants adopted local practices, changed the ways they identified themselves, and represented themselves in Greek ways and even in the Greek language, while also continuing to identify themselves as immigrants and foreigners especially in the first generation. Their presence led host communities to become familiar with and even formally accept the worship of foreign gods, live among monuments that included inscriptions in a foreign language and unfamiliar iconographic motifs, and incorporate foreigners and immigrants into their institutions. Over time, this process resulted in polities whose civic bodies were made up of a diverse population with different religions, languages, and institutions, in which immigrants and citizens alike were integral members who contributed to and increasingly identified with their new societies.

2

Phoenician Trade Associations

IN A TEMPLE in the bustling ancient neighborhood of Peiraieus, the harbor area of Athens where many immigrants lived, stood a rectangular marble slab, over one meter in height and thirty centimeters wide, inscribed in Greek (Fig. 2.1). The text records that in 333/332 BCE, a group of Phoenician traders from Kition approached the Athenian state to request the right to own property, a right known as *enktesis* and usually reserved for citizens, for the specific purpose of establishing a sanctuary—a sacred space that often had a temple—dedicated to Aphrodite. The inscription indicates that they presented this request to the Athenian council as a collective and, to make their case, cited a precedent in which the council had previously granted the same right to Egyptians living in Athens to build a sanctuary dedicated to the Egyptian goddess Isis. The record also shows that the Athenian council invited the Kitian traders to address the Athenian assembly, another right usually reserved for citizens, and present their request, which the assembly accepted.[1] When the Kitian traders proceeded to build their sanctuary in Peiraieus, where the stone was discovered in 1870, they inscribed the council and the assembly's decision on a stone, publicizing to Kitian immigrants and anyone else passing by their sanctuary both the legitimacy of the group's request and its service to its members. As this surviving record reveals, this group of Kitian traders had formed a professional association to organize and represent the interests of its members and the broader community of Kitian immigrants in Athens and had gained the legal standing and political authority to influence their host state's decisions and policies.

---

1. *IG* II³ 1 337. The inscription specifies that the assembly should decide what to do after hearing the Kitians regarding the sanctuary, as well as any Athenian who wanted to speak (ἀκούσαντα τὸν δῆμον τῶν | Κιτιείων περὶ τῆς ἱδρύσ|εως τοῦ ἱεροῦ καὶ ἄλλου Ἀθηναίων τοῦ βουλομένο|υ), implying that the Kitians directly addressed the assembly.

Phoenicians among Others. Denise Demetriou, Oxford University Press. © Oxford University Press 2023.
DOI: 10.1093/oso/9780197634851.003.0003

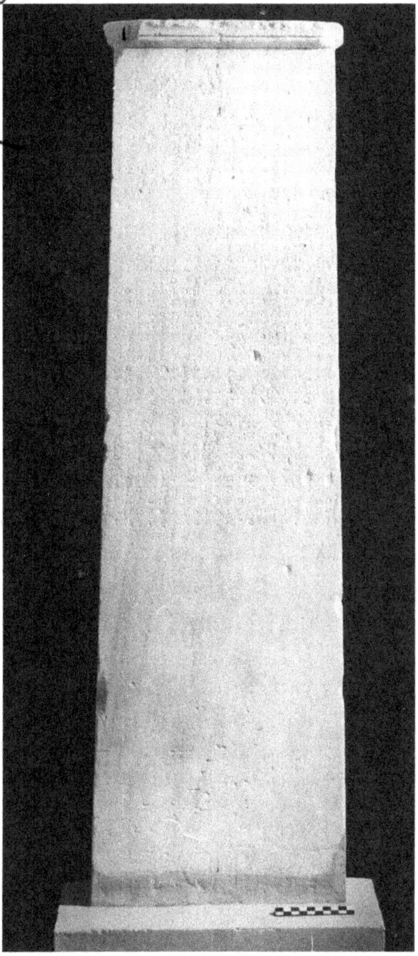

FIGURE 2.1 Stele with the Kitian traders' request for the right to own property, 333/332 BCE (*IG* II³ 1 337)
Athens, Epigraphic Museum 7173. © Hellenic Ministry of Culture and Sports / Hellenic Organization of Cultural Resources Development.

The Kitian example was neither unique nor unusual. As several surviving texts from Athens reveal, trade associations appeared for the first time in the fourth century BCE, and most were founded by Phoenician immigrants. Although the general phenomenon of voluntary associations was not new in Greek communities in this period, most of the existing associations were primarily religious, such as the religious associations of the Thracian goddess Bendis, those of Dionysus (the *technitai*, or artists), or even the religious associations of demes and phratries, two of Athens' administrative units.² Unlike those better-known examples, the Phoenician professional associations in Athens emerged specifically to represent the interests of Phoenician-speaking immigrants before the Athenian state and to provide them a social and physical space for maintaining religious and cultural ties to their home state. The originality of these Phoenician associations is reflected in that when they first appeared, they did not refer to themselves by any of the Greek words used at that time to describe private associations—*thiasoi, orgeones, eranoi*—despite their also having a religious character.³ As this chapter will show, these fourth-century BCE Phoenician trade associations were different not only in name but also in being structured around their members' state of origin and serving as quasi-state associations, representing immigrants before their host state.

Nor was the establishment of Phoenician trade associations limited to fourth-century BCE Athens. They were also founded on second-century Delos, especially after 166 BCE, when Rome declared the island a duty-free commercial center under Athens' jurisdiction.⁴ Like the earlier Phoenician trade associations in Athens, the ones on Delos had a strong religious character, evident in their theophoric names, as, for example, the Herakleistai of Tyre and the Poseidoniastai

---

2. For associations in general, see Ascough, Harland, and Kloppenborg 2012: 1–7 and the accompanying database: http://philipharland.com/greco-roman-associations/. For the Roman equivalent of professional *collegia* of merchants, see Verboven 2011. Most discussions of associations focus on their legal status and public functions. See, for example, Rauh 1993; Kloppenborg and Wilson 1996; Arnaoutoglou 1998 and 2003; Steinhauer 2014; Gabrielsen and Thomsen 2015. A notable and recent exception is Venticinque 2016, who treats trade associations in Roman Egypt not as religious or social groups but as economic operators. For associations in Athens, see Jones 1999 and Ismard 2010, and for associations in Rhodes, see Thomsen 2020.

3. *Thiasoi* first appeared in the sixth century BCE and with increasing frequency from the fourth century BCE onward. They were often associated with the worship of Dionysus and Herakles, Spartan feasts, cult-associations of Athenian phratries, and worshipers of foreign divinities, among others. See Arnaoutoglou 2003: 60–70. *Orgeones* were almost exclusively Athenian and organized groups of worshipers of specific gods and heroes, including foreign gods, such as the Thracian Bendis. See Ferguson 1944 and 1949 and Arnaoutoglou 2003: 31–60. *Eranoi* initially referred to feasts whose costs were shared by the participants before acquiring, in the fourth century BCE, the sense of loans given by friends. Only after the first century BCE in Attica was the related term *eranistai* associated with priests and cult-associations. See Vondeling 1961 and Arnatoutoglou 2003: 71–87.

4. Delos was home to many Phoenicians and other immigrants: Baslez 2013; Rovai 2020: 173–174. In addition to the texts discussed in this book, a seal with Greek and Phoenician texts was discovered from the House of Seals on Delos, a private house that held an archive of commercial transactions (Boussac 1982: 444–446 and 1992: 16–17). The seal with the bilingual inscriptions is of a joint tribunal responsible for adjudicating legal conflicts among the citizens of different cities. For Semitic names in texts discovered on Delos, see Rovai 2020: 178–179.

of Berytos (probably translations of the names of the Phoenician gods Melqart and Baal, the patron deities of Tyre and Berytos respectively); they were organized around a city-state of origin and represented their members before their host state's authorities.[5] Whether the examples on Delos were direct descendants of the earlier ones in Athens is unknown, but both are consistent with evidence that suggests that, from the Early Iron Age, Phoenician trading ventures around the Mediterranean were highly organized, often by city-state rather than by ethnicity, even though the particular form of organization into associations first appears in the fourth century BCE.[6]

In prosperous commercial centers such as Athens and Delos, which were inhabited and frequented by individuals of different ethnicities from all over the Mediterranean who collaborated in trading ventures, numerous institutions developed to facilitate cross-cultural trade. Professional associations, as, for example, of bankers, olive oil and wine merchants, sailors, and others related to trade, were one such institution, even if the intricacies of how they operated in long-distance cross-cultural trade have largely been lost.[7] Yet the surviving records inscribed on stone and the material remains of their buildings indicate that the professional associations established by collectives of Phoenician traders in Athens and Delos represent another adaptive strategy developed by Phoenician immigrants, complementing those created by individual Phoenicians discussed in the previous chapter, to work around the legal and other restrictions imposed on them by the migration and membership regimes of their host states. Without the ability to own land, immigrants could not build their own temples or bury their dead in public cemeteries; without the right to participate directly

---

5. One inscription, discussed below, records the existence of the Herakleistai of Tyre (*I.Délos* 1519), and several document the Poseidoniastai of Berytos (*I.Délos* 1520, 1772–1796, 2323–2327, 2611, and 2629). See also McLean 1996: 188 and Nielsen 2015: 145–148. A fragmentary text may also record a synod of Aradians (*I.Délos* 1543), but the reading of "Aradian" is not secure. Other professional associations on Delos were also named after gods, as, for example, the Apolloniastai (*I.Délos* 1730), Hermaistai (*I.Délos* 1731–1750), Poseidoniastai or Neptunales (*I.Délos* 1751–1752), and Competaliastai, named after the Hellenized form of the name of the festival for the Lares known as *compitalis* (*I.Délos* 1760–1771). The Apolloniastai, Hermaistai, and Poseidoniastai often gave dedications together (*I.Délos* 1753–1759). Rather than a state, these associations represented a specific social group or status of Italians (e.g., freedmen, enslaved persons, or free men). See Adams 2002: 108–115. The family names (*gentilicia*) on these inscriptions include Romans, Latins, Etruscans, Campanians, Apulians, and Samnites, as well as Greeks who identify as citizens of Taras (Tarentum) and Neapolis (Naples). See Rauh 1993: 30–32. For Italians on Delos, see Hasenohr 2007 and 2008.

6. Terpstra 2019, chapter 2, discusses Phoenician trade institutions (45–49 discuss early Phoenician trade).

7. Inscriptions record these other associations: bankers (*I.Délos* 1715), olive oil and wine merchants (*I.Délos* 1711–1714), and sailors (*I.Délos* 2401). See also Rauh 1993: 252.

in government, they could have little political say over the conditions in which they lived. While some immigrants, especially the wealthy ones, managed to find ways to bypass these limitations individually, organizing into groups served much the same purpose as today's special-interest groups and nongovernmental organizations: working as a collective, groups of foreigners were able to pool their resources and gain access to avenues through which they could petition their host state and negotiate privileges for themselves and other immigrants.

This chapter's examination of a series of inscriptions and material remains reveals that the trade associations that emerged from Phoenician diasporic communities in Athens and Delos facilitated the personal and professional lives of immigrants and integrated them as essential members of their host societies by maintaining good relations with their host state, providing a cultural locus for communities of Phoenician immigrants, and serving as quasi-state organizations that were officially recognized by the host state and even included in its political apparatus. This they did by fulfilling three main functions: lobbying the host state, maintaining the traditions of the home state, and honoring the host state.

Lobbying the Host State

The existing evidence makes clear that a chief way in which these professional organizations served the interests of their members was petitioning the host state for honors and rights that were not generally available to foreigners or noncitizens. Indeed, the earliest inscription alluding to Phoenician trade associations, a decree from the 360s BCE, singled out a subset of Sidonian citizens residing in Athens. Although not the first time in the ancient Mediterranean that a state treated foreign traders as a group, this appears to be the first time a Greek polity dealt with traders from a specific city-state as a group in its legislation.[8] On its face, this honorific decree records the Athenian state's decision to reward the king of Sidon, Abdashtart (365–352 BCE), known in Greek as Straton, for services he provided to an Athenian embassy on its way to the Persian king by awarding him hereditary *proxenia*, or the privilege of representing Athenian citizens in Sidon.[9] The text also records that Athens rewarded the king's envoy with an official

---

8. For instance, in 570 BCE, the Egyptian pharaoh Amasis granted areas on which to erect temples to Greek traders who did not wish to live permanently in Naukratis, one of the most famous Greek commercial settlements of antiquity on the Nile delta (Herodotus 2.178). Phoenicians probably also resided in Naukratis. See Demetriou 2012: 105–152, with bibliography, for more on trade institutions in this settlement.

9. *IG* II² 141. I discuss this text further in chapters 3 and 4. Chapter 3 uses this decree to show how the authorities of Phoenician city-states managed migration and maintained connections

dinner at the state's expense and attempted to forge a political alliance with Sidon. But what most discussions of this decree overlook is that it also includes an amendment, appended as a rider at the end of the main text, that formally recognized Sidonian traders as a group and granted them special privileges in the form of tax exemptions. More specifically, it declares that Sidonian traders whose domicile and citizenship were in Sidon and who resided in Athens on commercial business would not be required to pay metic taxes (*metoikion*) or capital taxes (*eisphora*) or finance a chorus in dramatic contests (*choregeia*), thereby allowing all Sidonian traders to remain in Athens without incurring any of the taxes ordinarily paid by metics and to continue their commercial operations without significant restrictions.[10] Although treating individuals from the same city-state and the same profession as a single group may seem an efficient way to pass legislation regulating migration, at the time this was not common practice in Athens and thus may reflect that the Sidonian traders had already organized themselves into a trade association or were seen as one by Athens.

By the 320s BCE, as an Athenian inscription from 325/324 BCE demonstrates, organized groups of Phoenician traders were successfully representing their members' interests before the Athenian state and provided a way to bypass the restriction that noncitizens could not directly address Athenian governing bodies. This inscription records that an association of traders and shippers who were possibly Sidonian had approached the Athenian state and declared that Apollonides, the son of Demetrios, a Sidonian, was worthy of awards from the state because of the goodwill he had shown to Athens.[11] In most recorded cases, such worthy

---

to their citizens abroad. Chapter 4 discusses the use of honorific awards both to Straton and to the Sidonian traders in the context of how host states facilitated migration through the awards and privileges they granted to foreigners.

10. *IG* II² 141, lines 31–36: ὁπόσοι δ' ἂν Σιδω|νίων οἰκῶντες ἐς Σιδῶνι καὶ πολι|τευόμενοι ἐπιδημῶσιν κατ' ἐμπορ|ίαν Ἀθήνησι, μὴ ἐξεῖναι αὐτὸς μετ|οίκιον πράττεσθαι μηδὲ χορηγὸν | μηδένα καταστῆσαι μηδ' εἰσφορὰν | μηδεμίαν ἐπιγράφεν (however many Sidonians live and are citizens of Sidon who reside in Athens for the purposes of trade, the metic tax shall not be exacted from them, nor shall any of them be appointed a *choregos*, nor should they be registered for any capital tax).

11. *IG* II³ 1 379. For a good edition of this inscription, see Culasso Gastaldi 2004: 185–187. Culasso Gastaldi 2004: 189 restores the name of the proposer as Isokrates from the deme of Anagyrous, because Isokrates is a common name in this deme. Lambert (2002: 79 n. 20 and 2006: 135 n. 90) suggests instead that the proposer of the decree was Polykles, a man also known from Demosthenes' oration *Against Polykles*. How one dates the inscription depends on how one reconstructs the beginning of the text. If it lacked the formula of approval of the decision by the council, it might belong to the period between 347/346 and 325/324 BCE, when most inscriptions without the formula of approval appear (Henry 1977: 44–45). Schweigert 1940: 342–343 has argued that the person who put the proposal to the vote, Epameinon, should be identified as a man of the same name who served as the chair of the presiding officers of the council (*proedroi*) in 323/322 BCE (*IG* II³ 1 378), thereby dating both *IG* II³ 1 378 and 379

foreigners were sponsored by individual Athenians who submitted a request to honor them to the Athenian council (*boule*), the main deliberative body in Athens, which would discuss the request and decide whether to present it to the assembly (*ekklesia*) for a vote.[12] Yet texts such as the decree honoring Apollonides suggest that associations—even if they were made up of immigrants—were also allowed to put forth candidates for state awards.

By helping to ensure that their members would benefit from having served their host state, such associations brought prestige both to the individual honorand and to the trade association that advocated on his behalf, especially because the inscription recording their actions served to publicize the actions of both in the center of the city. In this case, the Athenian assembly voted in favor of this recommendation and granted Apollonides a gold wreath worth a thousand drachmas, awarded him the title of proxenos and hereditary proxenia, named him and his descendants benefactors (*euergetes*), and even gave him the right to own property. It also decreed that this decision should be memorialized by inscribing, at public expense, the honors and privileges given to Apollonides (whose Greek name and that of his father, Demetrios, were common among Phoenicians who lived in Greek communities) on a stone stele to be erected on the Acropolis, one of the most public spaces in Athens. That text, which today survives in two adjoining fragments excavated from the area east of the Erechtheion, a temple on the Acropolis, offers evidence that a professional group of foreign traders was able to exercise enough organized clout to influence Athenian state decisions.

Functioning as voluntary collectives, associations of traders and shippers seem to have gained a quasi-state status in that they had the authority to appear before governmental bodies to act as mediators between their members and their

---

to the same day in 323/322 BCE. Culasso Gastaldi 2004: 188–191 finds this theoretically possible but difficult to accept, as the name Epameinon was common, although she, too, prefers a date in the last quarter of the fourth century BCE.

12. In later periods, associations of traders or traders and shippers in Athens could mete out their own awards without involving the political apparatus of the host state, as several decrees suggest. Two of the honorands on these decrees had served as generals: one in 97/6 BCE in Peiraieus (*IG* II² 2952) who in another inscription, a dedication to Aphrodite Euploia, recorded his service as a general there (*IG* II² 2872); the second had provided for the safety and security of traders in 15 CE (*SEG* 17 71). A third decree honors a man who had served as an *agoranomos* (*IG* II² 3493; 27 CE). A series of decrees from Delos dating to the second and first centuries BCE records dedications by an association of traders and shippers: *I.Délos* 1526, 1642, 1645, 1647–1649, 1652, 1657–1663, 1665, 1702–1705, 1726, 1729. *I.Délos* 1725 records honors given by a group of traders. In first-century CE Palmyra, Palmyrian traders (*I.Estremo oriente* 83, 149, 150), traders from Phorathos and Ologasias (*I.Estremo oriente* 91), and Skythian traders (*I. Estremo oriente* 412), among others, gave dedications to gods or patrons.

host state and facilitate their presence and activities in their new homes. The phrasing of the state decrees that record their actions suggests that trade associations framed their requests that individual immigrants be honored in terms of how those foreign individuals had benefited their host state. Although the state decrees that stemmed from such requests usually simply state that the honorand was a good man who had shown favor to the host state, they periodically provide more details about the specific service a person had performed, such as selling grain at low prices or below market prices, importing grain in times of shortages, donating funds to states with which they could purchase grain, or rescuing citizens and transporting them back to Athens, among others.[13] Such services and gifts to the immigrants' host state benefited both the government and all the state's residents, rendering individuals such as Apollonides valuable and at times essential members of the communities in which they resided. And such public acknowledgments of the beneficial and often vital contributions of members of these foreign trade organizations reflected positively on the immigrant community more broadly.

The host state's willingness to grant such honors that were of significant monetary and cultural value indicates that doing so could also procure further benefits to the host state. In this case, the specific honors and privileges that Athens chose to grant Apollonides would have both encouraged migration and capitalized on existing trade networks to increase Athens' tax revenues and secure a grain supply. The right to own property, which was a citizen privilege, would have facilitated his business affairs and his continued presence in Athens; the monetary award of a gold wreath would have encouraged him to continue to engage in trading activities that would serve Athens' interests; and the title of proxenos would have tied him to Athens in an official diplomatic capacity, as he would be legally responsible for Athenians in Sidon. Such awards and privileges were commonly awarded to traders in the 330s and the 320s BCE, especially under the tutelage of Lykourgos, the famous orator who held the office of the financial administrator of Athens four times (and in that capacity was also the person who presented to the Athenian assembly the previously mentioned Kitian request for the right to own land).[14] During this period, Athens also passed legislation

---

13. For example, *IG* II³ 1 367, 430, 432. Although the text does not specify the service that Apollonides had provided for Athens, since he was represented by traders and shippers it is likely he was involved in the shipping and trade industry. Some scholars have also argued that Apollonides was a trader (e.g., Isager and Hansen 1975: 207 n. 55; Hopper 1979: 115); others think it is unlikely that he was either a trader or a shipper (Reed 2003: 94–95 n. 7). Engen takes no position on whether Apollonides was a trader or not (2010: 310–311).

14. Several decrees from this period gave similar awards to grain traders: for example, *IG* II³ 1 367, 430, 432. Another decree, *IG* II³ 1 454, honored a man from the island of Kos because he

that ensured that commercial trials (*dikai emporikai*), which gave non-Athenians access to the Athenian legal system, were heard monthly and began to grant the right to own property to immigrants much more frequently.[15] This expansion in the granting of awards to Phoenician and other traders and associations has been generally explained as an attempt to facilitate trade and encourage economic growth, perhaps to alleviate the grain shortages reported throughout the eastern Mediterranean in this period.[16] Indeed, state revenues in the Lykourgan era were unprecedented in the history of Athens, and this efflorescence may have been due to Athens' encouragement of trade through a variety of policies, including honoring individual traders and trade associations.[17] Less attention has been given to the ways in which host states became more actively involved in matters of mobility and migration by recognizing professional associations as entities with collective bargaining power and rewarding traders who had performed unofficial services for the state.

Maintaining the Traditions of the Home States

In addition to their activities facilitating trade and lobbying the state for awards related to the commercial activities of their members, most trade organizations also had a specific civic identity and were engaged in practices intended to advance their collective as well as individual members' interests. A major one of these interests was immigrant communities' desire to maintain their religious traditions in their new homes, as reflected in the Kitian request to the Athenian state to own property for the purpose of establishing a sanctuary for worshiping

---

took care of both traders and shippers (perhaps an association) and ensured that an abundance of grain was shipped to Athens. The group that proposed this award was one of traders, but the decree is fragmentary, and although the reconstruction offered is that Athenian traders, Samians, and everyone else present, Athenian and otherwise, made this proposal, such an identification is far from certain. See also Engen 2010: 298–299.

15. For commercial trials, see E. E. Cohen 1973: 184–185. For the frequency of *enktesis* awards, see Gauthier 1976: 223–225.

16. Lambert 2006: 117. In addition to honoring traders, honorific inscriptions show that Athenian foreign policy in this period tried to cultivate positive relations with Macedon following the battle of Chaironeia in 338 BCE and the subsequent conquest of the Aegean world by Philip and Alexander of Macedon.

17. See Burke 1985 and 2010. Faraguna 1992 places the emphasis on the state's overseeing better and more efficiently various sources of income, including leasing of sacred property, sale of public land, and mining at Laureion, but Faraguna 2003 acknowledges that revenues from Peiraieus were important. For Lykourgan Athens, in general, see Mitchel 1973; Will 1983; and Hanink 2014.

Aphrodite mentioned in the opening to this chapter. Although the text specifically mentions that this site would be dedicated to the Greek goddess Aphrodite, the Kitians most probably intended to set up a sanctuary to Astarte, the most prominent divinity in the predominantly Phoenician-speaking Kition, and simply translated their deity into her Greek equivalent.[18] As discussed earlier, translations of deities from Phoenician into Greek were common, and both Greeks and Phoenicians who resided in Greek-speaking cities often translated Astarte into Aphrodite.[19] Both goddesses were worshiped as patrons of sexuality, fertility, navigation, and even warfare, making their equation with one another easy.[20] By translating Astarte into the Greek Aphrodite, the Kitian traders framed their request in more easily comprehensible and perhaps palatable ways for an Athenian audience, even though they clearly intended to form their association around a cult of a divinity from their homeland. In turn, as several fourth-century BCE dedications associated with this sanctuary offered by women suggest, both the Kitian trade association and their cult seem to have afforded all Phoenician Kitians living in Athens the opportunity to perform their traditional religious practices and retain their civic identity.[21] Such associations and both their religious and commercial operations would have allowed the wider immigrant communities from each city-state to forge links with one another, strengthen their community, and maintain cultural links to their home of origin.

The Kitians were not the only group of Phoenicians or other foreigners in the region who found ways to maintain their religious traditions by working around restrictions that came with their status as immigrants. As discussed elsewhere in this volume, Phoenicians in Athens also worshiped the Phoenician gods Nergal and Sakon, and a Sidonian association in Athens was formed around the worship

---

18. Pirenne-Delforge 1994: 309–369; Ulbrich 2008. *CIS* I 86A–B attests to a temple of Astarte in Kition. See also Karageorghis 1969: 517–527; Masson and Sznycer 1972: 21–67.

19. Greek literary sources relate the two goddesses: Herodotus claims that the cult of Aphrodite Ourania came from Phoenician Ashkelon (1.105). See also Bonnet and Pirenne-Delforge 1999; Budin 2004; Wallensten 2014. Examples of Phoenicians equating the two deities include *I.Délos* 2132 and *SEG* 36 758. The later Phoenician organizations on Delos, the Herakleistai of Tyre and the Poseidoniastai of Berytos, also translated the Greek names of the Phoenician patron deities of their city-states and turned them into the names of their associations.

20. Aphrodite was not the only Greek goddess associated with Astarte but was the most frequent.

21. *IG* II² 4636–4637. One of these dedications specified that the dedicant was a Kitian (*IG* II² 4636: Ἀριστοκλέα Κιτιὰς Ἀφροδίτηι Οὐρανίαι εὐξαμένη ἀνέθηκεν (Aristoklea the Kitian, praying, dedicated [this] to Aphrodite Ourania). All were discovered from the vicinity of the findspot of the decree recording the Kitian request, suggesting that the sanctuary was open to all Kitians (not just traders) and perhaps even non-Kitians.

of that city's patron god, Baal.[22] Whether the worship of these gods was enabled by the same kinds of concessions as those given to the Kitian traders is unknown, but existing records show that the worship of two other foreign gods—the Egyptian Isis and the Thracian goddess Bendis—was made possible by similar grants of the right to own property.[23] That the Athenian state was willing and able to accommodate such requests suggests that it was aware of the ways in which it benefited from the presence of both immigrants and the professional associations that represented them and that those professional associations were able to mediate between their immigrant members and the host state and to ensure that they could continue to enact the cultural practices and religious traditions of their homelands.

The available evidence also shows that the associations themselves were eager to publicize how their mediating role was instrumental to the lives of their members and fellow immigrants. The text of the decree regarding the Kitian request, for example, includes several peculiarities that suggest the inscription was actually erected by the association of the Kitians rather than by the Athenian state as would have been expected, as it contains no mention of the secretary of the Athenian council, no instructions on how to pay for inscribing the text, or any clauses regarding where to erect the decree, all details that are usually included in state-issued texts. All this strongly suggests that the Kitian trade association itself chose to bear the expense and responsibility for erecting the inscribed stone,

---

22. In addition to these gods, a second-century BCE inscription records that a Sidonian man gave a dedication to the Athenian hero Pankrates (*SEG* 16 182), who may have been worshiped as Palaimon/Melikertes in Athens, a divinity who bears connections to the Phoenician Melqart. The worship of this deity may have been imported to Athens by Phoenicians. See Vikela 1994: 81–108. Palaimon/Melikertes was also worshiped in Corinth, where he also had Semitic connections (Pausanias 2.2.1). See Astour 1967: 204–212. Moreover, Dionysios of Halikarnassos preserves among the list of speeches by the fourth-century BCE speechwriter Dinarchos a suit, now lost, brought by the Athenian deme of Phaleron against the Phoenicians concerning the priesthood of Poseidon, perhaps recording another group centered around a religious cult (possibly of Baal, since this Phoenician god was often translated into the Greek Poseidon). See Shoemaker 1971.

23. For the worship of Isis in Athens, see Simms 1989. It is not clear whether the Egyptians who received this right were also traders, but trade with Egypt was a staple of the Athenian economy in the fourth century BCE. The only other known example of Athens' granting *enktesis* to non-Athenians for the purpose of establishing a sanctuary is to the Thracian residents of Athens so that they could establish the sanctuary of Bendis (*IG* II² 1283). See Simms 1988 and Wijma 2014: 126–155. The worship of Bendis in Athens was organized by and around religious associations known as *orgeones*. There is no indication that the latter were professional groups. See Ferguson 1944 and 1949.

probably in the very sanctuary the association helped establish.[24] By erecting this record of the Kitian request and the Athenian grant, the trader organization publicly declared—to its members, the wider Athenian community, and everyone else who could read Greek or could recognize the erection of an inscribed stele as recording an official act of a collective—that it had the political influence to represent its members' collective interests and functioned as an organization through which Kitians could retain cultural links to their home state. *Cyprus*

Moreover, the specific wording of this decree demonstrates that the Kitian traders were an organized group defined not only by profession but by civic identity. In the phrase on the decree used to describe the Kitian traders, "the Kitian demos," the term "demos" intimates that the group had a political structure and some degree of independence, much like the later *politeumata* of the Jewish and other communities in Ptolemaic Egypt and other areas under Ptolemaic control.[25] This Kitian association and the group of traders and shippers that honored Apollonides appear to have been innovative institutions that could be incorporated into the administrative structure and political apparatus of the Athenian state. The internal political organization of Phoenician trade associations and the ways in which their semiautonomous nature allowed them to interact with the authorities of their host state can also be seen in a lengthy second-century BCE inscription in Greek produced by the Herakleistai, a Tyrian trader and shipper association from the island of Delos, which records, among other things, a request that the Tyrians made of the Athenian state for a place where they could worship their patron god Herakles. This text, dated to 153/152 BCE, when Delos was technically a free port within the jurisdiction of Athens but under the control of Rome, demonstrates that the Tyrian Herakleistai were similar to the fourth-century BCE trade associations of Athens in that they, too, offered a locus for a community of immigrants from the same city-state and facilitated their lives as immigrants by enabling them to continue worshiping their own gods and representing their collective interests to their host state. The inscribed text is an honorific decree issued by the association granting various awards to a member of the association, Patron, the son of Dorotheos, because he had led an embassy to Athens, represented the association before the Athenian authorities, and successfully petitioned them for land on which they would construct a sanctuary to

---

24. See comments on *IG* II³ 1 337 on https://atticinscriptions.com and Bonnet 2015: 427–428. The exact findspot in Peiraieus of the decree was not recorded by the excavator.

25. The phrase in Greek is δῆμος τῶν Κιτιείων (*IG* II³ 1 337, lines 20–21). For Jewish *politeumata*, see Préaux 1958; Kasher 1985 and 2008; Zuckerman 1985–1988; Sänger 2013. Gruen 2023 discusses Jewish immigrant communities throughout the Mediterranean, which he argues were self-governing, sanctioned by the cities they lived in, and even had some political rights.

Herakles (lines 11–14).²⁶ Although the text does not call it such, this was a request for *enktesis*, the right to own property, like the successful one made by the Kitian traders in Athens. Herakles' Phoenician equivalent, Melqart, was the patron deity of Tyre, who is described as the founder (*archegos*) of Tyre (lines 14–16), the association's homeland.²⁷ Athens presumably granted this request to the Tyrian association, since the inscription goes on to mention the existence of a sanctuary of Herakles on Delos (lines 43–44). Such a grant allowed a cult prominent in the association's home state of Tyre to also be established in the host state and helped maintain the members' cultural ties to their home state. The Tyrian trader and shipper association of the Herakleistai thus acted as a cultural conduit between its members and the city of Tyre even as it facilitated its members' immigrant status in their host state of Delos and mediated their presence there by negotiating privileges on behalf of their immigrant community.

Unlike the inscription regarding the Kitian association, this record provides insights into how the association discussed this request and the procedure for presenting it to Athens. As such, it reveals information about both the inner workings of second-century BCE Phoenician professional associations and how host states influenced those institutions, including their adoption of Athenian political culture and epigraphic practices. The text indicates that the Tyrian association had a synod (*synodos*), a body like an assembly that made decisions about association matters.²⁸ Like Athenian state decrees, the text begins with a preamble that provides the Athenian archon of the year, the month in which the deliberations happened, and the name and title (*archithiasites*) of the member of the association who had proposed the honors for Patron. It adopts a phrase that often appears in Attic texts recording acts of benefaction (*euergesia*) in which the issuing authority specifies that the reason for the erection of the decree is so everyone will know that honors are granted to those who strive to benefit the group (lines 27–34), thereby emphasizing the benefits of belonging to the association.²⁹ Similarly, the awards granted to Patron by the association were those typically given by Greek states to noncitizens for their exceptional service,

---

26. *I.Délos* 1519. For a brief discussion of this text, see Terpstra 2019: 69–70.

27. Ancient Greek authors identify the two divinities (e.g., Herodotus 2.44; Arrian 2.24.5), and bilingual dedicatory texts translate Melqart as Herakles (e.g., *KAI* 47 = *IG* XIV 600 = *CIS* I 122bis). For more on the identification of the two heroes, see Bonnet 1988, 2009, and 2012 and Bonnet and Bricault 2016: 35–43. Melqart was worshiped as a founder of city-states. See Malkin 2011: 119–141 and Bonnet 2015: 486–488.

28. For synods in general, see Arnaoutoglou 2003: 132.

29. For example, *IG* II² 1214.

including a commendation, a gold wreath, a statue of him to be placed in the sanctuary of Herakles on Delos, and exemption from membership and service fees (lines 36–45). Finally, Patron, who was sent as the association's representative to Athens, is described as an ambassador (*presbeutes*), the Greek term used to describe official diplomats (line 16). This adoption of standard Attic political culture and language and its expression on the records of state decrees may have made it easier for the association to approach the authorities of the host state—in this case Athens, the city that administered Delos—and to be integrated into the host state's political infrastructure, even if the bodies of the association may have mimicked Phoenician political practices.[30] Despite these imitations of Athenian (and more generally Greek) practices, the Phoenician character of the association is detectable in the purpose of the request, which was to allow the Tyrians to worship their ancestral god on Delos, and local Delian influences are visible in the predominantly religious character of the association, which was typical of other Delian professional associations. Such amalgamations as the structure of institutions such as professional associations seem to have been common among Phoenician immigrants living in the Greek world and were an adaptive strategy that helped facilitate their lives as immigrants.

Honoring the Host State

In addition to adopting or accommodating the practices of their host states, Phoenician professional organizations also found ways to directly honor their host states. Similar documentation is lacking for the right of the Phoenician association of Berytian traders, shippers, and warehouse workers, who called themselves the Poseidoniastai, to own property on which to build a sanctuary dedicated to their patron god, Baal (translated into the Greek Poseidon). Nonetheless, there is evidence that they had a building on Delos—the only building connected to a Phoenician association that has been identified as such anywhere in the Mediterranean.[31] This evidence, which includes the material

---

30. Bonnet 2015: 483 notes that the koinon of the Herakleistai on Delos acted as a miniature polis. For more on how these associations may have adopted Phoenician political structures, even while borrowing Greek political language, see chapter 3.

31. The building was constructed soon after the declaration of Delos as a free port in 166 BCE. One of the earliest financers of the building was the Roman banker Marcus Minatius, who had given the association interest-free loans and a monetary contribution to complete the building. In return, the Poseidoniastai honored the Roman banker by setting up his statue and portrait anywhere he wanted in the courtyard of the building except for its sacred spaces, accompanied with inscriptions for the statue and portrait recording this benefaction and the honors granted to him, as well as a dining couch during all festivals of Poseidon. Further, the association ordered

64   PHOENICIANS AMONG OTHERS

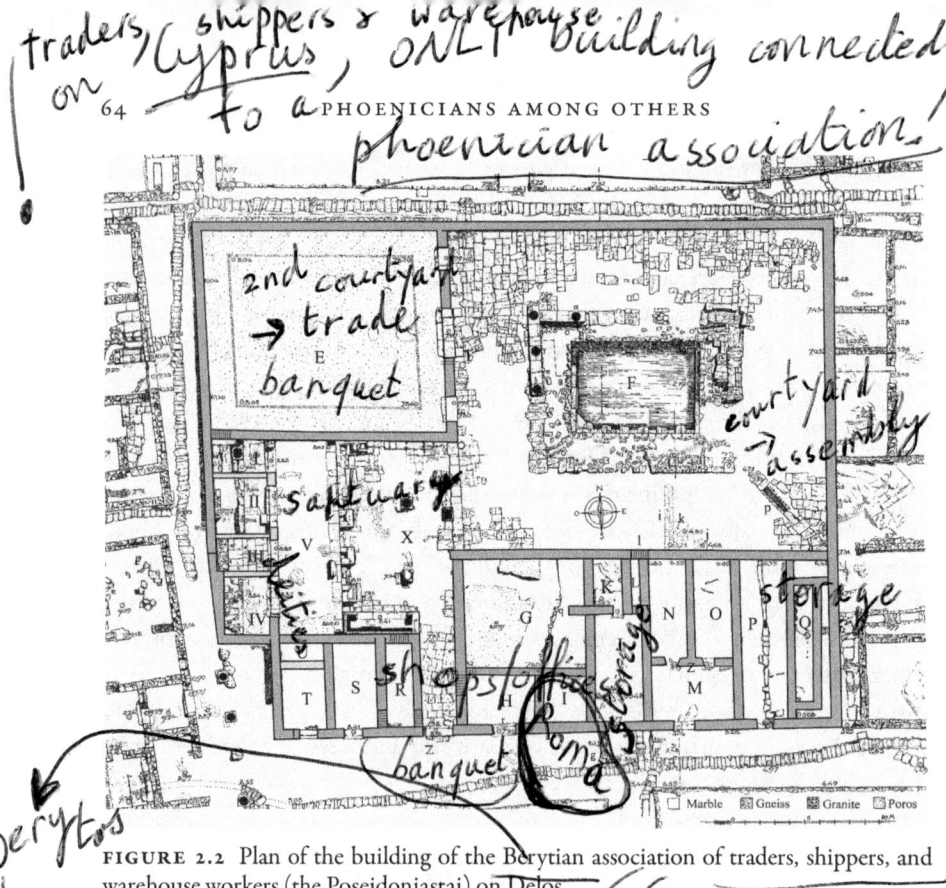

FIGURE 2.2 Plan of the building of the Berytian association of traders, shippers, and warehouse workers (the Poseidoniastai) on Delos. Trümper 2011, 82 fig. 2. Courtesy of Monika Trümper.

remains of this building and thirty-three mostly honorific inscriptions excavated from within it dating from 153/152 to 90 BCE, offers a glimpse into not only the association's operations but also the ways it attempted to maintain positive relations with its host state (Fig. 2.2).[32] This building was located adjacent to the city

---

that one day in the year be dedicated to Marcus Minatius. Proclamations of his goodwill were to be made during festivals and monthly meetings of the committee (synod) administering the association, and a bull sacrificed in his name. Finally, these honors could never be changed, and several prohibitions and curses were put in place to punish anyone who violated the prescriptions described in this award. The text that records his contributions, *I.Délos* 1520, dates to 153/152 BCE and contains very similar language to *I.Délos* 1519, which records the honors granted to the Tyrian Patron by the association of the Herakleistai. Similarities between *I.Délos* 1519 and 1520 include the commissioning of a portrait of the honorand to be placed in the building of the association, the award of a gold wreath, and exemption from membership fees and service requirements. That a Roman could become a member suggests that non-Berytians could be included in the membership of a Phoenician association, perhaps if they had performed an extraordinary service for the association, as Marcus Minatius had.

32. The inscriptions are *I.Délos* 1520, 1772–1796, 2323–2327, 2611, and 2629. *I.Délos* 2611 is a subscription list of individuals who had made contributions to the association, whose Greek

center, suggesting its relative importance to the island and its commercial operations. Large and complex, it covered an estimated fifteen hundred square meters and included a big peristyle courtyard that could house the assembly of the association (F), a second courtyard where some of the trade operations were carried out (E), a sanctuary (X and V), several smaller rooms reserved for the worship of specific deities (V.I–IV), storage facilities (J and P), shops or offices (H, I, R, S, T), and banqueting space (E and Z).[33] The plan of the building indicates that it provided space for the political, commercial, and religious functions of the association, which probably had a membership of about a hundred, given the size of the banqueting rooms and the number of banqueters they could accommodate.

The sacred areas of the building, only some of which have been securely linked to the worship of specific gods, reveal that it honored not only the Phoenician ancestral gods of the Berytians but also the city of Rome, which was the dominant polity in the Mediterranean in the second century BCE and was the political entity that had made Delos a free port under Athenian jurisdiction. For example, several dedications, mostly of statues or architectural elements incorporated in the building of the Poseidoniastai of Berytos, specify that the offerings were in honor of their ancestral gods, probably Baal (translated into Poseidon) as evidenced by the name of the association and other dedications, and perhaps Astarte, worshiped in rooms V.II and V.III, respectively.[34] If the Berytians had originally requested from Athens the right to own land to create a place where they could worship their gods, it most likely would have been for those deities. But the presence of a statue of Roma (the personification of Rome), the earliest

---

names are extremely common among Phoenicians living in Greek communities (among others, Zeno, Herakleides, Dionysios, Apollodoros, Mnaseas). *I.Délos* 2629 is a member list with similarly commonly adopted Greek names among Phoenicians (among others, Asklepiades, Asklepiodoros, Herakleides, Antipatros, Dionysios, Apollonios). For a discussion of the dossier of inscriptions of the Berytian Poseidoniastai, see Bonnet 2015: 490–498.

33. Trümper 2011: 53–58, with bibliography, discusses the layout of the building and the functions of its various parts. Terpstra 2019: 67–69 follows Trümper's analysis. See also Bruneau 1970 and 1978 and Steuernagel 2020: 71–75. The plan of this building both resembles a sanctuary complex dedicated to Eshmoun in Bostan esh-Sheikh, in the outskirts of Sidon (Stucky 1997: 923 and 2005: 165–166) and exhibits Italian architectural traditions (Tang 2005: 63–65), demonstrating its hybrid character.

34. *I.Délos* 1774, 1776, 1781, 1783, 1785, 1789, 2323, 2326, 2327 record dedications to the ancestral gods (θεοῖς πατρίοις). *I.Délos* 1786–1788, 1790, 1793, 2324, 2325 record dedications to Poseidon. Trümper 2002 and 2006 offer recent discussions of this building of the Poseidoniastai and the possible identification of the deities. See also Baslez 1986: 294, who proposed several alternatives, and Martin 2017: 157 for a discussion of the possible divinities worshiped in these spaces and the famous statue group of the Slipper Slapper found in this building. The Slipper Slapper depicts Aphrodite (who could be read as Astarte) holding her sandal, Pan holding on to her, and Eros flying above Pan, holding one of Pan's horns.

extant image of the goddess, in the furthermost room from the public entrance of the building (I) indicates that these sacred areas were specifically remodeled c. 130 BCE to ensure that there was now a space dedicated for the worship of that newly introduced deity. The creation of this new space for Roma's worship suggests an attempt to become better and more fully integrated into the local society of the island and Roman culture in general.[35]

Just as the adoption of the worship of foreign divinities common among the practitioners of the polytheistic religions of the ancient Mediterranean had made it easy for this Phoenician group to translate its theophoric name into a Greek one, it also seems to have made it fairly simple to worship a Roman goddess. Although that worship would have been carried out in the interior of the building and was thus not viewed by the general public, it would have been observed by the associations' members and any dignitaries, including Athenian and Roman representatives visiting the building. One dedication to Roma by the whole association of the Berytians explicitly calls her a benefactor and notes that the dedication was offered because she had shown favor not only to the association but also to their homeland, Berytos.[36] As this evidence shows, the Phoenician trade association of the Berytians found a way to both maintain the religious traditions of their homeland and adopt the worship of Roma, most likely as a way to maintain good relations with the powerful state of Rome that would eventually make the whole of the Mediterranean part of its empire.

Several dedications within the association's building show that the Berytian association on Delos also found ways to recognize and honor both the Roman and the Athenian administrative authorities of the island. Some of these dedications mention the ruling Athenian archon, the officer whose name was used to date the year of the offering, albeit at the end of the text rather than in the beginning as was the custom in Athens, or honor Roman or local officers, as, for example, the Roman praetor Gnaeus Octavius, following Greek and Roman

---

35. Several dedications to the goddess were inscribed: *I.Délos* 1778–1779. The exact date of the renovations to the building is not known, but they took place before 88 BCE, when activity from this building stops, following the attacks on the Greek peninsula by the Pontic king Mithridates: see Trümper 2011: 55–56.

36. *I.Délos* 1778: Ῥώμην θεὰν εὐεργέτιν | τὸ κοινὸν Βηρυτίων Ποσειδωνιαστῶν | ἐμπόρων καὶ ναυκλήρων καὶ ἐκδοχέων | εὐνοίας ἕνεκεν τῆς εἰς τὸ κοινὸν καὶ τὴν πατρίδα. | ἀρχιθιασιτεύοντος τὸ δεύτερον | Μνασέου τοῦ Διονυσίου εὐεργέτου | [Μένανδρος] Μέλανος Ἀθηναῖος ἐποίει (To Roma, the benefactor goddess. The association of the Berytian Poseidoniastai of traders, shippers, and warehouse workers [dedicated this] because of her favor toward the association and its homeland. In the second time that Mnaseas, son of Dionysus, the benefactor, was an *archithiasites*. [Menandros] the son of Melas, the Athenian, made this).

cultural practices.[37] Such a habit was also common among other associations on Delos, practiced both by the Tyrian association of the Herakleistai mentioned above and by various Italian associations.[38] In addition to adopting the Athenian and more broadly Greek habit of dating texts, in the late second century (122/121 BCE) the Berytian association also constructed a public monument to honor the people of Athens, who were, after all, the administrators of the island and its commercial operations, and awarded wreaths to the Athenian people, which were engraved on the stone recording that award.[39] The Berytians also participated in the procession, sacrifices, and banquet of the annual festival to Apollo, the patron god of Delos, and held a festival for their own Poseidon, their association's namesake god. As this evidence demonstrates, the Berytian association served three masters besides its own civic corporation—Delos, Athens, and Rome—and recognized all of them in the dedications and language used on these records, thus maintaining excellent relations with these host states while enabling Berytian immigrants to retain their religious traditions and links to their home state.

The development and political character of the Tyrian Herakleistai and the Berytian Poseidoniastai over time can also be better understood by examining the terminology associated with those professional organizations as it was used in texts inscribed on stones. Whereas the fourth-century BCE Kitian association in Athens referred to itself only as the "demos of the Kitians" and the "Kitian traders," and the association that proposed the honors for Apollonides of Sidon in Athens called itself only "the traders and shippers," by the second century BCE such groups were describing themselves in more elaborate ways. On Delos, both the Herakleistai and the Poseidoniastai used different terms to describe different organs of the association—*koinon*, possibly a general term for association; *synodos*, most likely the assembly that discussed and made decisions; *archithiasites*, a title often recorded as a way of marking time on the texts that suggests the existence of a *thiasos*, perhaps a part of the association that had religious

---

37. *I.Délos* 1777 and 1782.

38. The Competaliastai often mention who was consul in Rome (*I.Délos* 1763), as does a dedication to Apollo, the deity to whom the whole island of Delos was sacred, by the association of the Hermaistai, Apolloniastai, and Poseidoniastai (*I.Délos* 1758), who was the archon in Athens (*I.Délos* 1760), or even the Athenian supervisor of Delos at the time of their dedication (*I.Délos* 1761–1763). These were all common dating formulae on inscribed texts, demonstrating that these associations had integrated the Roman, Athenian, and Delian administrative practices. The Competaliastai, too, had dedicated a statue of Roma (*I.Délos* 1763), as the Berytian Poseidoniastai had done.

39. *I.Délos* 1777 and *I.Délos* 1780. *I.Délos* 1781 also has engraved wreaths underneath the text of the inscription. The engraving of wreaths on stelae was common in Athens.

functions; and *hiereus*, a priest mentioned in conjunction with dating formulae.[40] The Tyrian Herakleistai seem to have had, in addition, an *ekklesia*, perhaps a reference to a meeting or a meeting place rather than an administrative organ of the association, as well as a secretary and treasurers.[41] All these details regarding the structure of these associations show that they operated as semiautonomous entities with their own political bodies that made decisions regarding the association and its members, interacted with their host state and other dominant powers, and represented their immigrant members.

Conclusion

As the evidence presented in this chapter demonstrates, Phoenician trade associations were an innovative adaptive strategy developed by immigrants. They facilitated migration by organizing immigrants into groups that availed them of more power than would likely have been available to them as individuals. While such organizations played a potentially important role in commerce, they also allowed migrants to administer aspects of their respective immigrant communities with some autonomy even while living under the jurisdiction of their host state. In so doing, they helped immigrants maintain a sense of civic identity within their host lands, retain their cultural traditions, keep good relations with their host state, and influence their host state's policies. Their internal organization into assemblies that made decisions and officers who ran meetings granted them authority among both the immigrant communities they represented and their host states. Their ability to lobby their host states for awards or petition them for special grants that bypassed restrictions normally placed on immigrants suggests that those states recognized Phoenician trade associations as having the political standing to make suggestions of a political, economic, or diplomatic nature, such as the award of honors to traders and the requests to establish sanctuaries to maintain the traditions of their homelands. In this respect, the professional associations in Athens and Delos resembled the better-studied private associations on Rhodes, which were able to interact with public associations, political elites, and the Rhodian state and ultimately shape Rhodian politics.[42] Although

---

40. All these terms appear on *I.Délos* 1519, the only text recording the existence of a Tyrian association on Delos, and *I.Délos* 1520, and various combinations of these terms also appear on the other inscriptions produced by the Berytian association.

41. The *ekklesia* is mentioned in line 5, the secretary and treasurers in lines 46–47.

42. The number of private associations discovered on Rhodes is close to an astounding two hundred. Thomsen 2020 provides the most recent analysis of this Rhodian institution. See also Baslez 1977 (whose claims that associations were based on ethnic exclusivity, common

the Rhodian associations comprised a mix of both citizens and noncitizens, both they and the professional organizations of Athens and Delos provided foreigners the possibility of upward social mobility, a direct link to the authorities of their host state, and integration into the social structures of their host polis.[43] Over time, these Phoenician innovations of the fourth century BCE became institutions that were politically and socially integrated into their host state, changing the fortunes of both their members through the support they provided them and the host states that incorporated these foreign associations in their political infrastructure.

Abdashtart: King of Sidon

---

profession, and common cults have now been debunked); Gabrielsen 2001; Benincampi 2008: 244–52; Maillot 2015. Of these associations, only one may be Phoenician, that of the Aphrodisiastan Basileias Aphroditas (Maillot 2015: 139 with bibliography). Thomsen 2020 dubs private associations on Rhodes a "corporate polis," namely, a polity made up of various associations that crisscrossed Rhodian society and constructed networks across families, professions, cultic groups, foreigners, citizens, and enslaved persons, among others.

43. See also Maillot 2015: 155–156, who argues that through associations, foreigners in Rhodes created a framework for social life that could help newcomers integrate into their host societies.

3

Managing Migration

AN INSCRIPTION NOW in the Ashmolean Museum in Oxford records that in the mid-360s BCE, Athens, in gratitude for the help King Abdashtart of Sidon had provided to Athenian ambassadors on their way to an audience with the Persian king, awarded him the honor of proxenia, invited his envoy to a meal at the Prytaneion (a building that symbolized the city's religious and political center), and explored the possibility of establishing diplomatic relations between the two city-states. Of particular interest to the concerns of this book is a rider or an amendment to the main decree, which appears to suggest that Abdashtart had also taken steps to negotiate privileges for Sidonian traders living in Athens, mostly tax exemptions that facilitated their stay there while also ensuring that they retained their citizenship in Sidon (Fig. 4.2). Presumably through these negotiations, the rider reveals, a community of Sidonian traders living in Athens received an unprecedented combination of tax exemptions by the Athenian state that allowed them to bypass some of the legal restrictions typically placed on long-term immigrants and remain in Athens indefinitely. These Sidonian traders were granted exemption from metic and capital taxes and from being liable for financing a chorus, a form of indirect taxation imposed on wealthy Athenian residents, regardless of their citizenship status.[1] Although such tax exemptions were typical of awards given to foreign individuals who had provided valuable services or benefactions to their host state or that had been negotiated by their trade associations, these Sidonian traders in Athens appear to have been the only immigrant community, in Athens or other Greek polities, to have been awarded such extensive privileges.

These awards were also unique among those recorded in extant sources in that they were specifically granted only to those Sidonians who had lived in and were

---

1. *IG* II² 141, lines 29–36. For the Greek text and its translation see chapter 2 n. 10.

citizens of Sidon and had emigrated to Athens specifically because they were traders.[2] Whereas these provisions safeguarded Athens against the blurring of boundaries between citizen and noncitizen while allowing the Sidonian traders to stay in Athens for as long as they wanted to, they also ensured that Sidon would not lose those citizens and their obligations to their home state to emigration abroad. Although the decree does not state whether Abdashtart's envoy had negotiated these specific privileges or they were a unilateral grant by the Athenian assembly, the lively debate at the assembly must have included input from the Sidonian envoy (whether in person or through a citizen agent), who, as the inscription records, had come to Athens specifically to request something.[3] This rider thus indicates that the envoy may have come to Athens not just to seek the establishment of diplomatic relations but to negotiate benefits for Sidonian citizens who lived in Athens, suggesting that Sidon had a foreign trade policy that included staying actively involved in the affairs and citizenship of Sidonian citizens living abroad.

Similar attempts by Phoenician city-states to maintain the citizenship of their citizens who lived abroad and to negotiate agreements with their host states on behalf of their citizens can be found in a variety of literary and epigraphic sources. In Livy's famous history of Rome, for instance, the ancient historian records a debate that took place in the Carthaginian senate in the early second century BCE over how to deal with foreigners in its midst—in that case, a Tyrian whom they viewed with suspicion. Although the final outcome of the debate is unknown, Livy's account makes clear that the senators were fully aware that whatever action they decided to take regarding this man—including apprehending him—was likely to also have repercussions for Carthaginian citizens frequenting Tyre and other markets.[4] Similar concerns are suggested by a clause in an Attic decree from the middle of the fourth century BCE that honored Orontes, the provincial governor (or satrap) of the Persian Empire's province of Mysia in northwest Asia Minor, with citizenship and a gold wreath for his goodwill and favor toward Athens. According to the fragmentary text of that clause, negotiations between Athens and Orontes had led to an agreement that Athenians traveling or living in Orontes' territory would be liable to legal proceedings under unspecified,

---

2. The Greek text specifies that these exemptions would be given to those who were domiciled and citizens of Sidon (οἰκõντες ἐς Σιδῶνι καὶ πολιτευόμενοι) and who were in Athens for commercial business (ἐπιδημῶσιν κατ' ἐμπορίαν Ἀθήνησι).

3. The phrasing of the amendment, which was proposed by a different man than the one who proposed the main decree, suggests that both decrees were most likely debated only at the assembly without first having been discussed at the council.

4. Livy 34.61. This anecdote is also discussed in chapter 5.

agreed-upon judicial conventions, implying a reciprocal agreement regarding citizens of Mysia who were residents or visitors in territories under Athenian jurisdiction.[5] As such texts reveal, widespread mobility and migration in the region during this period led states to take steps to clarify the legal standing of their citizens who traveled or lived abroad.

Although such provisions and concerns for citizens living abroad may appear to have been an afterthought in discussions among states that traded with one another and operated within the same international political arena, an examination of bilingual or exclusively Greek inscriptions commissioned by state actors in major Greek religious sanctuaries indicates that such state-sponsored acts were intended to manage as well as facilitate the migration of their mobile populations. These inscriptions show that, just as Phoenician immigrants developed individual and collective ways to advance their opportunities and improve the quality of their lives across the Mediterranean region, the Phoenician polities from which these migrants originated were not merely disinterested parties in the relationships between migrants and their host states. Rather, they employed multiple methods to both maintain the citizenship of their citizens who lived abroad and make it easier for them to succeed in their host societies. As the chapter will also show, the ties between immigrants and their home states were bolstered by immigrants living in Greek communities, whose own actions and contributions to Phoenician trade organizations helped sustain those long-distance relationships and boost the image of their city-states of origin.

Creating Enduring Relations with Their Citizens Abroad

During the period that is the focus of this book, states intervened in the affairs of their citizens living abroad in a variety of ways, including through diplomacy

---

5. *IG* II³ 1 295. The text is composed of four fragments that seem to record two separate decrees, the first of which dates to the 360s and the other to the 350s or 340s BCE. For a discussion of the date of the inscription, the various problems associated with it, and bibliography, see Demetriou 2020: 111–117. The text reads (fr. a, lines 13–17): τοὺς μὲν Ἀθηναίους δίκας <δ>ιδόναι ἐν τοῖς συμβόλ[οις – – – – – – – – –] | [. . .] εἰσὶν ἐκ τῆς Ὀρόντου ἀρχῆς ΕΤ ΠΑΙ[– – – – – συ]μμαχ[– – – – – – – – – – –] | [. . .] ἐξεῖναι τῶι ἐγκ(λ)ήματι ΩΙΑΛΣΕΠ [– – – –] ΑΝ [– – – – – – – – – – – – – –] | [. . 5 . . .]υσιν· τὴν δὲ βουλὴν τὴν [– –] | [. . . 6 . . .] καὶ τῶι δήμωι [– –] (the Athenians on the one hand shall be liable to legal proceedings under the judicial convention . . . from the territory governed by Orontes . . . allies . . . it shall be possible . . . for the complaint in law . . . and the council . . . and to the people . . .). We only have the μέν part of a μέν + δέ construction in line 13, suggesting that there was a reciprocal agreement for Mysians in Athenian territories.

at the state level, direct communication with their citizens by means of bilingual dedications inscribed on offerings given in the Greek sanctuaries frequented by those citizens, and enhancing their prestige and renown through contributions to international Greek sanctuaries. Although the outcomes of such efforts are not always known, the numerous texts that record their home states' diplomatic actions, benefactions, and admonitions suggest that their underlying intention was to both help their citizens who had migrated and remind them of their citizenship and fiscal obligations.

Diplomatic actions such as those undertaken by Sidon and the other states mentioned above were one way in which city-states acted to advance their interests and activities of their own citizens living and traveling outside their home state. Such efforts are illustrated in even higher relief in the text of a later, second-century BCE decree from Teos, a Greek city on the coast of Ionia in Asia Minor, intended to memorialize that Tyre had sent ambassadors to Teos to negotiate a renewal of the friendship between the two city-states and to reaffirm all other previous agreements, concessions, grants, and privileges.[6] Although the decree does not provide the details of the previous agreements between the two cities, it nonetheless makes clear that these diplomatic ties, privileges, and grants were extended not only to the state and officials of Tyre but to its citizens as well.[7] Such agreements, which often addressed commercial or military alliances, freedom of travel to and from each place, the inviolability of personhood and belongings, and even the right of property ownership or citizenship, would have profoundly shaped the affairs and living conditions of Tyrians living in Teos, and thus such diplomatic actions undertaken by representatives of a state played an important role in how states managed mobility and migration.

Such concerns about citizenship and the rights and obligations of the Phoenician diaspora are also demonstrated by a bilingual Phoenician and Greek inscription dating to the last quarter of the fourth century BCE that was found

---

6. *SEG* 4 601 (lines 3–4: καὶ ἀνανεῶται τ[ὴν φιλίαν καὶ τὰ ἄλ]]λα τα προϋπάρχοντα ταῖς πόλεσι πρὸς ἑ[αυτὰς φιλάνθρωπα]). The decree also announces the Tean officials' intention to make the ambassadors' stay in Teos pleasant, dignified, and worthy of the standards of the two cities, including following the customs of hospitality by inviting them to dinner in the Prytaneion.

7. A different inscription from the late fourth century BCE from Athens, *IG* II² 418, records the presence of Carthaginian ambassadors, whose names were Hellenized to Synalos and Bodmilkas, who were invited to a meal at the Prytaneion, one of the honors granted to foreign individuals. Whatever else had been decided regarding these men and their state no longer survives on the stone, but that the decree was recorded on stone for posterity and at the state's expense indicates the importance of the diplomatic action that had taken place. Walbank 1985 suggests that these two Carthaginian ambassadors were ferried to Athens by the father and son team of Hieron and Apses, whom Athens honored with proxenia, as discussed in chapter 4.

FIGURE 3.1 Bilingual dedication by the Sidonian royal family on Kos, late fourth century BCE (*IG* XII.4 2 546 = *KAI* 292).
Kos, Museum of Kos, Inv. No. E6. © Hellenic Ministry of Culture and Sports / Hellenic Organization of Cultural Resources Development.

on the Greek island of Kos in the southeastern Aegean Sea, famous as the birthplace of the ancient physician Hippokrates. That inscription, like the rider to the decree honoring Abdashtart, reveals that taxation was a major issue of mobility and migration from the perspective of Phoenician city-states. Although the left side of the stone is damaged and the first few letters of all four lines of the Greek text are missing, this inscription, discovered in the town of Kos in 1982, records a religious dedication made by the Sidonian royal family (Fig. 3.1).[8] As with most bilingual inscriptions discussed in this book, the Greek and Phoenician texts follow Greek and Phoenician epigraphic practices, respectively; the two texts are not direct translations of each other; the Phoenician text is longer and more detailed; and consequently, the two texts, despite their similarities, convey different kinds of information to potential readers.[9] The Greek text, which is the only one of the

---

8. *SEG* 36 758 and now *KAI* 292 and *IG* XII.4 2 546. Kantzia 1980 and Sznycer 1980 first published the Greek and the Phoenician texts, respectively. For an updated reading of the Phoenician text, see Sznycer 1999. For a different reading of the last line, see Lipiński 2004: 149–155. For more on the Phoenician presence on Kos, see Bourogiannis 2013 and 2020.

9. Briquel-Chatonnet 2012: 636–637.

Managing Migration   75

two that preserves the name of the dedicator, states simply that Diotimos, the son of the Sidonian king Abdalonymos (a Hellenized version of his Phoenician name), made a dedication in honor of Aphrodite on behalf of those sailing.[10] The Phoenician text similarly records that the son of King Abdalonym dedicated a maritime monument to Astarte for the safety of all sailors and then also mentions some taxes owed, presumably by sailors, to the Phoenician god Eshmoun, one of the patron divinities of Sidon.[11] Selecting Astarte and Aphrodite as the recipients of a dedication for sailors would have been a natural choice, given that the Phoenician Astarte was a deity of mariners and sea travel and that the Greek Aphrodite was often worshiped as a patron of navigation. On the island of Kos in this period, Aphrodite was worshiped as both Aphrodite Pandamos (of the People) and Aphrodite Pontia (of the Sea) in a temple located on the coast next to shipyards.[12] That through this dedication the Sidonian royal family was requesting blessings for all those who sail would have been clear to readers of both texts despite their respective cultural settings, given the flexibility of polytheistic systems resulting from the movement and migration of peoples in the region.

Although travel and migration had made the two goddesses translatable into one another and ensured that both Greek and Phoenician audiences would have

---

10. *IG* XII.4 2 546: [Ἀφρ]οδίτηι ἱδρύσατο | [. . .]τιμος Ἀβδαλωνύμου | [Σιδ]ῶνος βασιλέως | [ὑπ]ὲρ τῶν πλεόντων ([Dio]timos, the son of the king of Sidon Abdalonymos, established [this] for Aphrodite on behalf of those sailing). The Greek name Diotimos is not identified as the name of a Phoenician king in any other source, Phoenician, Greek, or otherwise. Lipiński 2004: 153 suggests Gerbaal, a direct translation of Diotimos, as a possibility for his Phoenician name. This text is the only epigraphic attestation of Abdalonymos, who was placed on the Sidonian throne in 332 BCE by Alexander the Great when he conquered Sidon, known from various ancient literary sources: Diodorus 17.46.6–17.47; Plutarch, *Moralia* 340d; Quintus Curtius 4.1.15–26; Pompeius Trogus in Justin, *Epitome* 11.10.8.

11. *KAI* 292: (1) lrbty lʾštrt pʾlt t[ʾ] l z ʾ[nk – – – –] (2) bn mlk ʾbdʾlnm mlk ṣdnym ʾl ḥy k[l mlḥm] (3) ʾš[– –12– –] ʾl kl msʾt ʾš lʾšmn ln[– – – –] (To the lady Astarte, I have built this maritime monument, the son of King Abdalonym, the king of the Sidonians, for the safety of all sailors, who [. . .] for all taxes owed to Eshmoun . . .).

12. For the worship of Aphrodite on Kos as Aphrodite Pandamos and Pontia, see Parker and Obbink 2000 and Parker 2002. For Astarte as a maritime deity, see Baslez 1986; Bonnet and Pirenne-Delforge 1999; Ruiz Cabrero 2010. See also *I.Délos* 2132, a dedication to Isis Soteira Astarte Aphrodite Euploia where Astarte and Aphrodite are identified with one another and with Isis, as well as with smooth and safe sailing, as the goddesses' epithets, Soteira (Savior) and Euploia (Smooth-Sailing), show. For Aphrodite as a patron of navigation, see Demetriou 2010; for Isis as a maritime divinity, see Bricault 2019. Paul 2013: 91–93 also argues that Diotimos gave this offering because of Aphrodite's protection of sailors. Neither the Greek nor the Phoenician text specifies whether "those sailing" did so for military or commercial purposes. Sznycer 1999: 113–114 thinks that Diotimos sailed to Kos on a diplomatic or military mission. Baslez and Briquel-Chatonnet 1991b: 239 call Diotimos a "nauarch," an admiral. Hauben 2004: 32 n. 29 rejects the hypothesis that Diotimos held the title of a nauarch. For a general discussion of Sidonian kings and their role in the Persian and Ptolemaic navies, see Hauben 1970.

understood the connotations of this dedication, the additional information provided for Diotimos' Phoenician audience, which referred to a different deity altogether, was apparently intended to remind Sidonian citizens visiting or living on Kos of their obligations to their home state. The third line of the Phoenician text, although poorly preserved, refers to taxes or payments owed to the god Eshmoun. Some scholars have attempted to explain this reference by suggesting that these taxes refer to the means by which Diotimos paid for the maritime monument,[13] yet other evidence from Phoenician city-states indicates that acts of benefaction were paid for exclusively by kings or royal families.[14] Although some scholars have proposed that the Sidonians chose to invest in a large-scale monument on Kos because it was home to a famous international sanctuary of Asklepios, who was often translated into the Phoenician god Eshmoun, both the Greek and Phoenician texts emphasize that it was dedicated in honor of Aphrodite/Astarte on behalf of sailors.[15] All this suggests that the references to taxes owed to the god Eshmoun, one of the patron deities of Sidon, were mentioned in the Phoenician text as a reminder to Sidonians who traveled for business to pay their dues to their own gods and their own cities. The taxes owed to Eshmoun might well parallel some monetary payments and ritual regulations that "those sailing" were expected to observe toward Aphrodite Pontia on Kos, as recorded on two inscriptions from this temple that detail that sailors and soldiers serving in warships were required

---

13. Briquel-Chatonnet 2012: 623; Bonnet 2013: 48–49. Lipiński 2004: 154 reads the last line of the Phoenician text altogether differently, translating it as "who [should pay attention] to all the beacons of oil lights for those ap[proaching the harbour]," and thereby identifying the maritime monument as a lighthouse. This leads him to translate *mš't* as *beacons* rather than *taxes* and to read in *'šmn* not Eshmoun's name but rather the noun for oil lights. Indeed, Eshmoun's name is in the same semantic field as oil. Xella 2010: 89–90, followed by Amadasi Guzzo 2013: 167–172 and Bonnet 2015: 255, assesses this interpretation as possible but highly hypothetical.

14. The rich epigraphic material from the sanctuary of Eshmoun at Bustan esh-Sheikh, an extra-urban complex two miles from Sidon in southwestern Lebanon, provides ample evidence of the Sidonian royal family's patronage from the sixth to the fourth centuries BCE. See Stucky 2005.

15. Bonnet 2013: 48–49. For the identification of Asklepios with Eshmoun, see Ribichini 2009. Pausanias 7.23.7–8 and Strabo 16.2.22 both equate Eshmoun with Asklepios. *CIL* 10 7856 = *IG* XIV 608 = *KAI* 66 = *CIS* I 143 is a trilingual inscription, in Latin, Greek, and Phoenician, that records a dedication to Aesculapius in Latin, Asklepios in Greek, and Eshmoun in Phoenician. For more on this inscription, see chapter 5. As to what the monument could have been, Bonnet and Lipiński (in Lipiński et al. 1992: 121 s.v. Cos) suggest either a jetty or a monumental work of art that would serve the sailors; Sznycer 1999: 111 proposes it was an embankment or mole at the entrance to the harbor; Lipiński 2004: 149–155 argues that it was a lighthouse; Xella 2010: 87–90 suggests that it was some kind of large structure. Such public works would have taken a long time to complete, making it possible that Diotimos was present on Kos for a significant amount of time (Sznycer 1999: 113; Hauben 2004: 30).

to sacrifice to Aphrodite Pontia when they completed their voyage, fishermen and shipowners were expected to make annual monetary offerings to the goddess calculated per ship, and traders and shipowners were obligated to perform requisite sacrifices to Aphrodite Pontia when they had returned safely from their ventures.[16] It may have been customary for even non-Greeks such as the Phoenicians to make offerings to Aphrodite, but the taxes owed to the god Eshmoun would have been taxes that the Sidonians were expected to pay at the temple of the god back in their home city-state. While the dedication to Aphrodite suggests the Sidonian royal family's desire to maintain friendly and respectful relations with a Greek city-state in which its citizens lived and worked, the reminder of taxes still owed by those citizens to their home state appears to indicate that such efforts were also motivated by a desire to maintain connections with immigrants living elsewhere who still bore financial obligations to their home state. Ultimately, both the soft diplomacy exemplified by the religious dedication offered by the royal Sidonian family on Kos and the formal diplomacy of the king of Sidon to negotiate tax privileges that ensured that Sidonians would not be burdened by double taxation may have been largely motivated by a desire to maintain state revenues received from citizens even if they lived elsewhere.

Although the intended purpose of several other inscriptions that record gifts offered by Phoenician states or Phoenician kings—mostly dedications of monuments in famous Greek sanctuaries such as Delos—is not as explicit as those of the previous examples, at least one of their functions appears to have been to offer gathering spots and maintain cultural connections with Phoenician citizens who traveled extensively or had migrated to various Greek city-states. In one such example, a bilingual inscription in Greek and Phoenician from Delos accompanying a dedication that represented both the states of Sidon and Tyre suggests that, although the actual dedicator is not known, it was commissioned with the direct involvement of the royal authorities of those two city-states (Fig. 3.2).[17] While the Greek text simply announces the dedication of some statues of Sidon and Tyre to the Greek god Apollo by a group called the Tyrian *hieronautai* (sacred sailors), the more fragmentary Phoenician text begins with the typical Phoenician dating system, which includes the regnal year of the Sidonian king, in this instance

---

16. *I.Cos Segre* ED 178; *SEG* 50 766. Although these inscriptions date from 196/195 BCE, these regulations may well have been in place even earlier, given the often fixed sacred laws that governed Greek religious practices.

17. *I.Délos* 50 = *CIS* I 114. The block of marble was originally described as an architectural element (an epistyle or architrave placed on top of the abacus of a column), and more recently Elayi 1988: 550 has suggested that the block was reused as a statue base for the Tyrian and Sidonian dedication.

FIGURE 3.2 Bilingual dedication in the Sanctuary of Apollo on Delos by the Tyrian *hieronautai*, 340s–330s BCE (*I.Délos* 50 = *CIS* I 114). Athens, Epigraphic Museum 1862. © Hellenic Ministry of Culture and Sports / Hellenic Organization of Cultural Resources Development.

another Abdashtart who ruled from 342 to 333 BCE, emphasizing the authority of the king of the Phoenician city-state of Sidon and again suggesting the two states' involvement in giving this offering on Delos.[18] Just what the statues or images might have represented and who the *hieronautai* were remain something of a mystery; still, this offering to Apollo, discovered close to his temple and located in one of the most frequented sanctuary complexes in the ancient world, was undoubtedly intended to proclaim the power and status of Sidon and Tyre to an international audience, maintain good diplomatic relations with Delos, and strengthen the bonds between the migratory Sidonians and Tyrians and their home states by emphasizing the prestige of those states.[19]

The political nature of the dedication is also evident in the specific statues that were placed on the stone base with the inscribed text and in the peculiar title of the Tyrians who made this joint dedication. First, the size of the stone would have been sufficient for the mounting of two statues, one from Tyre and the other from Sidon, perhaps personifications or an emblem representing each

---

18. The Greek text reads Τύρου καὶ Σιδῶνος | [εἰκ]όνας οἱ ἐκ Τύρου ἱεροναῦται | Ἀπόλλωνι ἀνέθηκαν (The Tyrian *hieronautai* dedicated images of Tyre and Sidon to Apollo). The Phoenician text reads *bšt . . . [l] mlk[y] ʿbd ʿ[štrt] mlk [ṣdnym . . .] l [. . .]* (In the Nth year of the reign of Abdashtart, king of the Sidonians). The Greek letterforms suggest a date from the third quarter of the fourth century BCE, when a second king by the name Abdashtart ruled Sidon. For the regnal dates of Phoenician kings, see Elayi 2006: 20 and 33–34 and 2018: 296–297 Table 2. For the paleography of the Greek text, see Elayi 1988: 551 and 555.

19. See Homolle 1878: 9–10 for the location of the dedication.

of the two polities in an international Greek sanctuary.[20] Second, the title of the dedicators—the Tyrian *hieronautai*—suggests that this was a religious association that may have operated among immigrant communities in Greek polities. It is also one of only two attestations of the word *hieronautai*, which scholars have usually translated as "sacred sailors" and assumed were official pilgrims traveling to sanctuaries, whom the Greeks would have called *theoroi*; such travel was a common practice in the Near East and among Phoenicians.[21] This reading of the institutional role of these sailors is supported by the only other occurrence of the term, which, although much later (from the third century CE), describes an association, and the mention of a sacred ship (a *hiera naus*) on the tombstone of Shem——, discussed earlier in the book. The later text appears on an inscribed stele from Histria, a state near the mouth of the Danube River on the Black Sea coast in present-day Romania, and records a dedication in honor of the son of a certain Menekrates and his wife made and paid for by the *hieronautai*, a religious association (or *koinon*) of admirals affiliated with the worship of the goddess Isis.[22] As discussed in the first chapter, the men who sailed on a *hiera naus* to bury Shem——, a Phoenician immigrant in Athens, may have been an official group of professionals who represented the interests of their members living in Greek communities. Whoever the Tyrian *hieronautai* may have been, this evidence suggests that they had an official capacity as religious ambassadors who represented both Tyre and Sidon and performed religious acts to serve immigrants from those home states while also performing diplomatic acts to maintain good relations

---

20. Renan 1880: 70 suggested that these statues were personifications, similar to the personification of Tyche of Antioch. But personifications became common in Phoenician polities only after the end of the second century BCE. Nonetheless, Bonnet 2015: 502–503 n. 96 thinks that the absence of earlier examples of personifications is not detrimental to the argument that these statues were personifications of the city-states of Tyre and Sidon, a hypothesis that has recently been revived by Hermary 2014, who argues that parallels of personifications may be found on Cypriot coinage from Salamis from the last third of the fourth century BCE (the same period as when these statues were dedicated). Elayi 2015 resists using Greek prototypes to propose the form of a Phoenician monument. Bonnet 2015: 502 suggests that εἰκόνας might be a direct translation of the Phoenician *šrn 'rṣ*, which appears on an inscription (c. 500 BCE) recording a dedication to Astarte by King Bodashtart of Sidon, signifying a city emblem (see Bonnet 1995 and 2008). The meaning of this phrase has been contested by Zamora 2007: 102–103 and 109–112, esp. 109 n. 51, who argues that it was a monumental structure that belonged perhaps to a temple rather than an emblem of the city.

21. Elsner and Rutherford 2005: 26–27; Rutherford 2013: 276 and 379–380. For Phoenician pilgrims, see Polybius 31.12.11–12, who mentions Carthaginian pilgrims who visited the temple of Melqart in their mother city of Tyre. Barbanera 1992: 94 and Stager 2005: 438 propose that the sacred ship that came to provide Shem—— with the appropriate burial rituals carried a sacred *theoria* based on the evidence of the dedications of the Tyrian *hieronautai* on Delos.

22. *IScM* II 98. For this text, see Vidman 1970: 76–87, esp. 78, and Takács 1995: 190–191.

with their host states. In so doing, they helped make it possible for migrants to maintain their cultural and religious traditions while living elsewhere and to feel proud to maintain their civic identity as citizens of home states that appeared to be major actors in international sanctuaries.

The international recognition and prestige of Sidonians both at home and abroad were similarly boosted by diplomatic acts that served Greek states and dedications made in the sanctuary of Delos by the last king of Sidon (c. 310 and 279/278 BCE). Philokles, who is known only by his Greek name and is best known for his military cunning while serving as a general in the navy of the Greek-installed Ptolemaic dynasty that ruled Egypt, was also honored for diplomatic services he rendered to various Greek states, including Athens, Delos, Thebes, and polities in the Aegean and the southeastern coast of Asia Minor.[23] The various awards granted to him by those states almost always identified him as the king of Sidon, projecting a positive image not only of Philokles but also of his city-state. The reputation of his city-state was also enhanced by Philokles' many dedications recorded on the temple inventories of Delos, which included sponsoring choruses and offerings of gold wreaths of myrtle and laurel to the temple.[24] Some of those inventories also include dedications made by Iomilchos, described

---

23. In Athens he probably helped liberate the city from Demetrios Poliorketes in 287/286 BCE, and, with the help of one of his subordinates named Zenon (a typical Hellenized Phoenician name), he supplied the city with grain supply. For these acts, he received a gold wreath and citizenship (*IG* II³ 1 868) and a bronze statue (*IG* II² 3425), and Zeno was honored, too (*IG* II³ 1 863). Philokles had also helped the Delians recuperate a loan they had made to the League of Islanders—a federal league of ancient Greek city-states on the Cycladic islands in the Aegean Sea—for which he received a gold wreath worth a thousand drachmas (the only recorded recipient of such an honor on Delos), among other honors (*IG* XI.4 559). In Thebes, Philokles may have been one of several foreign benefactors who had helped rebuild the city with a hefty monetary contribution (*IG* VII 2419). For a discussion of the contributions to the refoundation of Thebes, including those of Philokles, see Kalliontzis and Papazarkadas 2019 (esp. 300–304 and 309). His connection to Thebes was further reinforced when he and a Theban officer of the League of Islanders (a *nesiarch*), Bacchon, embarked on several diplomatic expeditions to Keos and Samos (*IG* XII.5 1065 and *IG* XII.7 506) for which they were both honored. He carried out further diplomatic activity in Aspendos c. 301–298 BCE (*SEG* 17 639), Telmessos in 282 BCE (*SEG* 28 1224), and Samos and Myndos c. 280 BCE (*IG* XII.6 1 95). Philokles is not identified as "king of the Sidonians" on the inscriptions from Aspendos and Telmessos. He had also captured Kaunos while in the service of the Ptolemaic navy, a feat later commemorated by the erection of a statue in his honor: Polyainos, *Stratagems* 3.16; *I.Kaunos* 82. For brief discussions of most of these texts, see Hauben 1987 and 2004, the two most comprehensive articles on Philokles and his career, with bibliography. See also Huss 2001: 171–172, 204–205, 209, 211–212, 239.

24. *IG* XI.2 161, 193, 203, 208, 219, 223, 287 and *I.Délos* 296, 298, 313. Philokles' name has also been reconstructed on two other inscriptions as a dedicant at the sanctuary: *IG* XI.2 162 and 191. The reasons for these dedications and whether they were accompanied by dedicatory texts are not recorded.

as the king of Carthage, probably a Greek translation of the Phoenician term *suffete*, a high office in Carthage.[25] The dedications of Philokles and Iomilchos were listed among those of such other Hellenistic kings as Ptolemy I, who ruled Egypt from 305/304 to 283 BCE; Demetrios Poliorketes, the king of Macedon in 294–288 BCE who founded Demetrias; Antipater, who briefly served as the regent of all of Alexander the Great's empire in 320–319 BCE; and Seleukos I, king of the Seleucid Empire in 306–281 BCE, the largest of the Macedonian kingdoms that bordered India in the East and Syria in the West. The names of this Phoenician king and Carthaginian leader were thus recorded at the time and for prosperity as among the company of Alexander's successors, implying that their respective city-states were comparable in renown to the empires of Hellenistic kings.

Whereas Sidon and Tyre were represented on Delos by their royal authorities in the fourth century BCE, temple inventories show that by the third century BCE, the Phoenician city-state of Byblos was making dedications at this Greek sanctuary as a state, reflecting constitutional changes occurring in Phoenician city-states in this period. Although Byblos and the other Phoenician states continued to have kings for several decades after Alexander's conquest of the region, sometime in the first quarter of the third century BCE hereditary kingship was abolished in Tyre, Sidon, Byblos, and Arados and replaced by constitutional democracies.[26] The temple inventories of Delos, which record at least two different dedications (a strigil and a fillet) by the Byblians as a collective rather than by their king, confirm these changes.[27] Just as Philokles' diplomatic acts and many dedications on Delos probably bolstered Sidon's reputation both at home and abroad, Byblos' offerings on Delos functioned to represent Byblos and its citizens within this international setting. This was one of the ways in which city-states declared their legitimacy, power, and strength and their citizens as active participants worthy of respect in the international theater of the island of Delos and in the larger Mediterranean world. In this way, they both facilitated Phoenician

---

25. *IG* XI.2 161, 199, 203, 208, 223 and *I.Délos* 298, 313, 442, and 1439, 1450, and 1457. Iomichos is called a king only on *IG* XI.2 223 but appears in the company of the other kings in the other inscriptions. *I.Délos* 1439, 1450, and 1457 specify he was a Carthaginian. See also Masson 1979 and Manganaro 2000: 259–260.

26. For more on these changes, see Millar 1983: 61–63; Apicella and Briquel-Chatonnet 2015: 10–12; Bonnet 2019: 103–104. As these authors demonstrate, although these changes have traditionally been interpreted as signs of "Hellenization," the elimination of kings from the constitutions of Phoenician city-states actually resulted in new forms of government built on preexisting infrastructure and were inspired as much by Carthage as by Greek polities.

27. *IG* XI.2 164, 199, 287 and *I.Délos* 313.

migrants' stay in their host state and engendered in them a sense of pride in being citizens of their home state.

Investing in One's Home State

In addition to such efforts by Phoenician city-states and their representatives to maintain bonds with their citizens abroad and to ensure that they fulfilled their obligations, Phoenician immigrants themselves—as individuals and as groups—also engaged in activities to help publicly promote their home states, maintain their identities, and preserve their cultural traditions. These activities included their previously discussed efforts to continue the religious traditions and increase the visibility and prestige of their home states and to provide practical and cultural support for one another within their host states, particularly through their participation and investment in professional associations centered around their city-state of origin. Like expatriate communities and cultural organizations today (such as the National Hellenic Society or the Alliance Française), Phoenician professional associations enabled immigrants not only to maintain their cultural traditions but to represent and advance the interests of their members and city-state of origin, as is evident in various epigraphic texts recording immigrants' benefactions to their associations and the home state with which they were affiliated.

A prime example is the Berytian association of traders, shippers, and warehouse workers on the island of Delos that was known as the Poseidoniastai. This organization not only mediated between its members and the officials of Delos, Athens, and Rome, as discussed earlier, but provided an avenue through which Berytians living on or visiting Delos could themselves invest in and proclaim their ongoing relationship with their home state of origin. In the second century BCE, many immigrants from Berytos made various benefactions in support of the association that indirectly helped to promote their city-state before an international audience. Dedications within the large building that housed the association's activities indicate, for example, that one benefactor, Dionysios, who identified himself with a multiancestor genealogy in the traditional Phoenician style, contributed to the financing of several stoas and other features.[28] Another such contributor was Mnaseas, the son of Dionysios, whose name and patronymic are names often associated with Phoenicians living among Greeks and who was one of the main officers of the association called the *archithiasites*.[29] Among those identified as making dedications to Poseidon within the association's building

---

28. *I.Délos* 1772, 1783–1785.

29. *I.Délos* 1773, 1775. That Mnaseas served as the *archithiasites* is recorded on *I.Délos* 1778.

was Demetrios, the son of Apollonides;[30] Zenon, the son of Dionysios, who also gave an offering to the ancestral gods;[31] Dionysios, the son of Zenodoros;[32] and a man whose father's name was Hieron, who among other things dedicated an altar—all of whom also bore names common among Phoenicians who Hellenized or translated their names in Greek.[33] It is possible that such gifts as the construction or refurbishment of stoas and other structures that were part of the building that housed the Poseidoniastai and represented the Berytians on Delos reflect a form of indirect taxation to benefit the association itself and their home state of Berytos. Such wealthy Berytian immigrants living on the island ensured through their contributions that their association had a strong presence on Delos, enhanced their home state's prestige, acknowledged their ties to their homeland, and expressed their identity and status as Berytians.

A late fourth- or early third-century BCE bilingual inscription in Phoenician and Greek found in Peiraieus, in Athens, that honors a Sidonian man for benefactions he made to his Sidonian association offers more insight into the mutually beneficial relationship between such associations and their members. Unlike the inscriptions just discussed, this bilingual inscription is almost exclusively concerned with the relationship between the association and its members, its only engagement with the larger world around it being the extremely terse Greek text that follows the much longer Phoenician text (Fig. 3.3).[34] Whereas that Greek

---

30. *I.Délos* 1786–1787.

31. *I.Délos* 1788–1789.

32. *I.Délos* 1790.

33. *I.Délos* 1791–1792. Several other similar dedications do not preserve the name of the dedicator: *I.Délos* 1776, 1793–1794.

34. *KAI* 60 and *IG* II² 2946. The earliest publications of the inscription used the internal date provided in the Phoenician text—that is, the fourteenth year of the Sidonian era, which traditionally is set to have begun in 112/111 BCE (Honigmann in *RE* 2 A 2, 2225–2226; Bickerman 1968: 74)—to date the inscription to 96/95 BCE: Cooke 1903: 94–99 no. 33. Later scholars dated independently both the Phoenician and Greek letterforms to the third century BCE (for the Phoenician letters: Teixidor 1980 and Gibson 1982; for the Greek text: Köhler, *CIA* Suppl. IV.2 1335b), and suggested that the internal reference to a date must refer to another Sidonian era that began in the late fourth or early third century BCE: Ameling 1990: 190–192 and Lipiński 2004: 171–172. Baslez and Briquel-Chatonnet 1991b have suggested 320/319 BCE as a date for this bilingual text based on several criteria, including that the epigraphic habit of inscribing numerals on inscriptions in Athens is common only in the latter half of the fourth century BCE and that a monetary value associated with gold wreaths appears only before 303/302 BCE. Taking the beginning of the reign of Abdalonymos, the man Alexander the Great placed on the Sidonian throne, to be the beginning of the Sidonian era referred to in this text, they arrived at the specific date of 320/319 BCE. I suggest that an alternative way of dating this text is to consider Year 1 as being the year after Sidon had abolished kingship (sometime c. 280 BCE, when the last attestation of Philokles, the last king of Sidon, appears in epigraphic texts).

FIGURE 3.3 A Sidonian koinon honoring one of its members in Athens, late fourth / early third century BCE (*IG* II² 2946 = *KAI* 60)
Paris, Musée du Louvre AO 4827. © Musée du Louvre / Thierry Ollivier.

text merely identifies the honorand by his Greek name, Diopeithes ("he who obeys Zeus" or "he who persuades Zeus"), and the entity responsible for granting the awards, the Sidonian association, the longer Phoenician text explains that the association had decided to honor this member, whose Phoenician name was Shama-Baal ("Baal listens," appropriately translated as Diopeithes in Greek), not only because he had benefited the association by providing its sanctuary with a court and performing various other tasks entrusted to him, but also to publicize how well the association treated those of its members who became the association's benefactors.[35] Recording on stone the honors they granted Shama-Baal

---

Other Phoenician states, after the conquest of Alexander the Great and once they abolished kingships, started to use a dating system in which Year 1 was the first year after the last king (see Millar 1983: 61). This would date the text to the mid-260s BCE.

35. The Greek text (*IG* II² 2946) reads τὸ κοινὸν τῶν Σιδωνίων | Διοπείθ⟨η⟩ν Σιδώνιον (The association of the Sidonians for Diopeithes the Sidonian). The translation of the Phoenician text (*KAI* 60) is "On the fourth day of the *marzeaḥ*, in the fourteenth year of the people of Sidon. It was resolved by the Sidonians, members of the assembly (*ṣdnym bn 'špt*): to crown Shama-baal,

offered the koinon of the Sidonians an opportunity to publicize itself as a social institution that allowed its immigrant members to maintain religious practices that were common in their home state of Sidon. That this Sidonian association was centered around the cult of Baal is suggested by several details in the text, which indicated that the association was in charge of the temple, the cost to inscribe the decree was paid by the temple's treasury, the temple's courtyard served as the location where the inscription was erected, and the decision to honor Shama-Baal was made on the fourth day of the *marzeaḥ*, a ritual feast.[36] Like the Berytian benefactors of their association on Delos, Shama-Baal, by carrying out the refurbishments of the temple complex and performing his other duties as the president of the association, helped make it possible for the Sidonian association to retain its Phoenician character and for himself and the other members to celebrate their religious traditions and reinforce their ties with their homeland Sidon.

This bicultural monument, while exhibiting the same name-changing practices, translations of divinities, and amalgamations of political practices as those described in previous chapters, also hints at the possibility that the home state used such associations to exercise some level of control over its citizens living in Athens. The Phoenician text is difficult to read and interpret both because several of its words appear only on this particular inscription and because it makes little sense in terms of Phoenician practices and becomes comprehensible only when read as a Phoenician translation of Athenian honorific practices. In the Phoenician text, the Sidonian association is said to have met as an assembly and made a decision (just as the Athenian assembly would have done); to have granted Shama-Baal a gold wreath of appropriate cost (which would have been a typical Athenian award); and to have ordered the association's decision to be inscribed on a stele in the temple of Baal (just as the Athenians often erected decrees in temples). As to the specific wording, neither the verb *tm*, usually translated as "decided" based on a parallel with the Greek ἔδοξεν, nor the word for "decision," *r't*, exist

---

son of Magon, who is the president of the association (*gw*) in charge of the temple and the construction of the court of the temple with a gold wreath of twenty legal darics because he built the court of the temple and he fulfilled all public functions conferred on him. Those who are the leaders of the temple should inscribe this decision on a cut stone and they should erect it in the portico of the temple for everyone to see. The association (*gw*) shall appoint the guarantor of the stele: they will take from the silver of the god Baal of Sidon twenty legal drachmas. In this way, the Sidonians will know that the association (*gw*) rewards men who fulfill public functions for the association."

36. On the *marzeaḥ* in Near Eastern sources, see McLaughlin 2001: 42–43. On the *marzeaḥ* and its connections to Greek cultural practices, see Nijboer 2013 (especially 99–101) and Martin 2018 (especially 298–299 for its occurrence on the bilingual inscription from Peiraieus). See also Baslez and Briquel-Chatonnet 1991a: 386; Baslez 2001: 242–243 and 2013: 231–232; Bonnet 2015: 449–450.

in any other known Phoenician or Punic text, which suggests that they represent a Phoenician translation of Greek words used in the Athenian decision-making process.[37] The very last sentence of the Phoenician text is likewise a translation of a phrase that often appears in Attic texts recording acts of *euergesia* (benefaction), and is similarly used in a decree by the Tyrian Herakleistai on Delos that records the honors given to a member who had represented their request for land on which to build a sanctuary of Herakles and publicizes the association's rewarding of members who strive to benefit the group.[38] The seeming Greekness of this text does not stop with the word choices and the practices they describe: the grammar in the Phoenician text is distinctly that of Attic epigraphy and is unusual in Phoenician, reinforcing the suggestion that in this dedication the Sidonian association translated language recorded on Attic honorific decrees just as it had translated Shama-Baal into Diopeithes.[39] The visual representation of a wreath on the stele similarly reflects the Athenian practice of engraving images of wreaths on decrees that record the grant of an actual wreath to individuals. All these oddities in the language of the text highlight the hybridity of artifacts such as this one produced in the context of migration.

Although the language used on this decree may have been borrowed from that of Athenian honorific decrees, it appears that the internal operations of the Sidonian association did represent Phoenician practices, as they are similar to those of the Phoenician trade associations operating in second-century BCE Delos, such as the Berytian Poseidoniastai and the Tyrian Herakleistai. The organization of the Sidonian association mimicked that of a political entity in that some of its apparatuses were similar to those of a state, perhaps even those of Phoenician states, as is evident in two different phrases in the text that indicate an organization akin to that of a political entity: *ṣdnym bn 'spt* (Sidonians, members of the assembly), and *gw* (association, perhaps a translation of the term *koinon*, used to describe the association in the Greek text).[40] The multiple terms

---

37. Ezra 5.17 uses *r't* to indicate a "royal decision."

38. The decree from Delos: *I.Délos* 1519. See also Donner and Röllig 1973: 74 no. 60. This phrase appears especially in decrees issued by the local authorities of demes, the Athenian administrative districts, when honoring their demarchs (their highest officers) for their supervision of deme affairs. See Matricon-Thomas 2011: 283; Bonnet 2015: 448–449.

39. For example, the presence of infinitives and conjugated verbs follows Greek rather than Phoenician grammar. Donner and Röllig 1973: 73–74 no. 60; Baslez and Briquel-Chatonnet 1991a: 375; Bonnet 2015: 451.

40. Baslez 2001: 244; Bonnet 2015: 449. The word *koinon* followed by the genitive of a civic group is a phrase that occurs frequently in Greek, including in inscriptions set up by Phoenician and Syrian associations in various Greek polities: Ameling 1990: 194–198.

used to describe the political organization of the association are reminiscent of the varied Greek terminology used by the trade associations of the Berytians and the Tyrians on Delos to describe themselves, including the words *koinon*, *synodos*, and *thiasos* to refer to the deliberative and decision-making apparatuses of those associations. While it is possible that such an internal structure, with varied bodies that had deliberative and legislative authority within the association, was borrowed from Greek political practices, it may also have derived from political structures common in Phoenician city-states. The city-state of Carthage, for instance, had a republican form of government composed of the high office of the suffetes (which originally served judicial functions), a senate that served as the main deliberative body, and an assembly that ratified decisions, among other administrative bodies and offices.[41] Most evidence regarding the governments of other Phoenician city-states suggests that they were hereditary monarchies, though they also included a civic community that implies the existence of an assembly with some power.[42] In fact, one scholar has interpreted the term *ṣdnym bn 'spt* (Sidonians, members of the assembly) on the honorific inscription by the fourth-century BCE Sidonian koinon as indicating an actual legislative body of Sidon rather than one of the association.[43] Although such an interpretation is unlikely, given the similarities between the associations' honorific practices and those of Athens and the parallels with the Phoenician associations on Delos, which seem to have operated autonomously even within the jurisdiction of their host state, some intervention in these associations on the part of their home states cannot be excluded.

However direct or indirect such an intervention might have been, a much later text dated to 174 CE from southern Italy in the western Mediterranean that describes the relationship between an association of Tyrians and their home state demonstrates a certain level of interdependence between such associations and their homelands. This inscription records two different texts in Greek. The first is a letter from Tyrian traders who lived in Puteoli, a port city known to the Romans as *Delus minor* (little Delos) just outside Naples (ancient Neapolis) in Campania and home to many foreign merchants, which was sent to Tyre to

---

41. Hoyos 2010: 20–38 describes the state and government of Carthage.

42. The existence of an assembly is implied by the use of the collective noun as a descriptor of the state, as for example in "king of the Sidonians," a phrase that appears on many inscriptions, including many cited in this book. For a summary of the political organization of the Phoenician kingdoms before Alexander's conquest in 332 BCE, see Sader 2019: 143–146, and for the changes that occurred in the early third century BCE, see Millar 1983: 61–62 and Apicella and Briquel-Chattonet 2015.

43. Teixidor 1980: 455; 460. See also Terpstra 2019: 51–52.

request help with paying the annual rent to maintain their station—the building housing this trading association and its activities—and the expenses for the sacrifices to the ancestral gods. The second is a partial record of the discussions of this matter by the council in Tyre.[44] In their letter, the Tyrians of Puteoli explained that their expenses had increased because local authorities had begun to exact another payment for a bull sacrifice at the games in Puteoli and the association had to prepare the station to celebrate the imperial cult, the latter an expense they claimed to have taken on so as not to burden Tyre further, implying that Tyre had been financially supporting this association. Moreover, they reported, even though their expenses had increased, their income had decreased because their membership numbers had been dwindling and no income had been accruing from the membership fees paid by shippers and traders. The record of the ensuing debate in the Tyrian council reveals that Tyre had the authority to make decisions over both the association's station in Puteoli and another one in Rome, which had previously assisted the station in Puteoli by paying its annual fees. The council discussed asking the Tyrian station in Rome to continue to help support the one in Puteoli and, if they refused, combining the leadership of the two stations. According to this text, the ultimate authority in these dealings, at least at a time of crisis, was Tyre, though the stations had some autonomy in making their own decisions even while being subject to the local authorities of Puteoli who imposed sacrifices on them and to the imperial authorities in Rome who forced them to celebrate the imperial cult. Although the actual decision of the Tyrian council is not recorded, that this text was inscribed on stone suggests that Tyre somehow managed to resolve the situation at Puteoli and ensure that the station continued to exist separately from the one in Rome.[45] In any case, this text shows that, at least in the second century CE, official authorities of Tyre were directly involved in the administration of their trade associations in Puteoli and Rome and exercised some control over and benefited from the trading activities of their members who lived there, who in turn benefited from the support of their homeland.

Individual immigrants showed their loyalty to their home state and cultivated ties with it not only through their benefactions to collective associations but also

---

44. *IG* XIV 830. Station is the translation of the Latin *statio* and στατίων in Greek. On associations in Puteoli in general, see Terpstra 2013: 51–93. On comparisons between this Tyrian station at Puteoli and the Berytian association of the Poseidoniastai on Delos, see Steuernagel 2020. The Roman author Lucilius called Puteoli *Delus minor*. On Tyrians in the Roman empire, see Aliquot 2011.

45. For a discussion of this inscription and what was at stake, see Sosin 1999, with bibliography, and Terpstra 2019: 52–53.

by their own dedications, as the story of Philostratos demonstrates, which can be stitched together from a series of inscriptions from the turn of the first century BCE. Philostratos, whose Greek name was common among Phoenicians living in Greek communities, was a Phoenician from Ashkelon who had risen to such prominence on Delos as a banker that he gave at least five different dedications on Delos and himself received several honors there, including the erection of a statue in his honor in the Agora of the Italians, a local building that housed the associations of the Italians (the Competaliastai, Hermaistai, Apolloniastai, and Poseidoniastai) and to which Philostratos was the only non-Italian donor.[46] All but one of Philostratos' dedications (c. 100 BCE) were made on behalf of himself or his family and "on behalf of the city of the Ashkelonites."[47] In addition to honoring the local god Apollo and the local association of the Italians, who probably employed him, these dedications indicate that Philostratos also worshiped a deity from his home state, perhaps Baal, whom he translated into Greek as the Ashkelonite Poseidon, as well as a specifically Semitic goddess, the Palestinian Astarte, who was syncretized with Aphrodite Ourania, demonstrating his multiple identities and allegiances to his home state, his host state, and the gods of both places.[48] Although Philostratos does not seem to have had an official role as a representative of Ashkelon and identified himself professionally only as a banker on Delos, his dedications in a major international sanctuary on behalf of his city-state of origin both solidified his connections to and performed a service for Ashkelon by reminding other Ashkelonites of the excellence of their home state and its citizens and by projecting a positive image of Ashkelon and its citizens within the wider international arena of Delos.

Philostratos' dedications on Delos on behalf of his home state of Ashkelon are even more striking since his success as a banker on Delos had led the Greek

---

46. *I.Délos* 1717–1724. Trümper 2014: 73–75 discusses the erection of his statue in a niche in the building known as the Agora of the Italians, recorded on *I.Délos* 1722 and *I.Délos* 2549. See also Rovai 2020: 179.

47. *I.Délos* 1717 (for Apollo and the Italians), 1719 (for Palestinian Astarte Aphrodite Ourania), 1720–1721 (for Ashkelonite Poseidon [Ποσειδῶνι Ἀσκαλωνίτῃ]). The Greek phrase used to indicate that his dedications were on behalf of Ashkelon is ὑπὲρ τῆς Ἀσκαλωνιτῶν πόλεως.

48. The syncretism of these two goddesses was common. Another Askhelonite gave an offering to Zeus Ourios and Astarte Palestina Aphrodite Ourania, the gods who had listened to his prayer (θεοῖς ἐπηκόοις) because he had been saved from pirates (*I.Délos* 2305), and another man, who did not specify where he was from, gave a dedication to Isis Soteira Astarte Aphrodite Euploia and Eros Harpokrates Apollo, equating Isis, Astarte, and Aphrodite, three goddesses who were frequently identified with one another (*I.Délos* 2132), as discussed in chapter 5. Astarte is also equated with Isis in a second-century BCE dedication by a Sidonian on Delos: *I.Délos* 2101. For these syncretisms, see Wallensten 2014.

city-state of Neapolis (most likely the one in Italy's Campanian region in the Bay of Naples) to grant him citizenship and, according to a text from the period between 102/101 and 92/91 BCE, Philostratos had indeed switched his citizenship. The dedication of the life-size statue of Philostratos by three brothers of the family of the Egnatii describes Philostratos as a banker on Delos and as a Neapolitan who had previously been an Ashkelonite businessman.[49] This rare honor of citizenship was probably granted to this Ashkelonite because he had helped Neapolis in a significant way, perhaps through his patronage of the Agora of the Italians and his various dealings with the Italian associations.[50] Yet the inscriptions on his own dedications, which are contemporary with the one referring to him as a Neapolitan, make clear that Philostratos continued to identify as at least a former citizen of Ashkelon and never forgot his home state, on whose behalf he had made several dedications. In the life story of this one individual as reconstructed from this epigraphic evidence, both the effects of migration and the persistent tug of identification with one's homeland are clear: even as the fluidity of the notions residency and citizenship allowed an Ashkelonite to live abroad (on Delos) among others for years and even to acquire citizenship in yet a third place (Neapolis), his ties to his homeland remained strong regardless of where he lived and he continued to identify as an Ashkelonite throughout his life regardless of his residency and citizenship. His dedications also hint at the possible irrelevance of switching citizenships: what appears more important is that, though a migrant among Greeks, he seems to have become relatively well integrated into his new host society and to have belonged both culturally and socially in his new home even while continuing to promote Ashkelon, his homeland.

---

49. *I.Délos* 1724: [Φιλ]όστρατον [Φ]ιλοστρά[του] | Νεαπολίτην | τὸν πρότερον [χ]ρηματί[ζ]ον[τα] | ['Ας[κα]λωνίτην, τραπεζιτε[ύοντα] | ἐν Δήλωι | [Π]ό[π]λιος καὶ Γάιος καὶ Γναῖος Ἐγνά[τι]οι Κοίντου Ῥωμαῖοι τὸν ἑαυ[τῶν] | εὐεργέτην Ἀπόλλωνι. | Λύσιππος Λυσίππου | Ἡράκλειος ἐποίει (For Philostratos the son of Philostratos, the Neapolitan, previously an Ashkelonite businessman, who is a banker on Delos, Publius and Gaius and Gnaeus, the Egnatii, sons of Cointus (Quintus), the Romans, [dedicated this] to Apollo because he was their benefactor. Lysippos the son of Lysippos from Herakleia made it).

50. *I.Délos* 1722 details the honors the Italians gave him and his sons for his justness and his love of goodness in his capacity as a banker. Another dedication made by an Ashkelonite honored Philostratos because he was his uncle, foster parent, savior, and benefactor: *I.Délos* 1723. Two other dedications were made on Philostratos' behalf by one of his friends: *I.Délos* 2253 and 2254.

Conclusion

As the epigraphic sources presented in this chapter reveal, Phoenician city-states and their citizens who lived abroad maintained a reciprocal relationship through a range of diplomatic acts and dedications in religious sanctuaries. For their part, authorities of Phoenician city-states attempted to regulate mobility and migration in the ancient Mediterranean by negotiating privileges for their citizens who lived abroad and enabling them to maintain both their cultural traditions and their citizenship in their home state, while Phoenician immigrants who lived in Greek communities preserved strong ties to their home states by investing in the activities of their trade associations and making various benefactions. By so doing, these immigrants helped project a positive image of their home state to both a Greek and a Phoenician audience and benefited financially and otherwise both their associations and their home state. A major motivation behind Phoenician city-states' desire to maintain the relationship between citizen and home state seems to have been to ensure that citizens paid taxes directly to their home states, and the investments of individual migrants in their professional associations and host city-states indicate that at least some of those immigrants had managed to acquire an abundance of money and resources. While mobility and migration were not experienced in the same way by all social strata and the available sources may indeed reflect inequalities of wealth, the actions undertaken by Phoenician city-states and wealthier Phoenicians to support the members of their communities abroad did result in managing migration, maintaining civic identities, and increasing the visibility of Phoenician immigrants and Phoenician city-states in Greek communities.

4

Honors, Privileges, and Greek Migration Regimes

MORE THAN 90 percent of the extant inscribed Attic decrees bestowing honors on individuals come from the Athenian Acropolis, one of the most public places in Athens. Among them stood a marble stele that offers the most extensive surviving record of honors given to a single individual by the Athenian state. The text contains five different decrees associated with two different instances in which the Athenian council and assembly discussed how to honor a man named Herakleides who had repeatedly served Athens (Fig. 4.1).[1] According to one of those decrees, in 330/329 BCE this man had been the first merchant to sail into Athens to deliver grain during a period of grain shortage and had donated three thousand *medimnoi* (a unit of volume for dry goods) of wheat to Athens at the regular price of five drachmas each at a time when prices had risen to sixteen drachmas.[2] Such grain shortages were common in the late 330s and 320s BCE, not just in Athens but throughout the eastern Mediterranean. As another of the five decrees inscribed on this stele states, in 328/327 BCE this same man donated three thousand drachmas to Athens to help the state purchase grain. In 325/324 BCE, citing both his previous gifts to Athens and his continued ambition (*philotimia*) and good deeds toward the Athenian state and its citizens, the Athenians decreed that the state should not only grant him several honors and

---

1. *IG* II³ 1 367. For a recent discussion of this text, see Culasso Gastaldi 2004: 167–182. Despite its extensive contents, the stele is of average size, about 0.97 meters tall and 0.37–0.40 meters wide.

2. Demosthenes, *Against Phormio* 39 records these price increases.

FIGURE 4.1 Stele recording the honors and privileges granted to Herakleides over the period of 330–325 BCE (*IG* II³ 1 367)

Athens, Epigraphical Museum 7219. © Hellenic Ministry of Culture and Sports / Hellenic Organization of Cultural Resources Development.

privileges but inscribe this and their previous decision to honor him on a marble stele.[3]

---

3. The five decrees inscribed on this text do not appear in order. The first and last texts inscribed on the stone were the assembly and the council's decrees, respectively, regarding the most recent awards of 325/324 BCE. The second and penultimate paragraphs, respectively, describe the council and the assembly's decrees regarding this man's actions in 330/329 BCE. The middle paragraph records the assembly's decree instructing the council to put forth a proposal to the assembly in that same year. In 325/324 BCE, when the Athenians decided to record their decree

This Herakleides, who had served Athens exceptionally well, was not an Athenian citizen but a Phoenician trader from the city-state of Salamis on the island of Cyprus. And he was one of several Phoenician traders who were granted honors and privileges by Athens in the last quarter of the fourth century BCE.[4] Immigrants like Herakleides, who were wealthy enough to be able to make generous donations and perform services for their host states, were recognized as instrumental to the well-being of those states and were frequently rewarded with honors. In 330/329 BCE, for instance, Athens honored Herakleides with a gold wreath worth five hundred drachmas and sent an envoy at the state's expense to Herakleia Pontica, a Greek city-state on the Black Sea coast about 150 miles east of ancient Byzantion (present-day Istanbul), to recover Herakleides' sails from the Herakleiots who had stolen them. The envoy was also to reprimand Dionysios, the tyrant of Herakleia, demanding that he and his people refrain from any wrongdoing against anyone sailing to Athens.[5] In 325/324 BCE, Athens honored Herakleides again, granting him another gold wreath worth five hundred drachmas and several additional awards, including the titles and responsibilities of a proxenos and benefactor, the right to own property, the privileges of participating in military service and paying capital taxes, and the honor of having all these awards inscribed on a stele erected on the Athenian Acropolis at the expense of the Athenian state. Although officials' decision to side with Herakleides in his dispute with the Herakleiots and undertake diplomatic actions on his behalf reflected how essential securing the safety of shipping along sea routes was to Athens' food supply, Herakleides' generous financial and material contributions to Athens appear to have been the primary factor in its decision to grant him these honors.

---

on a stele, they consulted the state archives and inscribed all the previous decrees regarding this man.

4. Although his name is Greek, the frequency with which the name Herakleides appears among Phoenicians on Cyprus and in Greek communities suggests that he was likely of Phoenician ethnicity. Moreover, Cypriot Salamis had many resident Phoenicians and connections to Phoenician city-states, including in the fourth century BCE, as ancient sources suggest. For instance, Hermesianax fr. 2 in Lightfoot 2009 recounts the story of Arkeophon, who was rejected as a suitor of the Salaminian king's daughter in the 330–320s BCE because he was Phoenician, and the fourth-century BCE Greek historian Theopompos *FGrHist* 115 F 114 points out the close relationship between the earlier (mid-fourth century BCE) Salaminian king Nikokles and the Sidonian king Abdashart (known in Greek as Straton).

5. In 335/334 BCE, Athens had honored the very same Dionysios for his gift of grain to the city with the right to pay capital taxes (*eisphora*) and participate in the Athenian military (*IG* II³ 1 439).

Honors such as those given to Herakleides were neither unusual nor granted only to Phoenician immigrants, though the available records indicate that Phoenicians received more awards than other non-Greeks. Further, all Greek states, not just Athens, granted combinations of these same awards, despite some variations contingent on the local geography and history of the grantor states. This common institution of award giving was not only a diplomatic tool that both encouraged foreigners to engage in acts that benefited the host state and expressed that state's power and prestige, as has been recognized previously, but also, this chapter argues, an essential part of Greek states' migration and membership regimes.[6] By granting such honors to foreign individuals, Greek states simultaneously delimited the rights of immigrants and enabled a prolonged and even permanent stay by foreign-born residents, sojourners, or visitors, including the Phoenicians. As the examples in this chapter will show, those awards included monetized gifts of gold wreaths, honorific grants of *proxenia* and *euergesia* (benefaction), and a wide assortment of legal awards, such as the right to own property (*enktesis*), tax exemptions (*ateleia*), the privilege of paying the same taxes as citizens (*isoteleia*), personal and property inviolability (*asylia*) and security (*asphaleia*) during travel, better seats at the theater at state expense (*proedria*), state-sponsored dinners alongside prominent citizens (*xenia*), and the rights to pay capital taxes (*eisphora*) and to serve in the military with citizens. Last, they also included awarding immigrants resident alien status, and the rare grant to enroll in the citizen body and partake in the political community of citizens. As this chapter will show, these awards explicitly and implicitly encouraged mobility and long-term relationships with a host state.

Yet even as these awards promoted mobility and migration, they also defined the rights of such privileged immigrants as Herakleides. As this chapter argues, each time a state granted a combination of monetized, legal, or honorific awards to a foreign individual, it created a distinct social status for that foreign resident to inhabit—a status that, as an individual acquired more privileges, freedoms, and legal rights, could shift along a spectrum of participatory memberhip in a political community, ranging from slavery at one end to citizenship at the other and the legal immigrant status of a metic in between.[7] The existence of this

---

6. For an essay on the purposes of inscribed honorific decrees in Athens, see Lambert 2011, who uses the decree honoring Herakleides as a springboard to discuss how publishing such texts would have urged others to perform similar acts of service to the state.

7. The similar range of privileges given to free foreigners could also be given to enslaved persons; likewise, citizens could be disenfranchised. See Jansen 2012: 726–732. For the idea of a spectrum of social statuses see Finley 1982: 116, who views social status as a continuum, and most recently Kamen 2013, who maps out the Athenian spectrum of statutes as encompassing the following: chattel slaves, privileged chattel slaves, freedmen with conditional freedom,

spectrum both made citizenship and residency more fluid notions than is generally recognized and regulated immigration by placing individuals on specific points along it.

Ancient Athenian commentators and politicians recognized that this system of award giving could be used to attract immigrants and increase mobility in ways that could serve the state. Such awards or changes in citizenship status were not haphazardly introduced or granted but carefully considered. In the fifth century BCE, for instance, Athens passed a naturalization law prescribing that the path to citizenship should be "impossible unless the candidate was deemed worthy of citizenship because of his good service," a stipulation that, while clearly intended to limit grants of citizenship, also facilitated such grants through the broadness of the terms under which one could potentially receive this award.[8] In particular, because such services for the people of Athens as those that prompted the awards offered to Herakleides could be measured in monetary terms, it was possible for wealthy ancient immigrants to indirectly buy privileges, tax exemptions, and even citizenship.[9] In his fourth-century BCE treatise on Athens' ways and means, the ancient historian, military commander, and philosopher Xenophon, who had been one of Socrates' students, acknowledged this relationship between money and citizenship when he proposed that more social and legal privileges be given to metics on the grounds that they had the capability to inject funds into the Athenian economy and could help make Athens a hegemon again.[10] In addition to the rights described above of *enktesis*, *proedria*, *isoteleia*, and *xenia*, Xenophon also proposed that wealthy immigrants should be exempt from serving in the infantry, granted the more prestigious right of serving in the cavalry, and offered a prompt settlement of disputes involving foreign merchants. He further suggested that the state should provide better housing and shops at the port, establish honor rolls for foreign benefactors who subscribed to a capital fund, and create a board of Athenian citizens whose responsibility would be to enroll

---

metics, privileged metics, bastards, disenfranchised citizens, naturalized citizens, female full citizens, and male full citizens. Kamen assigns two statuses to immigrants: those of a metic and of a privileged metic.

8. The law is quoted in Demosthenes, *Against Neaira* 89: πρῶτον μὲν γὰρ νόμος ἐστὶ τῷ δήμῳ κείμενος μὴ ἐξεῖναι ποιήσασθαι Ἀθηναῖον, ὃν ἂν μὴ δι' ἀνδραγαθίαν εἰς τὸν δῆμον τὸν Ἀθηναίων ἄξιον ᾖ γενέσθαι πολίτην.

9. See also M. Osborne 1983: 149 and the examples of citizenship awards given to metics or other foreign residents in M. Osborne 1981–83: T5, T9, T30–31, T48–50, T80–81 (metics) and T2, T19, T75–78, T85, D50 (foreign residents). As Jansen 2012: 730–731 observes, the majority of these foreigners were granted citizenship because of their economic contributions.

10. Xenophon, *Poroi* 2.1–3.14, 5.1–4.

aliens as residents and to reward those citizens who enrolled the most aliens.[11] According to Xenophon, the privileges, honors, and incentives he proposed—which were subsequently widely granted by Athenian state decrees—would allow the foreigners who acquired them to increase their profits, solidify their loyalty to Athens, and augment their benefactions to the state.[12] Those honors also made immigration to Athens more attractive and served to incorporate foreigners into Athenian society as active and contributing members of the city, demonstrating that states not only saw immigrants as integral members of their societies but implemented policies targeted specifically toward them.

At the same time, immigration policies like those advocated by Xenophon and adopted by the Athenian state in the late fourth century BCE were not universally popular among Athenians. The fluid and changeable nature of the supposedly fixed statuses of immigrants seems to have been a concern for some who argued that granting awards to foreign immigrants—especially those made in return for money—eroded the notion of citizenship. As current debates about immigration have shown, the apparent buying of privileges can create status anxiety among native-born citizens, become grounds for real or alleged corruption, and be weaponized by certain politicians or sectors of the population in debates about immigration. Similar debates were publicly carried out in court cases that survive from ancient Athens, such as Demosthenes' fourth-century BCE orations *Against Neaira* and *Against Euboulides*, the first accusing the freedwoman Neaira of illegitimately claiming the rights of Athenian citizenship and the second accusing Euboulides of unlawfully removing the plaintiff, a certain Euxitheus, from the citizen register.[13] While the evidence against Neaira and Euxitheus was flimsy and the court cases may have been motivated by personal reasons, these examples of disputed citizenship demonstrate anxiety regarding the permeability of the contours of citizenship that may have been used to pander to the jurors' prejudices. Similarly, in the late fifth century BCE, a conservative attack on Athenian

---

11. Xenophon, *Poroi* 2.5, 2.7, 3.3, 3.11.

12. Given the extraordinary similarities between the awards described in this treatise and those given to foreigners and immigrants recorded on state decrees especially from the 330s BCE onward, the influence of Xenophon's *Poroi* on Athenian state policies is undisputed. See Cawkwell 1963, who argues that Xenophon's *Poroi* was influential when it was first published in 355 BCE, as can be seen in the overlap between the text and Euboulos' policies from 355 to 342 BCE, and Whitehead 2019: 42–52, who argues instead that the impact of the work can be seen mostly in Lykourgos' policies in the 330s. The economic implications of the policies Xenophon advocates in this treatise have also been studied by Gauthier 1976; Dillery 1993; J. D. Lewis 2009; Jansen 2012; and most recently Whitehead 2019.

13. For an analysis of citizen-passing in Demosthenes' *Against Euboulides*, see Kasimis 2018: 145–167.

democracy and its principle of equality written by an unnamed author today known as the Old Oligarch complained that privileged metics and enslaved persons were practically indistinguishable from citizens in their looks, dress, and rights.[14] Even if such claims were rhetorical exaggerations aimed at redefining citizenship as belonging to the elites rather than the masses, they reflect antidemocratic opinions of the time held by the more conservative parts of the population of Athens. Indeed, the distinction between foreigner and citizen was blurred by many of the awards that states granted to foreign individuals that appeared to equate foreigners with citizens.[15] The tension between states' desire to both honor immigrants and draw sharp lines between citizens and noncitizens, this chapter argues, can be seen as a manifestation of states' migration and membership regimes that sought to attract as well as regulate the presence of immigrants.

Although literary sources from Athens reveal these different political and personal positions on immigration and its perceived perils and benefits, epigraphic sources such as that recording Herakleides' actions and rewards allow a fuller examination of how Athens and other Greek polities used a complex system of award giving to both manage and promote mobility and migration. All Greek states had this tool at their disposal and used it extensively to honor foreigners, but most of the honorific decrees that survive today come from the city-state of Athens and the international sanctuaries of Delphi, Delos, and Oropos (in the region of Boiotia). The overwhelming number of honorific decrees granted by Greek states from the fourth to the second century BCE were given to citizens of other Greek city-states, indicating the large numbers of Greek migrants within Greek communities. Nonetheless, it should not be surprising that the number of Phoenician recipients (twenty-seven) dwarfs that of other non-Greek honorands, three of whom were Thracian, one Babylonian, and one Pelagonian.[16] By

---

14. Ps.-Xenophon, *Constitution of the Athenians* 1.10–12.

15. Engen 2010: 175; Jansen 2012: 740–743.

16. Starting in the second century BCE Romans also became frequent recipients of such awards. Searches in the Proxeny Networks in the Ancient World database (http://proxenies.csad.ox.ac.uk/places/home) and the Packard Humanities Institute epigraphic database (https://inscriptions.packhum.org/) have yielded twenty-seven Phoenician recipients of proxenia (among other awards), from the fourth to the second century BCE. This number is small compared to the total number of awards (over a thousand) granted in this period, and, in general, awards granted to individuals from specific Phoenician city-states are not significantly greater than those granted to individuals from any other state. Still, the awards given to Phoenicians are representative of the types of awards given to all foreign individuals and thus offer a useful example through which to study the migration and membership regimes of Greek city-states. Of the awards granted to Phoenicians, fifteen are Sidonians (*IG* II² 141; *IG* II³ 1 379; *I.Oropos* 37 (=*IG* VII 4260); *I.Oropos* 210 (=*IG* VII 4262); *IG* IX.1² 1.24; *IG* XI.4 746; *IG* XII.6 1 81; *IG* XII.9 900A; *IG* XII.9 1187; Maiuri, *Rodi e Cos* 192 and 193 [these two record the same proxenos];

honoring and thus encouraging ongoing relationships with Phoenicians—most of whose professions are recorded on these decrees as being related to trade—Greek city-states could tap into trade networks that were not easily accessible to them, as no other group had a network as extensive as that of the Phoenicians, who had access to markets from the Atlantic Ocean to Mesopotamia and Africa and a diaspora that was fortified with permanent settlements or immigrant communities throughout this vast region.[17] The cases of the Phoenicians featured in this chapter thus reveal more broadly the ways in which host states employed four different varieties of rewards—monetized, honorific, legal, and residency and citizenship—to establish interstate diplomatic relations, regulate and attract immigrants, and create multiple social statutes that migrants could inhabit.

Monetized Awards

The extremely formulaic language and standardized awards recorded on the thousands of honorific inscriptions from Greek communities throughout the Mediterranean region during the many centuries in which this system was employed to honor foreigners may make it seem rather pro forma. But closer attention demonstrates that it was sophisticated, nuanced, and institutionalized within state procedures and processes. It also allowed input from foreigners themselves. That both those giving and those receiving these awards were aware of their monetary worth is clear from language such as "and it should be possible for him to obtain from the demos whatever benefit he can" that appears in the honorific decree recording the awards given to Herakleides and a later,

---

Milet I.3 180B; *FD* III.1 435; De La Coste-Messelière 1925: 89 n. 18; Le Rider, *Monnaies* 258; *SEG* 60 1000), six are Tyrians (*IG* II³ 1 468 [two Tyrian recipients]; *I.Oropos* 18 [=*IG* VII 397]; *I.Oropos* 210 [=*IG* VII 4262]; *IG* XI.4 777; *IG* XII.4 1 15), two are Aradians (*I.Iasos* 35; *IG* XII.1 32 and 104c; and *I.Lindos* II 120 [these three possibly record the same proxenos]), one is Berytian (*SEG* 59 1360), one is an Ashkelonite (*IG* XI.4 817), one is a Carthaginian (*IG* VII 2407), and one is a Kitian (*IG* XI.4 512). Eight are from the fourth century BCE, ten from the third, seven from the second, and two from the third or second centuries BCE. By contrast, in the fourth century BCE only two awards were given to other non-Greeks: one to the Thracian king Sitalkes (*IG* II² 22) and another to the king of the Pelagonians (*IG* II² 190). From the third century, a Babylonian (*IG* XII.5 715) and two Thracians (*FD* III.4 414; *IGBulg* I² 307) received proxenia. None are securely recorded from the second century, other than Phoenicians. The same situation was true in fourth-century BCE Athens. See Hagemajer Allen 2003: 204. Hagemajer Allen's study only takes into account the period from 404 to 336 BCE, but her findings broadly apply to subsequent periods.

17. Carolina López-Ruiz 2021 discusses the Phoenicians as connectors of these areas, the extent of the ancient world known to them, the trade networks they established, and their contributions to creating a common Mediterranean culture. For the geographic extent of their networks, see López-Ruiz 2021: 79–80.

third-century BCE (285–270 BCE) Attic decree honoring several men, including a Sidonian, with gold wreaths because of the goodwill (*eunoia*) they held toward the Athenian people and their ambition (*philotimia*).[18] Such language, although highly abbreviated, suggests that these recipients could seek to receive further benefits from the Athenian council and assembly, depending on what these governmental organs deemed the honorands' actions were worth or what the honorands thought they could get. A variation of this awareness can be seen in numerous inscriptions detailing the various awards granted to individuals who had been named a proxenos and benefactor and adding that they were also eligible for all other awards customarily given to such individuals.[19] Together, such references indicate a level of flexibility within this award-giving system that appeared to allow some input or negotiation from foreign honorands, much like that conducted by the trade associations discussed in earlier chapters.

As the repeated awarding of gold wreaths to Herakleides for his continued benefactions toward the Athenians demonstrates, host states thought of such monetized awards, which were both the simplest and the most expensive awards given to foreigners and immigrants, not as commercial transactions but rather as efforts toward building long-term relationships with the honorands and promoting migration. Indeed, awarding a monetized gift to a foreigner did not signal the end of the relationship between the honorand and the host state, as it would in the case of a sale, but quite the opposite: by reciprocating an act of service to the state, the state initiated a potentially permanent relationship with the honorand, who was encouraged to continue to serve the interests of that state. Nor was Herakleides an exception, as other foreign individuals in Athens also received multiple awards over the years.[20] Despite the monetized nature of these awards,

---

18. On the decree honoring Herakleides (*IG* II³ 1 367, lines 63–64) the phrase reads εἶναι δ' αὐτῶι καὶ εὑ|ρέσθαι παρὰ τοῦ δήμου ὅ τι ἂν δύνηται ἀγαθόν. On the third-century BCE decree (*IG* II³ 1 940, lines 8–10) it reads καὶ ἄλλο [ἀγαθὸν εὑρέσθαι παρὰ | τῆς βουλῆς καὶ τ]οῦ δήμου, ὅτ[ου ἂν δοκῶσιν ἄξιοι εἶ|ναι]. This phrase is reconstructed on this decree based on similar decrees from Athens on which the wording is preserved, as, for example, *IG* II³ 1 1145.

19. The most simplified form of the phrase that suggests this is καὶ τἆλλα ὅσα καὶ τοῖς ἄλλοις προξένοις καὶ εὐεργέταις, which occurs in close to a thousand texts.

20. In addition to the examples discussed later in the chapter, another is recorded on *IG* II³ 1 324, which details the successive honors given to a doctor from Akarnania in the late fourth century BCE. In 337/336 BCE he was granted proxenia and euergesia, by 322/321 BCE he had also been given the right to own property, and after that he and his descendants were awarded citizenship. All this he received for practicing his craft well for the Athenians and for a contribution of a silver talent (equal to six thousand drachmas) that he made to a public subscription fund.

they entangled the grantor and the recipient in what was potentially a long-term and even permanent reciprocal relationship.

Two inscriptions from Delos, which, with Delphi, was one of the most famous and frequented Greek religious centers throughout antiquity by both Greeks and non-Greeks, provide a further example of repeated awards given to individuals and the long-term relationships that polities sought to create through giving these and other forms of awards. Early in the second century BCE, a few years after Delos awarded an Ashkelonite named Aphrodisios, the son of Zenodoros, a combination of honorific (*proxenia* and *euergesia*) and legal awards (*enktesis*, *proedria*, and *prosodos*, a right specific to Delos that granted the honorand the right to attend political meetings), they honored him again with a laurel wreath because of his excellence and reverence for the Delian sanctuary and the favor he showed toward the Delians.[21] The order in which these awards were made was probably not accidental: the legal rights and privileges granted Aphrodisios by the Delians facilitated his visits and stays on Delos and invited him and his family to become residents, such as by granting him the right to own property, an inheritable right that would stay in Aphrodisios' family. Like Herakleides, the Ashkelonite Aphrodisios must have helped the Delians and their sanctuary repeatedly to warrant consecutive awards, though each time the honors granted were different and the degree to which they were publicly announced increased: whereas the second grants, like the first, were recorded on a stele, they were also announced during the young men's choral contests. The audience on Delos witnessing these awards and learning about this particular Phoenician's benefactions would have been enormous, multiethnic, and from all over the ancient Mediterranean, increasing the prestige and honor he received and perhaps even further enticing him to continue his benefactions for the Delians and the sanctuary at Delos.

As an inscription honoring yet another Phoenician shows, the system of award giving was especially important to major sanctuaries such as Delos, as it helped ensure that foreign wealthy benefactors would not only continue to make contributions but also help facilitate their day-to-day operations and financial arrangements. In this case, the individual involved was the last king of Sidon, Philokles, who as discussed previously had given numerous dedications at the sanctuary on Delos and even helped resolve one of its disputes.[22] In 280 BCE, the Delians

---

21. *IG* XI.4 817 and 818. Both Aphrodisios and Zenodoros are common Greek names adopted by Phoenicians. Both inscriptions honoring Aphrodisios are generally dated to the beginning of the second century BCE. Habicht 2002: 16 points out that laurel wreaths were only awarded to individuals who were already proxenoi.

22. I discuss Philokles' dedications and diplomatic activity on Delos, in chapter 3. See Hauben 1987 and 2004 for Philokles' career.

awarded Philokles a gold wreath worth one thousand drachmas—the only individual so honored, as others, including other sovereigns, received a laurel wreath instead[23]—and specified that this award should be proclaimed publicly in the theater of Apollo and followed by sacrifices carried out on his behalf for Apollo, Artemis, Leto, Zeus Soter, and Athena Soteira. A particularly telling detail in this inscription is that these honors were awarded not just because of Philokles' benefactions to the temple, the favor and ambition he demonstrated toward the Delians, and his reverence toward the Delian sanctuary, but also because he had helped the Delians recover a debt owed to them by the League of Islanders, a federal league of the Cycladic islands.[24] By honoring him for this diplomatic service with a generous and unusual monetized award, the Delians showcased how instrumental foreign individuals were to running one of the biggest, wealthiest, and most renowned Greek sanctuaries.

Honorific Awards

Whereas the gold wreath given to Philokles made the diplomatic function of monetized awards to Phoenicians and other foreign individuals explicit, the role that honorific awards played in Greek states' foreign policies and migration and membership regimes was more implicit but at least as important. The most widespread honorific award granted by Greek states throughout the Mediterranean region—with more than twenty-five hundred securely identified grants from the late seventh century BCE to the Roman imperial period—was that of the institution of proxenia, an inheritable position that made a foreign individual responsible for legally representing citizens of the grantor state in his home state.[25] In

---

23. Habicht 2002: 16.

24. *IG* XI.4 559. Sanctuaries often gave loans and acted as creditors to communities that participated in their cultic activities. The best documentation of the financial administration of a sanctuary is recorded on *IG* II² 1635, which details the finances of Delos from 377/376 to 374/373 BCE. For the administration of Delos, see Chankowski 2008. For the general economy of Delos, see Reger 1994 (on Philokles' role, 17–18, 32–33, 253, and 267–269). For the role of influential and wealthy citizens mediating their state's relations with foreigners, including the Delian Mnesalkos, who proposed honoring Philokles, see Paschidis 2008: 439–440, and more generally on the role of such citizens in mediating between their state and Hellenistic kings and the euergetism of the latter, see pp. 469–505.

25. The institution of proxenia took off in the fourth century BCE, which saw almost four hundred cases of proxenia grants, though it existed even earlier. The vast majority of grants date from the third and second centuries BCE, with more than twelve hundred cases. The most recent study of proxenia is Mack 2015. Marek 1984 had previously studied this institution. Wallace 1970 examines the origins of the institution. Walbank 1978 focuses on Athenian proxenia decrees from the fifth century BCE. Henry 1983: 116–162 discusses proxenia in

the fourth century BCE, Athens was responsible for about half of all proxenia decrees issued by Greek states, and in the third century BCE, Athens, Delphi, Delos, and Oropos together produced about half of the proxenia decrees from that century.[26] This honor effectively created a permanent relationship with the honored individual by making him a diplomat for the state granting him this honor.[27] Through such grants, grantor states also forged links between themselves and other city-states, as both ancient and modern commentators have observed. For instance, Demosthenes, the fourth-century BCE Athenian orator and politician, recognized that diplomatic ties with other states were initiated indirectly when Athens entered into a reciprocal relationship with foreign individuals from those states by honoring them because they had benefited Athens in a private capacity.[28] As its frequency suggests, proxenia was a useful tool for constructing networks within the political landscape of the Mediterranean region, which was made up of peer polities connected by custom, law, or shared cultural values and institutions.[29]

Although previous scholars have recognized the diplomatic tenor of such awards, they have paid less attention to how proxenia, which was often granted together with euergesia and a combination of other awards that enhanced mobility (*enktesis, asylia, asphaleia, ateleia, isoteleia*) also promoted migration. Just as giving a monetized award did not signify the end of a relationship with an honorand, proxenia—which came with attendant prestige and honor, the public

Athens (among other awards). Culasso Gastaldi 2002 investigates proxenoi from the western Mediterranean in fourth-century BCE Athens and in her 2004 book those who came from Asia Minor. Zelnick-Abramovitz 2004 studies the institution in the western Mediterranean. For other studies on proxenoi and proxenia as a diplomatic tool, see Perlman 1958; Lehmann 1994; and Ribeiro Ferreira 2004.

26. Mack 2015: 13–14.

27. Although there are more than twenty-five hundred examples of proxenia awards, only eight of these were bestowed upon female recipients: Cabanes 1976: 565 n. 43; *CEG* 877 C; *SEG* 38 464; *IG* IX.2 62; *FD* III.3 145; *FD* III.3 249–250; *Syll*[3] 689; *IG* II[2] 1136; *IG* XII.6 1.471. The first four cases involve grants made to women associated with a male recipient. In all the other cases except *Syll*[3] 689 each of the honorands had a male relative who was simultaneously named proxenos. See Mack 2015: 25 n. 8.

28. Demosthenes, *Against Leptines* 50–51. Low 2007 points out that the reciprocal nature of interstate relations mimicked social interactions among individuals. See also Mosley 1972 and Bolmarcich 2010.

29. For peer-polity interaction, see Ma 2003 and Giovannini 1994: 274–279 and 2007. Leaderless, equipollent networks of polities are known as anarchic interstate societies in the field of international relations. See, for example, Waltz 1979: 102–128; Bull 2012; Wendt 1999: 92–138. For the validity and application of anarchic international systems to the ancient world, see Eckstein 2006; Low 2007; and Mack 2015.

commemoration of the award on stone stelae, and certain obligations that involved the grantor state and the honorand in a permanent official relationship[30]—was not simply a way of paying off a state's debt to a foreigner who had carried out a benefaction for the state but a permanent honor that could entice the honorand to migrate to the grantor state. Despite the responsibilities that proxenoi bore toward citizens of the grantor state in their home state, the extant sources suggest that ongoing relationships between host states and proxenoi thrived, often ending in migration. One such example of how granting proxenia to an individual and his descendants could lead to migration has already been presented in an earlier chapter: a series of third-century BCE dedications in various temples on the island of Rhodes suggests that the award of proxenia attracted an Aradian by the name of Zenon to the city of Lindos, and although he himself may not have emigrated to Rhodes, his son appears to have done so and to have been integrated into Rhodian civic society by becoming a member of one of the private associations there.[31]

Honorific grants' dual purpose of establishing interstate relations and promoting migration can also be seen in a shift in the recipients of such awards in the last third of the fourth century BCE that reflects changes in Athenian foreign policy. Most Attic proxenia awards given in the 370s and 350s BCE suggest that the honorands' service had somehow benefited the military (generals, ambassadors, and naval ships are mentioned often).[32] Following the Greeks' devastating defeat at the battle of Chaironeia in 338 BCE, which signaled the conquest of the Greek peninsula by the Macedonians under Philip and Alexander and a time of severe grain shortages in the eastern Mediterranean, Athens used honorific awards to establish positive relations with Macedon and to honor traders or

---

30. Mack 2015: 48–81 and 104–130 discusses the awards that regularly accompanied proxenia.

31. *IG* XII.1 32 and 104c.

32. Of the hundred or so Attic proxenia decrees from the fourth century, five date from 387/386 BCE (immediately after the Corinthian War and the King's Peace), nine from 378/377 BCE (when Athens was setting up the Second Athenian Confederacy and struggling for hegemony against Sparta and Thebes), twenty from 355–352 BCE (the years of the Social War and its aftermath when Athens' allies and members of the Second Athenian Confederacy rebelled), and eighteen from the 330s and 320s. The rest are not clustered around specific dates. See Paarmann 2009 for the services proxenoi provided to warrant their awards. For the military nature of the services honorands had performed, see *IG* II² 29 and 53 and *SEG* 32 50 for the 380s and 370s and *IG* II² 133 and 162 and *IG* II³ 1 398 and 478 for the 350s. See also the discussion in Engen 2010: 150–153, who observes the change from granting proxenia for military or political services to privileging trade services, although his discussion also includes the end of the fifth century BCE.

individuals who helped Athens alleviate any grain shortages.³³ The latter group included several Phoenician traders, one of whom was Apollonides, the son of Demetrios of Sidon, who, as discussed in a previous chapter, was nominated by a trade association in 323/322 BCE as a candidate for the honors of hereditary proxenia, euergesia, and *enktesis*, and a gold wreath worth a thousand drachmas, the same awards given at around the same time to Herakleides from Salamis on Cyprus.³⁴ Another example is the father and son team of Hieron and Apses from Tyre, who shortly after 332 BCE not only brought grain from Carthage and Italy and sold it more cheaply to Athens but also promised that, if needed, they would do the same in the future. For these benefactions, Athens praised them for their excellence and goodwill toward the people and not only gave each a gold wreath but also made them and their descendants proxenoi and euergetai of Athens, and granted them the right to own property.³⁵ Similarly, in 334/333 BCE a man from Kos was granted proxenia because he had ensured there would be plenty of grain in Athens;³⁶ in the same period a man from Akragas on Sicily was honored with proxenia for the same reason;³⁷ and, in the 330s and 320s about twenty other inscriptions recorded honors and privileges granted to non-Athenian merchants for helping Athens with its grain supply.³⁸ Employing the system of award giving

---

33. Lambert 2006: 117. This is also the period when Phoenician trade associations first appear in Athens, as discussed in earlier chapters. Engen 2010 argues that trade played an important role in Athenian foreign policy and provides a detailed analysis of the various honors and privileges given to traders in the fifth and fourth centuries BCE. See also Burke 1992: 206–208. Delos, a major trading hub from the fourth century BCE onward, may also have pursued an active trade policy in honoring traders from the Black Sea area to ensure its grain supply. See Ziebarth 1932–33: 244–245 and Engen 2010: 148–149, who challenges this idea.

34. *IG* II³ 1 379. For more on *IG* II³ 1 379, see Culasso Gastaldi 2004: 185–192.

35. *IG* II³ 1 468. See Culasso Gastaldi 2004: 195–203. Walbank 1985 argues that Hieron and Apses helped transport some Carthaginian ambassadors to Athens, in addition to bringing grain to Athens.

36. *IG* II³ 1 454 and 496. In the second edition of *IG* II this inscription was composed of two fragments, the first part of which bore the name of the Koan and the declaration that this was a proxenia decree (*IG* II² 416a) and the second part detailing the reasons for the awards (*IG* II² 416b). In the third edition of the *IG* II the two fragments are listed as belonging to different decrees. *IG* II³ 1 454 is equivalent to *IG* II² 416b and *IG* II³ 1 496 is the new entry for *IG* II² 416a. Even if the two fragments do not belong together, *IG* II³ 1 496 would fall in the same group of inscriptions as those honoring traders in Athens not with proxenia but with other honors and privileges.

37. *IG* II³ 1 432. The honorand (Sopatros) did not receive a gold wreath, but in addition to proxenia, euergesia, and *enktesis*, he was offered a meal at the Prytaneion and a seat at that year's festival of the City Dionysia.

38. Engen 2010 collects thirty-four Attic honorific decrees that record honors and privileges given to foreign individuals for trade-related services. Of these, six are from the fifth century

to show favor to traders rather than military figures indicates that such honors were deployed by Greek states to exploit the Phoenicians' extensive trade networks to secure grain and feed their populations at reasonable prices by encouraging long-term relationships with those traders and their home states.

Although the connection between Athens' trade policy and such honorific awards to traders has been recognized by other scholars, less apparent have been the ways in which those awards also invited the individual honorands to serve and reside in Athens for the long term or even permanently.[39] The honorific award of proxenia on its own, for instance, was often given to traders who appear to have had long-term connections in Athens and perhaps already resided there.[40] Herakleides from Salamis on Cyprus is one such example: he had been active in Athens for several years before he was given proxenia, euergesia, *enktesis*, and a gold wreath, all of which strengthened his relation to Athens and effectively allowed him to acquire a residence of his own there. The same rights were also given to Apollonides and to Hieron and Apses and encouraged them to move to Athens. The inheritable right of property ownership, which was usually exclusive to citizens, was especially instrumental in inviting migration, as it allowed foreigners and their families to live in permanent housing in their host state.[41] With these awards, all four Phoenician traders moved along the spectrum of participatory membership in a political community in ways that facilitated both their stay in Athens and their trading operations in commercial strongholds. Just as Xenophon had argued, allowing foreigners to own land and a house led more and "better" men to desire to live in Athens, where "better" stood for more useful to the state or wealthy.[42] To curry the favor of Phoenician traders, states appear to have relaxed their exclusionary residency and membership rules and adapted their laws and regulations to accommodate visiting, resident, and immigrant traders.[43]

BCE and twenty from the 330s and 320s. See his Appendix I, pp. 225–229. *IG* II³ 1 430 honors another trader from Salamis on Cyprus with a gold wreath because he brought grain from Egypt, ransomed Athenian citizens from Sicily and sent them to Athens, and donated a talent of silver, perhaps to a public subscription fund sometime in the early 330s.

39. Engen 2010 has discussed the connections between Athens' trade policy and the awards it gave traders. See also Lehmann 1994. Contra: Marek 1977, 1984: 359–361, and 1985.

40. Engen 2010: 150. Metics are among recipients of proxenia awards.

41. For *enktesis*, see Pečirka 1966.

42. Xenophon, *Poroi* 2.6. The Greek phrase is πλείους τε καὶ βελτίους ὀρέγεσθαι τῆς Ἀθήνησιν οἰκήσεως.

43. The situation in Athens is not unlike that of the Venetian republic in the sixteenth and seventeenth centuries, when it accommodated Netherlandish merchants by adapting its laws,

Several kings, Phoenician and otherwise, were also recorded as such recipients of honorific awards, albeit much less often than nonstate actors such as Herakleides, Apollonides, and Hieron and Apses.[44] Xenophon's prediction that creating a roll of benefactors would lead even kings and despots to subscribe to the capital fund in order to earn recognition and form communal bonds with Athens is borne out by several honorific inscriptions that suggest that heads of state were perhaps even more desirable as benefactors than individual traders because of their more extensive resources and power to effect policies that might benefit the grantor state.[45] Sometime around 286 BCE, a few years before Delos granted King Philokles of Sidon the honors discussed above, Athens also commended him by crowning him with a gold wreath, awarding him and his descendants Athenian citizenship, and enrolling him and his descendants in the tribe, deme, and phratry of his wish, honors later followed by erecting a bronze statue of him in Athens.[46] These awards were probably granted for help that Philokles had provided in the liberation of Athens from Demetrios Poliorketes in 287/286 BCE and because one of his subordinates by the name of Zenon had assisted Athens by supplying it with grain.[47] Another example is a series of decrees starting in the early fourth century BCE (c. 395–389/388 BCE) and lasting for another century (285/284 BCE) in which Athens granted several privileges to the Spartokid kings of Bosporus, including commendations, gold wreaths, tax exemptions, bronze statues, and citizenship, aimed at creating and sustaining a reciprocal relationship with the kings who were given the awards and the communities they ran.[48]

---

including offering a specific route to citizenship to foreign merchants. Netherlandish traders customarily submitted petitions that sought economic accommodation, similar to the ones Phoenician trade associations requested from Athens, discussed in chapter 2. See van Gelder 2013.

44. Only twenty-five of more than twenty-five hundred decrees honor kings or dynasts of non-Greek polities. For a collection of these twenty-five cases, see Marek 1984: 335–339.

45. Xenophon, *Poroi* 3.11. The Greek phrase that describes the communal bonds that immigrants will form with Athenians appears in 3.4: ὡς πρὸς φίλους ἐπισπεύδοιεν ἄν. Jansen 2012: 744–745 points out the subversive nature of Xenophon's proposal, which would construct the same bonds between foreign merchants and Athenians as those that held citizens together.

46. *IG* II³ 1 868, lines 10–12: [εἶναι δ' αὐτὸν | Ἀθηναῖον κα]ὶ ἐκγόνους· [γράψασθαι δὲ φρατρίας κα]ὶ δήμου καὶ φ]υλῆς ἧς [ἂν βούληται.] The erection of a bronze statue of his likeness is recorded on *IG* II² 3425.

47. The awards granted to Zenon are recorded on *IG* II³ 1 863. For Philokles' actions toward Athens, see Hauben 1987: 419–420 and Hauben 2004: 41–42.

48. *IG* II³ 1 298 records the honors given to Spartokos II, Pairisades I, and Apollonios, the sons of Leukon, in 347/346 BCE and mentions the honors given earlier to Leukon (in 389/388 BCE) and his father (c. 395 BCE). This family was given a commendation, a gold wreath, *ateleia*, and citizenship. Isokrates, *Trapezitikos* 57 and Demosthenes, *Against Leptines* 33 also mention the

The Bosporan kings, who saw tangible financial benefits from the tax exemptions they received in Athens, reciprocated by giving exemptions from export taxes to anyone sailing to Athens carrying grain, effectively subsidizing trade to Athens and promoting migration within the region.[49] Such awards to kings and dynasts may seem notional rather than actual, but they were not: should any of these foreign dynasts have needed to exercise their right to live and emigrate to Athens, they could have.[50] At least one of the Bosporan kings who received the awards mentioned above, Leukon, did own property in Athens.[51]

The relationship established between Athens and the mid-fourth-century BCE Phoenician king of Sidon, Abdashtart, known in Greek as Straton, reveals even more clearly the role of honorific awards in forging diplomatic relations and promoting migration. This relationship is detailed on a text from c. 360 BCE whose very beginning is missing (Fig. 4.2) as the stone is damaged.[52] The surviving text starts by mentioning that King Abdashtart had helped an Athenian

---

benefactions the Bosporan kings had carried out for Athens over the years. *IG* II³ 1 870 records the dedication of bronze statues given to Pairisades III and his sons in 285/284 BCE and the earlier gifts of grain by their grandfather, Spartokos. On the relationship between Athens and the Bosporan kingdom as it emerges from the honorific inscriptions granting the awards, see Oliver 2007: 30–37.

49. Demosthenes, *Against Phormio* 36 recites the decree by Pairisades.

50. For political exiles who did exercise their citizenship rights in Athens, see M. Osborne 1983: 211–216.

51. Demosthenes, *Against Leptines* 40.

52. *IG* II² 141. For a discussion of this decree, see Culasso Gastaldi 2004: 105–123. The decree has been dated variously from the 380s BCE to the 360s. Most recently, Matthaiou 2016 has attributed this inscription to the letter cutter of *IG* II² 17, active until 386/385 BCE, suggesting a date of 394–386 BCE. www.atticinscriptions.com follows this dating. Other scholars have dated the inscription to the 370s and 360s: Böckh in *CIG* 87; Dittenberger in *Syll*³ 185; and Hicks and Hill 1901: 220–222 no. 111. Schaefer 1885: 94–95, followed by Judeich 1892: 198 and Tod 1948: 139, suggested 367 BCE as the date, based on identifying the embassy mentioned in the text with the same Athenian embassy sent to the Persian king known from Xenophon, *Hellenika* 7.1.33–38. Moysey 1976: 182 argues against this. Johnson 1914: 417–423 suggested 378/377 BCE as the date, based on the phraseology of the text, and Henry 1982: 108–112 and 1989: 254–255 dated the text to 364 BCE, also based on phraseology. The two proposers of the decree, Kephisodotos and Menexenos, were active from the 370s to the 340s and the 360s, respectively. See Hansen 1983: 170 and 173. Knoepfler 1995: 329–330 suggests a date no later than the 370s. Culasso Gastaldi 2004: 115–123 offers a discussion of the scholarship on the date of the inscription. Ultimately, these suggestions are based only on Greek evidence and completely ignore the actual regnal years of Abdashtart I, derived from Sidonian numismatic evidence, now accepted as 365–352 BCE. See Elayi 2006: 18–19 and Table 1, 2008: 105–106, and 2018: 296–297 Table 2, which provide a revision of the chronology of kings of Phoenician city-states, now accepted both in scholarship on Phoenicians and by the editors of *SEG* 55 136. See also Elayi 2005 for a history of Abdashtart I and Sidon.

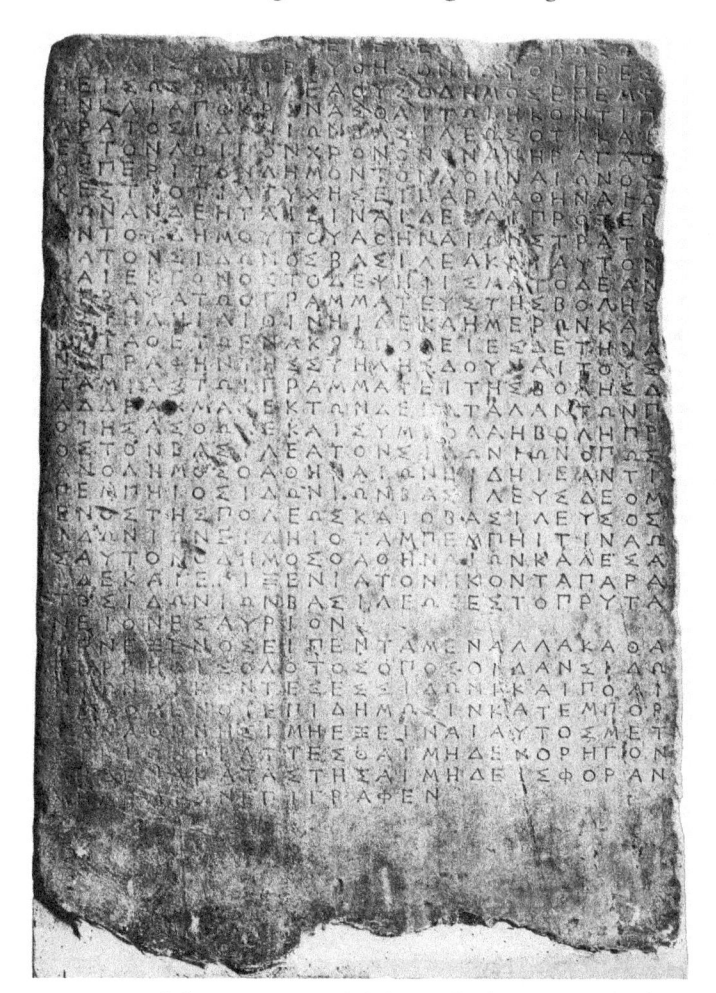

FIGURE 4.2 Attic stele honoring King Abdashtart of Sidon, c. 360s BCE (*IG* II² 141) Oxford, Ashmolean Museum AN Chandler 2.24. © Ashmolean Museum.

embassy make its way to the Persian king as splendidly as possible—a phrase used in decrees from Athens and elsewhere to describe religious processions, sacrifices, festivals, and dedications—and that he had sent an envoy to Athens to request something that is never made explicit in the text.[53] Contemporary texts indicate that Athenians went to great lengths to ensure that Athenian representatives

---

53. "As splendidly as possible" is the translation of the phrase ὡς κάλλιστα. For Attic decrees that use this phrase, see *IG* II² 380, 1039, 1125, 1186, 1242, 1330, 2492 and *IG* II³ 1 297, 856, 929, 1064, 1151, 1164. For decrees from elsewhere, see *FD* III.1 351; *FD* III.3 238; *IG* IX.1 683; *IScM* III 35; *I.Délos* 1518; *I.Cos Segre* ED 25; *IG* XII.4 1 79 and 339; *IG* XII.5 595; *IG* XII.7 44; *IG* XII.9 189;

made quite an impression on their peers, including embassies to the Persian king and choruses and sacred embassies to Delos.⁵⁴ By outfitting the Athenian embassy, a sacred and public representation of any polity, so as to help it impress the Persian court, the Sidonian king helped facilitate the Athenian diplomatic expedition and made its success a possibility. Such a service seems to have been sufficient cause for Abdashtart to send an emissary to Athens in an attempt to establish further official relations with that state, as the Athenian response to his envoy implies in the inscribed text, which stipulated that if the king ever approached Athens in need, he would obtain from the Athenians whatever he needed.⁵⁵ Athens further solidified its reciprocal relationship with Sidon by awarding Abdashtart hereditary proxenia (lines 9–12), granting his envoy a meal at the Prytaneion (lines 25–28), and tasking the Athenian council with exploring the possibility of exchanging *symbola*—objects that would guarantee the authenticity of envoys, embassies, or communications, and secrecy in communications between the two states—with the king of the Sidonians (lines 18–25).⁵⁶ Both the personal awards given to Abdashtart and the agreements struck between Athens

---

I.Magnesia 98; *I.Priene* B-M 64; *SEG* 4 598; *SEG* 19 569; *SEG* 41 1003; Wilhelm 1900: 54–55 no. 16; *MDAI(A)* 29 (1904) 152,1; *MDAI(A)* 32 (1907) 243,4; *MDAI(A)* 35 (1910) 409.3.

54. Aristophanes, *Acharnians* 65–89 describes an Athenian embassy to the Persian king in similarly decadent terms. Socrates describes Athenian choruses sent to Delos to participate in festivals as exceptional and their displays unmatched by any other city's choruses (Xenophon, *Memorabilia* 3.3.12). Plutarch, too, preserves the memory of magnificently extravagant *theoriai*—sacred embassies—sent to Delos in his biography of Nikias, and compares these with the poor, disorganized, and haphazard fashion in which other cities sent their *theoriai* (Plutarch, *Nicias* 3.4–6).

55. *IG* II² 141, lines 5–9: καὶ | ἐς τὸν λοιπὸν χρόνον ὢν ἀνὴρ ἀγαθ|ὸς περὶ τὸν δῆμον τὸν Ἀθηναίων οὐ|κ ἔστι ὅτι ἀτυχήσει παρὰ Ἀθηναίω|ν ὧν ἂν δέηται (and in the future, if he comes to the people of Athens, he will not fail to obtain from the Athenians whatever he needs).

56. *IG* II² 141, lines 18–25: π|οιησάσθω δὲ καὶ σύμβολα ἡ βολὴ πρ|ὸς τὸν βασιλέα τὸν Σιδωνίων ὅπως | ἂν ὁ δῆμος ὁ Ἀθηναίων εἰδῆι ἐάν τι | πέμπηι ὁ Σιδωνίων βασιλεὺς δεόμ|ενος τῆς πόλεως, καὶ ὁ βασιλεὺς ὁ Σ|ιδωνίων εἰδῆι ὅταμ πέμπηι τινὰ ὡ|ς αὐτὸν ὁ δῆμος ὁ Ἀθηναίων (let the council create *symbola* with the king of the Sidonians so that the demos of the Athenians may know if the king of the Sidonians sends some request when in need of the city-state, and the king of the Sidonians may know when the demos of Athens sends someone to him). This last clause should probably be understood as part of Athens' policy toward the provinces within the Persian Empire that had rebelled against it in the 360s, known as the Great Satraps' Revolt, of indirectly supporting the rebels without aggravating Athens' relationship with the Persians. See Demetriou 2020. The creation of *symbola* is decreed on only two other Attic inscriptions: the Kleinias decree of c. 425 BCE, which called for the creation of *symbola* with tributary cities within the Athenian hegemony to eliminate the possibility of states bringing the wrong tribute amount to Athens (*IG* I³ 34); and on a decree honoring Orontes, the satrap of Mysia, which mentions that *symbola* should be shown when representatives of the Athenian military purchased grain from him. See Demetriou, forthcoming b. See also Austin 1944: 100; Moysey 1976: 182; Culasso Gastaldi 2004: 111–112.

and Sidon reflected useful elements of the arsenal that Athens could deploy to effect diplomatic relations between states.

Moreover, the rider to this decree, discussed in the previous chapter, exemplifies how granting honors and awards to a king who was himself unlikely to emigrate nonetheless promoted mobility and encouraged migration within the region. This rider deals not with Sidon or the Sidonian king but with the community of Sidonian traders who lived in Athens on commercial business, granting them blanket tax exemptions from taxes that foreigners ordinarily had to pay when they stayed in Athens for longer than a month and were required to register as metics. According to these exceptions, the Sidonian traders were no longer liable for paying metic taxes (*metoikion*) or capital taxes (*eisphora*) or for financing a chorus for dramatic contests (*choregeia*), the latter an indirect form of taxation imposed on the wealthiest members of Athens' population, even though, as discussed in the previous chapter, the text makes clear that the traders were still considered citizens of Sidon who had acquired residency in Athens only for the purposes of conducting commercial business.[57] This new social status allowed Sidonian traders to prolong their stay in Athens, and perhaps even make it permanent, without incurring any of the financial obligations of either metics or citizens and without having to give up their citizenship in Sidon—a comfortable position to be in on the spectrum of participatory membership in a political community. Although the decree that records these awards was initiated to honor the Sidonian king, this rider demonstrates Athens' recognition that it benefited sufficiently from the presence of the Sidonian trading community that it was in its best interest to grant it those tax exemptions and a customized social status within a fluid spectrum of participatory membership in a political community.

Legal Awards

The honorific award of proxenia was typically accompanied by such legal awards as the right to own property, exemptions from certain taxes, and a guarantee of personal inviolability and security during travel, all of which were intended to facilitate the honorand's mobility, enhance his prestige and social status, and foster his sense of belonging within the host state. A case in point are the honorific awards from Oropos, a port city at the border of the regions of Attica and Boiotia located just across from the city-state of Eretria on the island of Euboia and home

---

57. *IG* II² 141, lines 29–36. On the *metoikion*, see Whitehead 1977 and Hesychius s.v. *metoikos*. I discuss the rider to this inscription in chapter 3.

of the famous oracular sanctuary of Amphiaraos. These were unique among those granted by Greek polities in that they regularly combined the award of proxenia with *isoteleia*, or the right to pay the same taxes as citizens did (including capital taxes, public subscriptions, and indirect taxes paid by wealthy individuals like financing military equipment or religious festivals), which, like the ability to own property, granted foreigners a right otherwise reserved for citizens.[58] Three such decrees honoring four Phoenicians, all from around 240–180 BCE, record that these men, two of whom were traders honored for importing grain and giving it to the city at a good price, were granted equality in taxation along with proxenia and other awards.[59] Several contemporary decrees from Euboia, Thessaly, Boiotia, and Athens, all of which date to c. 175 BCE and honor traders for importing grain or olive oil during a period of crop failure, suggest that grain shortages might have motivated these awards by Oropos to the Phoenician traders.[60] Although the right of equality in taxation meant that those immigrants granted this award actually paid more in taxes than foreigners who were in Athens for less than a month, had the legal status of a metic, or had been granted tax exemptions like the Sidonian traders discussed above, it also suggests that the honorands were residents of the host state, equal to citizens from at least the perspective of taxation, and presumably better integrated and more socially mobile within their host society than immigrants with a less permanent status.

In another demonstration of local variations in the Greek award giving system, the polities of Delos and Delphi frequently combined proxenia with

---

58. For the connection between *isoteleia* and proxenia at Oropos, see Knoepfler 2001: 59. The combination of proxenia with *isoteleia* was extremely rare in Athens; see Mack 2015: 56–57. Some scholars think that *isoteleia* was an inherent privilege that came with proxenia in Athens, and for this reason it does not often appear on honorific proxenia decrees. See Knoepfler 2001: 55–60, esp. 57. That may be so, but it does not explain why euergesia, for instance, was almost always awarded with proxenia. If euergesia were an inherent right that came with proxenia, it should also have been dropped from decrees.

59. *I.Oropos* 210 = *IG* VII 4262 records the two Phoenician traders, Dionysios, the son of Ariston, a Tyrian, and Heliodoros, son of Mousaios, a Sidonian. The Tyrian Diokles, son of Nisos, was honored because he saved the citizens of Oropos and gave them whatever they needed, both privately and publicly (*I.Oropos* 18 = *IG* VII 397). The reasons for honoring Straton, son of Apollophanes the Sidonian, are not mentioned (*I.Oropos* 37 = 4260).

60. The decrees recording the legal and honorific awards to traders are from Chalkis on the island of Euboia (*IG* XII.9 900A), Athens (*IG* II³ 1 1315), Gonnoi in Thessaly (Helly, *Gonnoi* II 41), Thespiai in Boiotia (*IG* VII 1719), and Chorsiai, a port city in Boiotia (*ISE* 66). For the grain shortages of this period and their relationship to these texts, see Knoepfler 1990: 490–91 and Walsh 2000.

exemption from taxation, or *ateleia*.[61] *Ateleia* is a broad grant that was applied variously in different polities and could mean anything from exemption on import and export duties to exemption from all taxation (*ateleia panton*), the latter of which was usual at Delphi and could be temporary, permanent, or inheritable, or even granted to associates of the honorands who received it.[62] In one example from Delphi from the first half of the third century BCE, the Phoenician Heliodoros, son of Dionysios from Sidon, indicates that he received, among several other privileges, exemption from all taxes.[63] All of the various tax exemptions that Athens granted to the Sidonian traders technically fell under the umbrella of *ateleia*, even though the text recording that award does not call them such.[64] In both cases, such comprehensive tax exemptions would have facilitated the commercial operations and migration of those so honored.

Such local variations in these awards reflect the different historical and cultural contexts of each polity and the flexibility of this system. Nowhere are such variations more visible than at the renowned Greek sanctuaries at Delphi and Delos, as can be observed in several of the legal awards these polities granted to honorands. At Delphi, for instance, proxenia was often accompanied by the awards of *promanteia*, the right to consult the oracle before others, and of *proedria*, the right to be seated in the theater at public expense, both of which were specific to polities that administered oracles, international sanctuaries, and athletic and dramatic contests, and the right of *prodikia*, priority of trial, which was a privilege granted almost exclusively by Delphi.[65] In the case of Heliodoros, mentioned above, all three of these awards were granted, along with comprehensive

---

61. Rubinstein 2009: 120–121 notes that two-thirds of *ateleia* grants given to proxenoi originate from Delos and Delphi.

62. For a study of what *ateleia* may have included in different poleis, see Rubinstein 2009. It is unclear what *ateleia panton* indicates; it could be the equivalent of granting *isoteleia* since it is often followed by the phrase "together with citizens," implying that *ateleia panton* signified tax exemption only on taxes paid by foreigners, thus making them equal in taxation to citizens. See Marek 1984: 157–160.

63. *FD* III.1 435. Delphi honored one other Sidonian in the second century BCE, but the stone is too fragmentary, preserving only the name, patronymic, and city-state of origin of the honorand: Apollodoros, son of Boiskos, the Sidonian. See De La Coste-Messelière 1925: 89 no. 18.

64. In other examples from Athens, *ateleia* could be limited to the metic tax or the one-hundredth tax (a harbor tax in Peiraieus, the port of Athens). See Engen 2010: 187–192 for *ateleia* as a grant given to traders in Athens.

65. Of over seven hundred occurrences of *prodikia*, only seventeen were issued by polities other than Delphi, and nine of these were issued by nearby Phokis. The *dikai emporikai* (commercial trials) of Athens (for which, see E. E. Cohen 1973) that gave prompt access to trials to foreigners and foreign residents of Athens may be an equivalent right.

tax exemptions and proxenia. Delos, home to a major sanctuary that was heavily visited by traders, especially after 166 BCE when the island became a duty-free commercial center under Athenian jurisdiction through a grant of *ateleia* by the Roman Senate, had its own regional variations in the otherwise formulaic language it used to record the honors it granted to foreign individuals. These often included giving those awarded with proxenia the additional right of *prosodos*, the right to attend the political meetings of the council and the people's assembly, thereby providing foreigners a privilege ordinarily reserved for citizens that allowed them access to the political apparatus of the state.[66] Among the four previously mentioned Phoenicians that Delos honored early in the second century BCE, three received this privilege alongside proxenia and the right to own property: Eudemos, son of Philokles the Tyrian; Basileides, son of Dionysios the Sidonian; and Aphrodisios, son of Zenodoros the Ashkelonite, who later received the further award of a laurel wreath, as discussed earlier.[67] Despite the local variations in the awards granted, the specific honors preferred at Delphi and Delos had the same effects of encouraging residency and enhancing social mobility among immigrants by granting rights that effectively equated them with, and at times placed them even higher than, citizens.

Particularly important among the legal awards given to Phoenicians was the commonly granted right of personal inviolability and security in travel (*asylia* and *asphaleia*) and the right to sail in and out of ports, which allowed foreign traders to be able to conduct their operations safely and safeguard their cargo, equipment, and even personal belongings.[68] These awards were frequently combined with proxenia especially by the islands of Kos, Kalymnos, Crete, and Samos, and to a lesser degree by states in Thrace, Asia Minor, and on the north shore of the Black Sea region, starting in the mid-fourth century BCE.[69] In 300 BCE, for instance, the island of Kos, off the coast of Turkey and home to one of the most famous ancient sanctuaries of the healing god Asklepios, honored

---

66. Habicht 2002: 15–16.

67. *IG* XI.4 777; *IG* XI.4 746; *IG* XI.4 817. The fourth Phoenician honorand was Heliodoros, son of Herakleides, from Kition, who received proxenia and euergesia: *IG* XI.4 512. In addition to the four inscriptions described here, two other texts from Delos record awards to two Aradians, but the decrees are fragmentary and what honors and privileges these men received is unclear: *IG* XI.4 776 and 816.

68. Engen 2010: 183–187 discusses Attic *asylia* grants.

69. Approximately two hundred inscriptions exist with variations of this phrase in different dialects. By contrast, *enktesis*, the right to own property, was never granted in proxenia awards from Kos. The local variant for Athens is "τὴν ναῦν ἥν δέται ἐκκομίσασθαι ... ἐκκομισθάσω καὶ ἐξεῖναι αὐτῶι πλέν καὶ χρήματα εσάγεν," as seen in *IG* I³ 174 and 175. See also Walbank 1978: 6–7, 280–286 (nos. 50 and 51), 385–392 (no. 75).

the Tyrian Theron, son of Boudastratos (a Hellenized form of the Phoenician name Bodashart) and his descendants with proxenia, the right of inviolability and neutrality for him and his goods, and the right to enter and exit the port in times of peace and war for rendering unspecified services to the people of Kos whenever they needed anything.[70] Likewise, the nearby island of Samos honored Metrodoros, the Sidonian, with proxenia and the right of inviolability and neutrality when sailing in and out of Samos during times of peace and war.[71] Polities that were located inland adapted this right to include travel by land, as when in the fourth century BCE the city of Thebes and the federation of the Boiotians honored Nobas, the son of Axioubos the Carthaginian, with tax exemptions and inviolability, probably on goods being transported, whether traveling on land or by sea.[72] Such rights that guaranteed security in travel enabled trade and encouraged migration, especially given that the right to sail in and out of a port was typically associated with a license to import and export with exemptions from custom duties.[73] Despite the formulaic language of these state decrees, threats while traveling were very real, as the theft of Herakleides' sails by the Herakleiots

---

70. *IG* XII.4 1 15, lines 7–12: ἐπαινέσαι τε αὐτὸν καὶ ἦ|μεν πρόξενον τᾶς πόλιος τᾶς Κώ|ων καὶ ἐκγόνους, ἤμεν δὲ αὐτοῖς ἔσ|πλουν καὶ ἔκπλουν καὶ ἐμ πολέμωι | καὶ ἐν εἰράναι ἀσυλεὶ καὶ ἀσπονδεὶ | καὶ αὐτοῖς καὶ χρήμασι.

71. *IG* XII.6 1 81. Sometimes the right to inviolability in times of peace and war was granted specifically on importing and exporting goods: for example, *SEG* 32 1586 (440–411 BCE, from Lindos on Rhodes); *IG* IX 1² 1 19 (300–250 BCE, from Aitolia); *SEG* 40 623 (fourth century BCE, North Black Sea); *I.Olbia* 12, 13 (fourth century BCE, from Olbia); *I.Labraunda* 42 (third century BCE, referring to a decree of Plataseis); *I.Priene B-M* 107 (330 BCE). In other cases, the right is abbreviated to that of exporting and importing goods with inviolability in times of peace or war, without mention of the right to sail in and out of a port: *I.Magnesia* 1, 2, 4, 5, 6, 9, 10, 12 (from the fourth century BCE to the second century CE); *I.Priene B-M* 15 (334 BCE), 27 (296–286 BCE); *I.Milet* VI.3 1028 (third century BCE).

72. *IG* VII 2407, lines 7–11: καὶ | εἰμέν ⟨Ϝ⟩οι γᾶς καὶ ⟨Ϝ⟩οικία|ς ἔ⟨π⟩πασιν καὶ ἀτέλιαν | καὶ ἀσουλίαν καὶ κὰ⟨γ γ⟩ᾶ⟨γ⟩ | καὶ κὰτ θάλατ⟨τ⟩αν καὶ πο|λέμω καὶ ⟨ἰ⟩ρά⟨να⟩ς ἰ⟨ώ⟩σας. This phrase occurs overwhelmingly on proxenia decrees from central Greece, including the federal state of the Boiotians, which had access to ports, but also included important urban centers such as Thebes that could be accessed only by land. The phrase also appears on a few Attic inscriptions that record military treaties and a few third-century BCE texts that record benefactions to Athens involving gifts of grain. Among the Attic military alliances that include this phrase is the famous decree of Aristoteles that records the constitution of the Second Athenian Confederacy (*IG* II² 43). Some of the other Attic decrees that use this phrase in military alliances date from the early fourth century BCE: for example, *IG* I³ 83, 376; *IG* II² 14, 15, 97, 105.

73. Bresson 2016: 289 discusses the association between grants of *asylia* and tax exemptions on imports and exports. Although the decrees honoring the Tyrian Theron and the Sidonian Metrodoros from Kos and Samos, respectively, do not mention specifically the profession of the honorand except in a few isolated cases, it is highly probable that both were traders (contra Reger 2003: 178).

demonstrates, and states' guarantees of inviolability were not empty, as Athens' decision to recuperate those sails shows.

Residency and Citizenship Awards

In addition to the awards discussed above, Greek states also granted the gifts of residency and more rarely of citizenship to individuals who had benefited the state, affording them the possibility of migrating permanently to the grantor state. As implied by inscriptions that granted foreigners tax exemptions from the metic tax, in Athens the legal status of a metic, or resident alien, was not officially assigned but automatically acquired by virtue of staying in a state longer than the prescribed period of a month, at which time migrants were required to register with the state, acquire a patron (*prostates*), and become subject to the metic tax.[74] Outside Athens, Greek polities recorded the names of those whom they had enrolled as metics, of metics who had made financial contributions to their host state, and of metics who had died in the service of the state. Such lists from second- and first-century BCE Rhodes and Iasos in Karia include Phoenicians from Arados, Sidon, Berytos, and Tyre.[75] Registers such as these were published in central areas of the city-states that commissioned them, and while they disambiguated the status of those immigrants listed, they also would have served the purposes of memorializing metics' benefactions, service, and loyalty to the host state, incorporating them into the polity and encouraging a sense of belonging and inclusion.

In Rhodes, where the spectrum of participatory membership in a political community appears to have had more legal categories for immigrants than in Athens and possibly most Greek states, records show that many recipients of awards related to residency had been previously granted other honors and privileges, reinforcing the supposition that such grants were intended to create long-term or even permanent relations with individuals and encourage their visits to or residence in the grantor state. For instance, at the turn of the second century BCE, the city of Rhodos granted Thraseas, the son of Mnaseas from Berytos, who

---

74. Sosin 2016 argues that the defining characteristic of a metic was the metic tax. See also Gauthier 1972: 122; Whitehead 1977: 9, 75–79, 89–92; Fisher 2006: 338–345. In Athens metics are also mentioned when discussing their contributions in the military and especially their participation in the resistance against the Thirty Tyrants, whom Sparta placed in charge of Athens after its defeat in the Peloponnesian War.

75. *I.Iasos* 408; *SEG* 43 526; *Clara Rhodos* 2 (1932) 177,6. *SEG* 43 526 is a list of metic women who made financial contributions to Rhodes. For a recent edition and a discussion of this inscription, see Migeotte 1997.

had already been made a proxenos, the grant of *epidamia*, the right to residency, an institution especially prominent on the island of Rhodes.[76] This award placed recipients further along the spectrum of participatory membership in a political community than metics and allowed them to reside in a state permanently, perhaps without having to pay the metic tax.[77]

The ultimate privilege was citizenship. Although Athens rarely granted citizenship in earlier periods, during and following the dire years of the Peloponnesian War and the subsequent struggle to restore democracy and overthrow the Thirty Tyrants (the Athenian oligarchs who had been placed in charge of the Athenian government by the Spartans), it granted citizenship to whole communities (such as Samos), citizenship or exemption from taxation to hundreds of metics who had fought alongside Athenians to restore democracy, and freedom to those enslaved who had done the same.[78] Starting in the fourth century BCE, states occasionally awarded citizenship to individuals who had performed extraordinary services to benefit the grantor state, as demonstrated by the example of the freedman Pasion and his son Apollodoros, possibly Phoenicians who worked as bankers in Athens.[79] Originally enslaved, Pasion worked as banker in Peiraieus. By 394 BCE he had been manumitted and acquired the status of a metic; by the 380s BCE, when he had become one of the wealthiest residents of Athens and had donated to the state a thousand shields and outfitted and manned five triremes (both immensely expensive gifts that only the most wealthy could afford) he and his descendants were granted citizenship.[80]

Upward mobility along the spectrum of participatory membership in a political community is also revealed in several third-century BCE citizenship grants given to Phoenician immigrants who had already previously received other awards or were honored with further privileges at the same time as they were awarded citizenship, reflecting the multiple combinations of awards that could be used to create different social statuses along that spectrum. In all these cases, the men who were awarded citizenship were said to have shown favor toward the state that

---

76. Maiuri *Rodi e Cos* 8. Thraseas might also have held citizenship on Chios since he identifies himself with a double ethnic as both a Berytian and a Chian.

77. Maillot 2015: 154–155.

78. For citizenship grants in Athens, see M. Osborne 1981–83. The block grant of citizenship to Samos is recorded on *IG* II² 1 and the enfranchisement of metics who had supported the coup against the Thirty on *IG* II² 10. See also Engen 2010: 202–211. Citizenship grants in general must have involved a citizenship switch rather than dual citizenship; see Savalli-Lestrade 2012 and Saba 2020.

79. Trevett 1992: 1; R. Osborne 2012: 331.

80. Demosthenes, *Against Stephanos* 85 and *Against Neaira* 2.

granted them this most prestigious right and to have done whatever good was possible to serve the citizens of that state. Among these were Hephaistion, son of Herakleides the Sidonian, and his descendants, who were given citizenship by the city of Ioulis on the island of Keos.[81] In another example, Iasos commended Theokles the Aradian for his excellence and favor toward the city and granted him citizenship as well as proxenia, euergesia, *proedria* in athletic events, *ateleia*, the right to sail in and out of the city in peace and war, and the right to participate as a citizen together with the other citizens.[82] Several third-century BCE lists of individuals who had been granted citizenship by Miletos include some Sidonians, among them Mnaseas, son of Theron, who was already a proxenos and an *euergetes*.[83] Although the specific reasons for granting this exceptional award are not mentioned on any of these inscriptions, the preponderance of evidence indicates that individuals who were granted citizenship had performed extraordinary services for the states that honored them and that in many cases they did so repeatedly and with each act of service were awarded a different and better social status than the one they held before, culminating in the very rare grant of participation in a polity as full-fledged citizens.

Conclusion

As these cases of Phoenician recipients of various monetized, honorific, legal, and residency and citizenship awards show, Greek states deployed a sophisticated and varied system of award giving not only as a diplomatic tool but as an essential part of their migration and membership regimes. Together, monetized awards that increased the wealth and prestige of those so honored, honorific awards that engaged them in a reciprocal relationship with their host state, legal awards that guaranteed their ease of mobility and safety, and residency and citizenship awards that added new and nuanced gradations to the social statuses that foreigners could occupy enriched the lives and livelihoods of both immigrants and the states in which they settled. At the same time, an examination of these honors also shows that these Greek states favored the wealthiest of foreigners, those who could afford to repeatedly bestow lavish gifts on their host states and help

---

81. *IG* XII.5 596.

82. *I.Cos Segre* ED 220 B: καὶ πολιτείαν μετέχοντι πάντων ὧν καὶ οἱ ἄλλοι πολῖται μετέχουσι.

83. *Milet* I.3 67, 79, 180B and *I.Milet* VI.3 1060. None of these lists record the reasons for the awards, though some indicate the age and legitimacy of the children. See Saba 2021 on citizen lists from Miletus and a suggestion as to why the age and legitimacy of children may have been of concern. LaBuff 2016: 191–198 argues that Miletos granted citizenship to individuals from neighboring communities to expand its territory and influence as a state.

ensure the survival of the host state's population. Such preferential treatment, still common among nations' immigration policies today, undoubtedly created inequalities within the migration and membership regimes of Greek city-states. Although the records do not reveal much about poorer immigrants living and working in Greek communities, we know from several court speeches given or perhaps even authored by the son of Pasion, Apollodoros, that even those who were granted citizenship, such as himself, could not fully escape the precarious position of immigrants.[84] Nonetheless, the evidence presented in this chapter demonstrates that as states granted these awards separately and in combinations, they not only created individual relationships with each honorand but also constructed a spectrum of participatory membership in a political community with different social statuses along which foreign individuals could move as they were given different awards and privileges. Over time, as this book will show, the ensuing social mobility and the public nature of these awards served to incorporate foreigners into a polity and create more cosmopolitan communities in which all their constituent population contributed to the survival, vibrancy, and intercultural connections of their societies.

---

84. Fisher 2006: 341–343 discusses this family and Apollodoros' preoccupations with citizenship. See also Trevett 1992. Six of the seven speeches written on behalf of Apollodoros are thought to have been written by him and attributed to Demosthenes: *Against Stephanos 2, Against Timotheos, Against Polykles, Against Kallipos, Against Nikostratos, Against Neaira*. Several speeches written by Demosthenes concern Apollodoros and his family: *Against Stephanos 1, For Phormio*. See MacDowell 2009: 99–126.

5
Phoenicians beyond Greek Communities

IN THE EGYPTIAN Museum in Cairo, Egypt, stands a stele from the ancient city of Memphis, twenty miles south of Cairo on the west bank of the Nile. Memphis was the capital of Egypt during the Old Kingdom (c. 2686–2160 BCE), a bustling center for commerce throughout its history, and the place where Alexander the Great was crowned king in 332 BCE and was buried after his death in 323 BCE. This black schist stele, which dates from the second or early first century BCE, is decorated with a representation of the Egyptian god Horus standing on crocodiles and holding scorpions, snakes, and other animals and is covered with hieroglyphic inscriptions of common Egyptian magical incantations for protection against such creatures. This typically Egyptian stele stands on a yellow limestone base containing a carved channel that runs around the stele and ends in a carved basin in front of it, presumably for performing a religious ritual involving the water that accumulated in this basin (Fig. 5.1).[1] Yet it also bears a four-line inscription in the Phoenician script and language, this one containing none of the magical incantations of the Egyptian texts but still appealing to a combination of Egyptian and Phoenician divinities—the Egyptian Isis, the Phoenician Astarte, and the gods more generally—to protect the dedicant, his four sons, and their mother.[2] In typical Phoenician practice, the text also provides a long genealogy

---

1. For a brief discussion of this stele, see Vittmann 2003: 74 and Thompson 2011: 104–105 and 2012: 82.

2. *KAI* 48. The Phoenician text reads: "I made this offering, Paalashtart, son of Bodmelqat, son of Benbaal, son of Abdmelqat, son of Benbaal, son of Abdmelqat. For my mistress, the glorious goddess Isis, the goddess Astarte, and the gods. May they bless me and my sons Abdosir and Benbaal and Abdshamash and Paalashtart, with their mother Hanashtart. May they give them favor and life before the gods and their children."

FIGURE 5.1 Dedicatory stele by Paalashtart with a Phoenician and hieroglyphic inscription, second or first century BCE
Cairo, Egyptian Museum CG 9402.

tracing the dedicant's ancestry for five generations and follows the adaptive strategies by which immigrants borrowed cultural practices of their host state: name changing, as one of the dedicant's sons is called Abdosir, a theophoric name that derives from the name of the Egyptian god Osiris; the adoption of the Egyptian goddess Isis as one of the deities to whom this offering was dedicated; and the use of two phrases that reflect Egyptian religious language—the request that the gods may give "favor and life" to the honorand and his family and the inclusion of the catchall category of "the gods" after specifically naming two of them.

Yet a closer look reveals several differences from the bicultural and bilingual monuments examined earlier in this volume that suggest that even though Phoenician immigrants in Egypt employed some of the same strategies as their counterparts in Greek communities, those strategies varied according to the cultural and historical context of the host society. In this stele, for instance, name changing was used in the Phoenician text but not in the Egyptian, as one might expect if the dedicant had been attempting to make his son's name more comprehensible to Egyptians, and it shows no effort to adapt his own name or that of his wife into Egyptian, as their names, Paalashtart and Hanashtart, are transliterated into hieroglyphic in the Egyptian text. Further, the name of his son, Abdosir (his other sons have the typically Phoenician names Benbaal, Abdshamash, and Paalashtart) was not a translation of an Egyptian name, an adoption of a purely Egyptian name, or an Egyptianized form of a Phoenician name; instead, it Phoenicianized the name of an Egyptian deity, Osiris, by incorporating it into a theophoric Phoenician name. Other peculiarities are that the Phoenician text mentions Isis, an Egyptian goddess, and Egyptian religious language is translated into Phoenician. That this Phoenician immigrant, like other Phoenician immigrants who lived in Egypt, worshiped Egyptian divinities, named his son after one, and proclaimed all this in his native language demonstrates this chapter's argument that, over time, immigrants' adaptive strategies and their host states' migration and membership regimes contributed to the creation not only of hybrid cultural identities but also of a more cosmopolitan Mediterranean world.

This chapter examines epigraphic texts from the fourth century BCE onward to investigate the presence and experiences of Phoenician immigrants in three settings beyond the Greek states explored in the previous chapters: fourth- to second-century BCE Carthage, which was first established by Tyre as a Phoenician settlement; fourth- to second-century BCE Egypt, which had a millennia-long history with Phoenicians and their predecessors, the Canaanites; and the central Mediterranean islands of Sicily, Sardinia, and Malta in the second and first centuries BCE, which were all home to Phoenician settlements from the eighth century BCE onward. The centuries of interactions between Phoenicians and the populations living in each of these locales provide a comparative perspective that reveals both similarities and differences in the adaptive strategies used by Phoenician immigrants across a wider extent of the Mediterranean and the long-term effects of mobility and migration across the region. As such strategies blurred the boundaries between citizen and immigrant and shaped cultural practices over centuries of settlement by Phoenicians in these societies, individuals became less recognizable as immigrants and more as citizens of a larger Mediterranean world. Mobility, migration, and adaptation, this chapter will argue, led polities to transform themselves from multiethnic societies in which both states and individuals were invested in distinguishing individuals according to their civic or ethnic identities into cosmopolitan environments in which such identities were less prominent and societies were more inclusive.

Carthage

Carthage (modern-day Tunis) was one of the most important trading centers and one of the wealthiest and most powerful cities of the ancient Mediterranean.

By the fourth century BCE, Carthage had become a hegemon in the central and western Mediterranean and remained so until 146 BCE, when it was razed to the ground and set ablaze and its citizens were sold into slavery after the conclusion of the Punic Wars with Rome, the rising power in the region at that time. Carthage, whose ancient name *qart ḥadasht* means "new city," was originally founded in the late ninth or early eighth century BCE by the Phoenician city-state of Tyre, and the two cities remained diplomatically and culturally connected to each other throughout their history.[3] According to the foundation legend of Carthage recounted by the Greek historian Timaeus in the fourth century BCE, Elissa, most widely known as Queen Dido from Virgil's *Aeneid*, fled the rule of her brother, Pygmalion, the king of Tyre, after he assassinated her husband.[4] Accompanied by other Tyrians, she sailed to the region of ancient Libya, where they established the new city of Carthage. Her tragic story ended when, despite pressure from her fellow Tyrians to do so, she refused to marry the king of the Libyans and killed herself by jumping into a funeral pyre.[5] Later Roman authors embellished the story with details influenced by familiar stereotypes of the Phoenicians that present them as crafty, deceitful, and perfidious. For example, the first-century BCE Roman historian Pompeius Trogus, summarized two hundred years later by the Roman writer Justin, claims that Dido tricked her brother into thinking she was only mourning her husband when she instead loaded the ships with money and sailed to Libya; that she tricked the local Libyans into giving her a bigger piece of land on which to settle; that her fellow citizens tricked her into accepting the Libyan king's offer of marriage; and even that she tricked the Libyan king and her countrymen by committing suicide rather than marrying the king.[6] The historian comments that her people exhibited the notorious *fides punica*, a Roman saying

---

3. For the foundation date of Carthage, see Dridi 2019a: 141–143 and Aubet Semmler 2019: 78.

4. Timaeus, whose account of the foundation of Carthage is the earliest in extant Greek sources, gives the Greek name of Elissa as Theisso, a combination of a translation of El, the first part of the compound name, into Theos, and a transliteration of *-issa* into *-osso*. See also Honeyman 1947: 77–78.

5. Timaeus *FGrHist* 566 F 82 probably followed Phoenician sources in constructing his account, as did Menander of Ephesos (Menander *FGrHist* 783 F 1, quoted in Josephus), and thus their presentation of the Phoenicians who settled in Carthage is neutral. See Haegemans 2000, who at 281–282 makes the case that Menander followed a Tyrian source, and Baron 2013: 223–224. Philistus, who is the earliest Greek source to discuss the foundation legend of Carthage, omits Elissa altogether and instead ascribes the foundation of the city to two men, Azoros and Karchedon, the Greek names of Tyre and Carthage (*FGrHist* 566 F 47).

6. Justin, *Epitome* 18.4.1–18.6.8.

that came to mean one was as treacherous and deceitful as the Carthaginians.[7] Stereotypes about their character seem to have accompanied the Phoenicians from the eastern Mediterranean, including the Tyrians who founded Carthage, and came to be applied to the Carthaginians.

Tyre had established numerous other cities in the western Mediterranean in the eighth and seventh centuries BCE.[8] In the fourth century BCE, Carthage actively attempted to solidify its control of areas in the central Mediterranean over which it had imperial ambitions by appealing to their common ancestry from Tyre and alluding to their common Phoenician past through the portrayal of a palm tree—a *phoenix*, the Greek word from which the term Phoenician derives—on the reverse of Carthaginian coins that circulated in the western Mediterranean.[9] According to the second-century CE historian Arrian, Carthage also attempted to maintain religious connections with its mother city by sending sacred ambassadors (*theoroi*) on a pilgrimage to Tyre to honor that city's patron god, Melqart, who was widely worshiped in the central and western Mediterranean as a founder of cities.[10] This special relationship between Carthage and Tyre provided a distinct set of circumstances that were different from those that Phoenician immigrants encountered in Greek communities, including that Carthaginians and Phoenicians from the eastern Mediterranean spoke the same language, albeit with slight dialectal variants depending on the city-state from which they came.[11]

Despite the close relationship between Tyre and Carthage and notwithstanding the presence of Phoenician and other immigrants in Carthage, ancient sources suggest that Carthage, like the Greek city-states discussed earlier, also had conflicting views regarding the presence of immigrants in the city. As recounted by

---

7. Justin, *Epitome* 18.6.2. For this and other Roman stereotypes of Carthaginians, see Starks 1999: 257–258. See also Bunnens 1979: 181–183.

8. On the Phoenician presence in the western Mediterranean, see Aubet 2001 and Celestino and López-Ruiz 2016. On the Tyrian colonial expansion, see Aubet Semmler 2019 and Martí-Aguilar 2019. On the presence of Phoenicians in the western Mediterranean more generally, see the essays by Hayne, Roppa, De Vincenzo, Vella and Anastasi, Costa, López Castro, Arruda, and Mederos Martín in López-Ruiz and Doak 2019.

9. Quinn 2018: 86–90.

10. Arrian 2.24.5. These ambassadors were caught in Tyre when Alexander the Great besieged and attacked it in 332 BCE. Alexander released them and sent them home to Carthage. For a common identity in Tyre and its colonies constructed around the figure of Melqart, see Bonnet 2009 and Martí-Aguilar 2019. For Melqart as a founder god and his connection to the Greek Herakles, see Malkin 2011: 119–141.

11. Even though scholars use the term "Punic" to describe the language spoken in Carthage, it was only a dialect of Phoenician that would have been comprehensible to any Phoenician speaker and vice versa.

the Roman historian Livy, for instance, a discussion in the Carthaginian Senate prompted by the arrival in Carthage of a Tyrian man named Ariston revealed the difficulties states faced in dealing with possible threats from foreigners and immigrants while also ensuring that their citizens were treated appropriately when visiting foreign states. Ariston had been sent to Carthage to deliver secret messages to the allies of the famed Carthaginian general Hannibal, who had gone into voluntary exile when his political and financial reforms aimed at paying off the war indemnity Rome had imposed on Carthage after the Second Punic War upset the Carthaginian elites. When Hannibal's enemies became aware of Ariston's mission, they brought the matter to the Senate, where some senators argued that foreigners (*advena*) like Ariston should be arrested and detained and others argued against it, pointing out that apprehending guests (*hospites*) might lead to reprisals against Carthaginians frequenting Tyre and other markets.[12] Although both the words *advena* and *hospites* were used to describe foreigners, they have different connotations, with the latter being a positive term implying that the host society would provide hospitality to such an individual and the former being more neutral or negative, like the words "foreigner" or "stranger" in English. In any case, Ariston was made to feel uncomfortable enough that he promptly absconded, boarding a ship and fleeing Carthage that same evening after the Senate had adjourned. Just as states worried about the presence of foreigners, foreign visitors often fretted over their possible reception in their host state, as in another example from Carthage reported by the historian Polybius. In this incident, Xanthippos, a Spartan mercenary who had orchestrated a Carthaginian victory in 255 BCE during the First Punic War against the Roman general Regulus, was said to have immediately boarded a ship to return home after his success rather than remain in Carthage because he feared the Carthaginians' envy, claiming that while a native could survive envy with the support of his friends and family, a foreigner without such support could easily be overpowered.[13]

Yet an examination of epigraphic evidence from Carthage left behind by Phoenician immigrants from the eastern Mediterranean reveals a more nuanced and balanced view of Carthage's migration and membership regimes. While literary sources allude to the presence of Phoenician immigrants in Carthage, such

---

12. Livy 34.61. The incident is summarized in Appian, *Syrian Wars* 2.8, where Ariston is described as a Tyrian trader. The Carthaginians, who evidently considered Hannibal's interference in Carthaginian politics serious, reported this incident to the Roman consuls and the Roman Senate. Livy's and Appian's accounts of Ariston's story, derived from Polybius, were written in the first and second centuries CE respectively and speak of events that took place in the early second century BCE (193 BCE) from a distinctly Greco-Roman perspective.

13. Polybius 1.36.

126   PHOENICIANS AMONG OTHERS

as refugees from Tyre or traders, epigraphic sources suggest not only a significant and multigenerational presence of eastern Phoenician immigrants in Carthage from the fourth to the second centuries BCE but also wide access to religious sanctuaries—places reserved for the worship of deities—across its resident population, regardless of class, gender, ethnicity, or place of origin, that helped create a more inclusive and cosmopolitan society.[14]

A tombstone in a Carthaginian cemetery that led to a chamber containing the skeletal remains of forty young individuals and children showcases the similarities between the adaptive practices and hybrid identities expressed by eastern Phoenician immigrants living in Carthage and in Greek communities. Its inscription, which was written in the Punic dialect of Carthage, recorded that the tomb belonged to Amran, the son of Gerashtart, and had been constructed by his Aradian wife, Kabedashtart.[15] Neither the name Amran nor Kabedashtart appears on any other Phoenician text, perhaps indicating that both names reflect the relatively unknown Aradian nomenclature and that some of the individuals buried in this tomb may have been members of an immigrant family. The text places equal emphasis on the deceased, whose civic identity is not stated, and the Aradian woman who erected the monument, a practice observed elsewhere only among Phoenicians living in Greek polities, such as Shem——, whose burial rites were performed by other Phoenicians.[16] Here, as elsewhere, it appears that the wider Phoenician immigrant community played an integral role in commissioning commemorative grave monuments for fellow Phoenician immigrants.

That immigrants in Carthage still retained some of the customs of their homeland is also indicated by a tombstone of a Phoenician immigrant from Kition

14. For the presence of Tyrians in Carthage generally, see Yon 2011 56–57. Several ancient historians mention that Tyre had reportedly sent women and children to Carthage for refuge from the impending attack by Alexander and his armies (Quintus Curtius 4.3.20; Diodorus Siculus 17.41; Justin, *Epitome* 11.10.14), and the novelist Heliodorus includes in his novel a Tyrian shipowner on his way to Carthage on commercial business who courts the protagonist, Charikleia (*Aethiopica* 5.19–23). That the author decided to make such a person a character in the novel suggests the type would have been familiar to the readers. Ps.-Skylax also refers to Phoenician merchants frequenting the coast of North Africa, which as he says (111–112) was littered with Carthaginian commercial settlements. Because of the distinction he makes between Phoenician and Carthaginian, these traders are more likely to have been Phoenicians from the eastern Mediterranean.

15. *CIS* I 5945 = *RÉS* 1226: *qbr ʿmrn bn gr*[*ʿš t*]*r*[*t*] | *hqbr ʿš pʿl ʾšt' kbd*[*ʾ*]*štrt h'rwdt* ([This is] the tomb of Amran, son of Gerashtart. [This is] the tomb that was constructed by his wife, Kabedashtart the Aradian). Ferjaoui 1992: 177–178 discusses this tombstone and the burial chamber it marked.

16. Ferjaoui 1992: 177 n. 38 notes that this practice did not become a custom in Carthage until after its fall to the Roman Empire in the second century BCE.

buried in the same cemetery as Amran. The Kitian's tombstone was inscribed with a single line of which only the end survives, recording the name of an ancestor and the deceased's place of origin.[17] Although such short genealogies were uncommon among either eastern Phoenicians and Carthaginians, who typically provided longer genealogies of ancestors, they were common on Cyprus, where Kition is located, suggesting that this was a hybrid practice that emerged among the bilingual population of Kition, which was predominantly Phoenician but also had a large Greek resident population. This tombstone was also unique in Carthage in that its inscription was carved on a gray marble stele—an uncommon material for Carthaginian tombstones—and its decoration was more typical of Greek rather than Phoenician tombstones, consisting of a floral relief above the epitaph, as in the tombstones of the Kitian immigrants Mahdash and Benhodesh in Athens discussed in the first chapter (Fig. 1.2).[18] These details suggest that the Kitian or his family had imported the funerary stone from Cyprus, which appears to have been unusual. In extant examples in Athens, Demetrias, and Rhodes, Phoenician immigrants from Kition and elsewhere used locally bought funerary stelae, sometimes engraved with imagery that borrowed from both Greek and Phoenician artistic repertoires. In no currently known instance did they import their own funerary stones, not even when someone from the homeland came for the specific purpose of conducting the appropriate funerary rites, as happened for Shem——, whose funerary stele was Attic in shape and form and purchased from an Attic workshop rather than imported from his home state of Ashkelon. The distinctiveness of the funerary stone of the Kitian immigrant in Carthage would have stood out in the cemetery and perhaps identified the deceased as a resident of Carthage who followed foreign cultural traditions. That such indications of one's foreign status were common throughout the Mediterranean region would seem to signify that immigrants did not find it necessary to hide their origins or identities as individuals who came from elsewhere even as they tried to fit into their host societies.

Epigraphic evidence also suggests that one way Carthage incorporated immigrants into its civic society was the tophet, the sanctuary dedicated to the goddess Tanit and Baal Hammon, which seems to have offered an avenue for all the residents of the city to participate in local rituals. This religious cult had first emerged in the middle of the eighth century BCE as a way for the Phoenician immigrants who founded the city to distinguish themselves from other Phoenicians through

---

17. *RÉS* 1225: *bn 'šmn'dny 'š kty* (. . . son of Eshmounadonai, a man from Kition). See also Ferjaoui 1992: 178.

18. *KAI* 55 = *CIS* I 117 = *IG* II² 9034 and *KAI* 57 = *IG* II² 9035.

their practice of religious rites not known in their eastern Mediterranean homelands.[19] Most of the burials in the sanctuary in Carthage and in those tophets in Sulcis on Sardinia, Rabat on Malta, and Motya on Sicily are of infants and children up to six to nine years old and a few of lambs and goats, and their remains suggest that what happened in these sanctuaries involved child sacrifice and not a normal burial of a deceased. Although the reasons for such practices are debated, it is accepted among scholars that children were indeed ritually killed and buried as part of vows made to divinities.[20] That no tophets have been found east of Malta suggests that the religious rites that took place in these sanctuaries originated in religious practices that were specific among the early founders of Carthage and among Phoenicians who had established settlements on Malta, Sardinia, and Sicily.

It is perhaps the immigrant origins of this cult that led to the inclusivity of the sanctuary of Tanit and Baal Hammon in Carthage, as evidence indicates that it provided access to the whole resident population of Carthage: citizens, immigrants, freedmen, and even enslaved persons. The multitude of dedicatory stelae from this sanctuary record the presence and participation of Greeks, Egyptians, Libyans, eastern Phoenicians, and others, in addition to Carthaginian cult participants.[21] Among the Phoenicians who made vows, offered dedications, and set up stelae to mark the burial places of their offerings in this sanctuary were several Sidonians. A third-century BCE dedication records a Sidonian woman Arishat, whose theophoric name derives from the Egyptian goddess Isis, as one such person who made a vow to these gods,[22] and another identifies a certain Abdes, who, depending on the reconstruction of the text, was either a Sidonian or a Tyrian.[23] Another thirty-four dedications from this sanctuary suggest

---

19. Quinn 2013.

20. The percentages of infant to animal sacrifices in each tophet varies. For recent debates on child sacrifice, see Xella 2013a and 2013b and McCarty 2019.

21. Amadasi Guzzo 1988: 148; Ferjaoui 1999; Xella 2008: 78; Crouzet 2012: 44–45. Sznycer 1975: 59–61 lists a series of dedications offered by individuals who say they come from *yrnm* (the island of Pantellaria), *ybšm* (Ibiza), *rš mlqrt* (Heraklea Minoa on Sicily), and *'ynṣm* (San Pietro, near Sulcis on Sardinia). These may have been official representatives of these communities who came to give their offerings to the sanctuary of Tanit and Baal Hammon in Carthage. Lapeyre 1939 also notes dedications by citizens from different places on Sardinia and one from Eryx on Sicily (296). See also Quinn 2013, who argues that the openness of the Carthaginian tophet and those in Motya, Sulcis, and Rabat demonstrates the networks created among these sites.

22. *CIS* I 308. The reconstructed name "Arishat" occurs three times in Carthage. See Ferjaoui 1992: 176–177.

23. *CIS* I 4914. The name "Abdes" occurs frequently in Sidon and Cyprus and on several tombstones of Phoenicians who lived in Athens and Demetrias. See Masson 1969: 689–690 for the Greek transcription of the name. See also Ferjaoui 1992: 175–177, who prefers to see Abdes as a

that Sidonian freedmen and freedwomen had access to this sanctuary and had adopted this cult.[24] Instead of recording the names of their ancestors, these dedicants often listed the name of their former masters, usually specified that they had legally been freed, and included a phrase that has traditionally been translated as "man from Sidon" (*'š ṣdn*).[25] Enslaved persons, on whose labor Carthaginian elites were dependent, especially for agricultural purposes, also used this same sanctuary, identifying themselves using the word *'bd* (servant) followed by their master's name, including one such individual who identifies himself as the slave of a Tyrian immigrant and may himself have been a Tyrian.[26] Carthage had a reputation for its extensive role in the ancient Mediterranean slave trade, and the presence of Tyrian slaveowners suggests that affluent Tyrian immigrants were among Carthage's resident population.[27] Whether enslaved or freed persons, free men or free women, citizens or immigrants, the dedicants appear to have all participated in this cult in the same way, and their inscribed stelae were of the same types, locally bought and engraved and inscribed with a formulaic text that appears on all the other similarly styled stelae dedicated in this sanctuary, indicating that the whole resident population of Carthage had equal access to the use of this sanctuary, which in turn may have served as a unifying force among all the residents of Carthage.

Tyrian. Another possible Tyrian offering a dedication in the same sanctuary of Tanit and Baal Hammon may be attested on *CIS* I 3139 (Ferjaoui 1992: 176).

24. *CIS* I 269–286, 289–293, 2998, 4901–4908, 5638, 5679. Some of these were offered by women: *CIS* I 273, 279, 280, 281. The ones that specify that the dedicant had had a master (*'bd 'dn*) are *CIS* I 269, 272, 276, 279, 280, 281, 290, 292, 293. For a discussion of these inscriptions and their implications on the freed status of the dedicants, see Février 1951–52 and 1961; Heltzer 1985: 79–81; Lemaire 2003: 221–222; D. M. Lewis 2018: 262–263.

25. A phrase that often occurs at the end of some of these texts (*CIS* I 269–275, 290, 291, 2822, 4908) and may have been included in the other inscriptions belonging to this series, has been translated as "people of Carthage" (*qrtḥdš 'm*) and indicates that the manumission of the enslaved person was official or had been registered with the Carthaginian government. More specifically, Février 1951–52: 18 has argued that it either records the payment received for freeing the man or the erection of the stele. Sznycer 1975: 56–59, followed by Lemaire 2003: 222, Heltzer 1985: 79 (but with qualifications on pp. 81–84), and Bonnet 1991: 159–160, has suggested it means that the enfranchisement of the enslaved was done according to the decree of the Carthaginian people (i.e., legally). The translation of *'š ṣdn* as "man of Sidon" is likely even though it is not the normal designation of "Sidonian," which is usually rendered as *ṣdny*. Nonetheless, the alternatives that have been proposed—a copper coin or an official legal status (Février 1951–52: 14)—are not sustainable. See Heltzer 1985: 79–81.

26. Lemaire 2003: 221. The text of the inscription (*CIS* I 4913) reads: *bn | brk' 'bd ḥml | kt ḥṣry* (…son of Bariku, servant of Himilkat, the Tyrian). The enslaved person's father bears a Semitic name, but it is unclear whether he, too, was Tyrian.

27. See D. M. Lewis 2018: 260–266.

The inscriptions of most first-generation Phoenician immigrants in Carthage, as in the Greek polities examined in the previous chapters, expressed an identification with their place of origin by saying that they were a "man from Kition" (*'š kty*) or "a Kitian" (*ḥkty*) or some other city-state of origin.[28] Yet a set of ten fourth- to second-century BCE inscriptions, one funerary and the rest dedications from the sanctuary of Tanit and Baal Hamon, illustrate that some second- and even third- or fourth-generation immigrants used a different form of identification, instead calling themselves sons of [the city of] Tyre (*bn ṣr*).[29] The texts inscribed on the stelae marking offerings in the sanctuary adhere to the same dedicatory formulaic incantations, followed by the identification of the dedicant, as illustrated in the following example: "To lady Tanit, the Face of Baal, and to the lord Baal Hammon, to whom *gdn'm* made a vow, daughter of Baalyaton, son of [the city of] Tyre" (Fig. 5.2).[30] The expression "son of" followed by a toponym is unusual enough that the editors of early scholarly collections of these inscriptions understood Tyre as a personal name rather than a toponym, listed as it was amid a catalog of ancestors of the dedicant.[31] But Tyre as a personal name is highly unusual and the expression "son of [toponym]" is not unknown; other inscriptions refer to a son of Tyre from Sabratha in North Africa, a son of Arqa (a site north of Byblos) from Tamassos on Cyprus, and two sons of Carthage from Tyre, all contemporary to the references to sons of Tyre in Carthage.[32] This phrasing is

---

28. *KAI* 55 = *CIS* I 117 (= *IG* II² 9034) and *KAI* 57 (= *IG* II² 9035), the two epitaphs for Benhodesh and Mahdash, immigrants in Athens discussed in the first chapter, and *RÉS* 1225, the funerary inscription for the Kitian immigrant in Carthage discussed above, use the expression "man from Kition." *Thess. Mn.* 290–291 no. 76 offers an example of the alternate mode of identification on an epitaph of a Kitian in Demetrias, also presented in the first chapter.

29. These ten inscriptions end with the name of the dedicant, his or her genealogy, and include the expression "son of Tyre": *CIS* I 617, 913, 1477, 2020, 3968, 5226, 5826, 5970, 6051 and Ferjaoui 2008. *CIS* I 5970 is the funerary inscription. *CIS* I 617, 913, 3968, 5526, 2020 and Ferjaoui 2008 all begin with the dedication to Tanit and Baal Hammon. *CIS* I 1477 and 5826 are fragmentary, with the beginning of the text missing. *CIS* I 6051 begins differently and was not discovered at the tophet. The most updated list of all inscriptions that contain this or similar phrases is in Amadasi Guzzo 2012.

30. Ferjaoui 2008: 184–185.

31. See Bordreuil and Ferjaoui 1988: 140–141 and n. 16 for a discussion of the different interpretations. Bonnet 1991: 154 n. 25 notes that we cannot exclude the possibility that *ṣr* in the expression *bn ṣr* is a personal name. In Greek, the name "Tyros" is only attested four times: *IG* II² 11415; *I.Beroia* 160; *SEG* 24, 504a–b; *TAM* I 115. The last text, from the fourth century BCE, records the name of a man as Phoinix, son of Tyre. This might be a parallel example to the Carthaginian cases, identifying a man from Tyre.

32. For the two sons of Carthage in Tyre, see Bordreuil and Ferjaoui 1988: 137–139; Sader 1993, who published one of these inscriptions; and Teixidor 1986, who published the other in the 1986 *Bulletin d'épigraphie sémitique*. Bordreuil and Ferjaoui (1988: 137) also mention

Phoenicians beyond Greek Communities 131

FIGURE 5.2 Dedication to Tanit and Baal Hammon by a descendant of a Tyrian immigrant in Carthage, fourth–second centuries BCE
Tunis, Carthage Museum.

also commonly used in the Hebrew Bible to indicate citizens of different cities, kingdoms, or members of tribes.[33] There is good reason, then, to believe that the expression in the ten inscriptions from Carthage refers to an immigrant from Tyre, meaning that Baalyaton would have been the individual who emigrated to Carthage from Tyre in the line of immigrant descent in the text cited above. The dedicants in these texts, who were probably Carthaginian citizens, appear to have traced their genealogy back to an ancestor who had been a citizen of Tyre as a matter of pride and a marker of their family's identity as having originally

---

that this phrase was used to refer to sons of Ugarit and Canaan and date from the Bronze Age. B. Kaufman 2009 provides a useful history of the various translations that have been offered by scholars and adds the inscription from Sabratha to the corpus. See also Quinn 2018: 222–223 n. 62 for more references. B. Kaufman 2009: 46–47 proposes that the phrase is used as a title based on the evidence of *CIS* I 6051 as the expression "son of Tyre" appears sandwiched between two titles: scribes and judges. Amadasi Guzzo 2012: 108 convincingly disputes this.

33. For example, Num 21:24 (Ammonites); Exod 1:1 (Israelites); Joel 4:6 (Jerusalemites; Judeans); Neh 12:23 (Levites); Ps 149:2 (sons of Zion).

emigrated from Carthage's mother city. Unlike Phoenician immigrants in Greek communities, who over generations progressed to using exclusively Greek instead of both Phoenician and Greek in their funerary or dedicatory inscriptions and gradually switched from identifying as members of their state of origin to using their host state's city-ethnic, in Carthage, multigeneration Tyrian immigrants began to claim descent from Tyrian ancestors when that identification became prestigious as Carthage mobilized its Tyrian roots as a tool of empire in the fourth century BCE.[34]

Egypt

Egyptians and Phoenicians had already been entangled in trade and war and belonged to the same political and economic networks for two millennia before the fourth to the first centuries BCE. For instance, some Semitic curses against "Byblite snakes," probably some pest that invaded Egypt after having been inadvertently carried by ships from Byblos, have been found rendered in hieroglyphs and embedded in Egyptian incantations on pyramid texts dating to the third millennium BCE.[35] Other evidence of travel between Egypt and Phoenician polities comes from the Egyptian *Tale of Wenamum*, which dates from 1090 to 1075 BCE. This fictional story recounts the adventures of a priest who traveled from Egyptian Thebes to Byblos to acquire timber for the construction of a ceremonial bark for the god Amun-Ra. On his way to Byblos, the priest Wenamun stopped in Dor, where one of his crewmen stole some gold and silver from the ship, and then conducted acts of piracy. Once in Byblos, the king of this city refused to give timber to Wenamun unless he paid—a reasonable request, of course, but the king spends a lot of time justifying why this was necessary—and Wenamun accuses him of haggling with the god Amun over the timber. Although it is Wenamun who haggles and tries to get out of paying for the timber, the accusation against the Byblite king and his insistence on getting paid contains seeds of later stereotypes of Phoenicians as crafty and deceitful traders found in biblical, Greek, and Roman sources. After he had secured timber from the king of Byblos, Wenamun found himself under pursuit by the ship he had looted, so he set on his way to Egypt, only to be driven to Alasiya (Cyprus) by the winds, where he met the

---

34. See, for instance, the Tyrian family of sculptors on Rhodes discussed in chapter 1, who eventually stopped identifying as Tyrians and switched to identifying as Rhodians.

35. Steiner 2011: 23–58 includes a presentation, translation, and discussion of the Semitic spells. Pages 79–80 propose the serpents were actual snakes accidentally brought into Egypt by ships from Byblos.

local queen, at which point the story breaks off.³⁶ This story and the inclusion of Semitic curses in Egyptian mortuary complexes reflect the interconnectedness of both the political elites and the common people of the eastern Mediterranean region. An examination of the evidence left behind by Phoenician immigrants in Egypt indicates that such cross-cultural interactions led to not only a close familiarity with each other's culture but also cultural influences and appropriations by both groups and reveals new adaptations, novel modes of identification, and the nascent cosmopolitanism of the Mediterranean region by the second and first centuries BCE.

The close contacts between Phoenician city-states and Egypt, especially through commerce, led to the popularity and prestige of Egyptian art among the elites of Phoenician city-states and to the adoption of Egyptian religious practices and iconography among both those elites and the common people. Phoenicians appropriated Egyptian religious symbols such as the lotus flower and the uraeus, which can be seen on their funerary stelae, as mentioned in the first chapter. They also worshiped Egyptian deities, as is evidenced in theophoric names such as Abdosir or Arishat, that are recorded among Phoenicians in Carthage, Malta, Egypt, and their homelands; the wholesale adoption of Egyptian gods, such as Bes, a male Egyptian god of fertility who was worshiped widely among the Phoenicians; and amulets and scarabs produced in Egypt bearing images of Egyptian gods that were used by Phoenicians in their homelands and in their settlements in the central and western Mediterranean.³⁷ Similarly, Phoenician kings of the early first millennium, perhaps in an effort to align themselves politically with Egypt rather than the Assyrians, the dominant power in their region at that time, offered dedications of Egyptian stelae and Egyptian statues in their city-states. The king of Byblos Yehimilk (c. 950 BCE), for instance, erected an Egyptian-style stele inscribed in Phoenician but depicting a seated Egyptian god and a king bringing offerings portrayed in Near Eastern fashion.³⁸ Two other kings of Byblos, Abibaal and Elibaal, who ruled in the last third of the tenth century BCE, dedicated and inscribed statues they brought from or commissioned in Egypt of the contemporary Egyptian pharaohs Shoshenq I (943–922 BCE)

---

36. *The Tale of Wenamun*, in Lichtheim 2006: 224–230. See also Sader 2019: 35–36.

37. For a survey of the influences by and adoption of Egyptian religion and religious art, see Aliquot 2004 and Sader 2019: 211–213, with references. For Phoenician theophoric names derived from Egyptian deities, see Bentz 1972: 269–272, 317, 396. For the worship of Egyptian deities by Phoenicians, see Lipiński 1995, chapter 11. For the adoption of Bes, see Mazar 2009–10. For scarabs and amulets, many of which bear Phoenician inscriptions, see Boschloos 2014 and López-Ruiz 2015: 63–70. See also Vittmann 2003: 76–80.

38. *KAI* 4.

and Osorkon I (922–887 BCE), respectively.[39] Similarly, the sarcophagus of King Ahiram (c. 1000 BCE) of Byblos was produced locally but included many elements inspired from Egyptian art, such as two sphinxes flanking the king's throne and a lotus held in the king's hand.[40] In later periods, Sidonian kings reused Egyptian sarcophagi (which they had perhaps looted) for their burials. Both King Tabnit (c. 490 BCE) and his son Eshmounazor II (c. 475 BCE), for example, were interred in basalt Egyptian anthropoid sarcophagi. Tabnit's sarcophagus, now in the Istanbul Archaeological Museum, includes a hieroglyphic inscription that identifies its original Egyptian owner (General Pen-Ptah) and a Phoenician inscription added at the bottom, while Eshmounazor II's sarcophagus, now in the Louvre, bears only a Phoenician inscription, and both Phoenician texts end with the admonition—ironic given that these are reused monuments—that whoever finds the sarcophagus should not disturb it.[41] Such evidence demonstrates that by the fourth century BCE, Phoenician art and religious practices had already incorporated Egyptian divinities and iconographic motifs.

In addition to the millennia-long interactions between Egyptians and Phoenicians, Phoenician immigrants are recorded as living in Egypt by the dawn of the Iron Age.[42] This evidence includes Herodotus' report that Tyrian mercenaries who had served in the armies of the pharaoh Psammetichos I in the seventh century BCE were given a land grant and settled in a camp in their own quarter in Memphis, and the preponderance of both Phoenician amphorae and inscribed ostraca (pottery shards) found in Tell el-Maskhuta in the eastern Nile delta that suggest a significant presence of Phoenician traders there in the late seventh and sixth centuries BCE.[43] Other examples include Phoenician graffiti scratched on the two colossal statues of Rameses II at the temple of Abu Simbel in the

---

39. *KAI* 5 and *KAI* 6. Alibaal's dedication records his genealogy, that he brought the statue from Egypt, and that he dedicated it to the Lady of Byblos. Elibaal's inscription notes that he commissioned the statue himself, in addition to providing his genealogy and explaining that he was dedicating it to the Lady of Byblos so that she would make long his reign over Byblos. For the identity of the Lady of Byblos and a discussion of both *KAI* 5 and 6, see Zernecke 2013. See also Vittmann 2003: 52–55.

40. Vittmann 2003: 52. See also Bondì 1988: 35 and pl. 127. For the inscription, see *KAI* 1.

41. The Phoenician inscriptions are *KAI* 13 and 14. Vittmann 2003: 58–61 discusses both these monuments.

42. Bresciani 1987 and Vittmann 2003: 44–83 both provide overviews of the Phoenician presence in Egypt. Phoenician texts from Egypt have been published in Derenbourg and Derenbourg 1885; Lidzbarski 1912; Aimé-Giron 1931; Magnanini 1973: 61–83; and Segal 1983.

43. For the Tyrians in Memphis, see Herodotus 2.112. A third-century BCE papyrus refers to ethnic neighborhoods in Memphis: *PSI* V 488. For the pottery shards in Tell el-Maskhuta, see Schmitz 2012: 43–53 and Calabro 2015: 97.

region of Aswan that identify the authors as mercenary soldiers in the armies of Egyptian pharaohs campaigning in Nubia in the sixth century BCE and evidence that Phoenicians were also present in the famous military fortress of Elephantine in the fifth century BCE, perhaps as soldiers, traders, or both.[44]

Despite the presence of Phoenician and other immigrants in Egypt over many centuries, numerous depictions in Egyptian art and literature, especially from New Kingdom Egypt (1550–1050 BCE) indicate that Egyptian attitudes toward foreigners were mostly negative: foreigners were portrayed as potentially dangerous yet alluring, as wealthy others who came mostly from the Near East and disrupted both the social and cosmic order of Egypt.[45] Yet the attitudes represented in these negative literary tropes, like similar ones from Athens discussed earlier, often appear to have been more complex when other types of evidence, including epigraphic, are taken into consideration. In the case of Egypt, official Egyptian policies both accepted and regulated immigrants' presence. State decrees regulating which ports foreign traders visited and where they disembarked and accounts by ancient Greek authors and evidence left behind by foreigners suggest that Egyptians segregated foreigners into quarters according to ethnic group and assigned foreign mercenaries into units separate from Egyptians. For instance, the twin stelae from Naukratis and Thonis-Herakleion, both commercial settlements on the Canobic branch of the Nile, bear a text that regulated trade into the Nile delta.[46] Herodotus corroborates this when he reports that Naukratis in the past had served as the only commercial center (by Herodotus' time, in the fifth century BCE, other sites, such as Memphis, also served as trading centers). Indeed, the Egyptian government forced traders who accidentally landed at other sites to sail back to Naukratis.[47] Moreover, both Herodotus and later papyri indicate that foreign residents lived in separate settlements or neighborhoods, as the Tyrian veterans did in Memphis, which besides the Tyrian precinct also had a Syropersian, Karian, and Greek quarter.[48] Such evidence suggests that the Egyptian state

---

44. For the presence of Phoenician mercenaries in the campaigns against Nubia, see Schmitz 2010 and 2012: 32–42. Becking 2017 makes the argument that the Phoenicians of Elephantine were traders rather than soldiers. For a complete list of the Phoenician inscriptions from Elephantine, see Lidzbarski 1912.

45. O'Connor 2003; Booth 2005; Di Biase-Dyson 2013; Anthony 2017.

46. See von Bomhard 2012 for a discussion of the twin stelae.

47. Herodotus 2.178–179.

48. Herodotus 2.112 specifies that Tyrian Phoenicians whom he describes as army veterans lived in their own precinct in Memphis. The third-century BCE papyrus, *PSI* V 488, refers to various ethnic neighborhoods in Memphis, such as the Syropersian, Karian, and Greek quarters. Greek graffiti scratched by mercenary soldiers on the colossal statues of Rameses II in Abu Simbel

tended to follow a policy of separating foreign populations from each other and from Egyptians, even when they lived in the same multiethnic town, such as Memphis. This policy, as this chapter shows, had tangible effects on the ways Phoenician immigrants living in Egypt identified themselves and interacted with their host state.

The highly bureaucratic nature of Egyptian royal and provincial administration and the long history of interactions between Egyptians and Phoenicians led to novel modes of identifications by immigrants. The example of Paalashtart's dedication from the chapter opening points to the wholesale adoption of Egyptian religion and Egyptian names alongside Phoenician ones, changes that could already be seen in a sixth-century BCE letter written in Phoenician on a papyrus discovered in Saqqara, the cemetery that served Memphis. This text not only showcases the name changing, worship of a mixture of Phoenician and Egyptian deities, and close collaboration between locals and immigrants common among the adaptive strategies of immigrants, but also demonstrates ways in which the presence of Phoenician immigrants changed Egyptian society.[49] The letter opens with the addressee's name, the Phoenicianized theophoric name of Arishat, which derives from the name of the Egyptian goddess Isis, followed by a benefaction from the sender, Bassa, a woman with a typically Egyptian name who was possibly Egyptian, that alludes to both the Phoenician god Baal Saphon and the Egyptian deities of Tahpanhes (Tell Defne), where Bassa was probably based.[50] The rest of the letter illuminates the economic activities of a business organization, probably a banking operation since the letter records transactions involving money, that seems to have been headed by Bassa in Tahpanhes and Arishat in Memphis and involved several other women with Egyptian names who were stationed at or sent to Memphis. Baal Saphon is a deity whose worship was actually introduced into Egypt by Phoenician immigrants, seems to have been adopted by Egyptians, had become one of the most prominent deities worshiped in Tahpanhes, and as such

---

suggest that foreign-speakers and Egyptian soldiers served in different contingents led by different commanders (*M-L* no. 7).

49. *KAI* 50. The papyrus was first published by Aimé-Giron 1940, who provided the first translation. Here I use Peckham's translation (Peckham 2014: 437–439). Another papyrus fragment in Phoenician records a letter with lists of goods and prices that dates from the fourth to the third centuries BCE of unknown provenance: *KAI* 51. See Aimé-Giron 1938: 1–18.

50. The beginning of the letter reads: "To Arishat, the daughter of Eshmounyaton, say to my sister Arishat: 'Your sister Bassa says: "I hope you are well: I too am well. I have blessed you by Baal Saphon and all the gods of Tahpanhes: May they keep you well."'" For a discussion of the opening of the letter see Greenfield 1984. Arishat was also the name of the Sidonian woman in Carthage who had given an offering in the sanctuary of Tanit and Baal Hammon mentioned above. Scholars have identified Tahpanhes with Tell Defne or Greek Daphnai.

was an appropriate deity for Bassa to mention to her Phoenician business partner.[51] Yet the mention of this Phoenician god is also combined with a reference to all the gods of Tahpanhes, most of whom were presumably Egyptian, a grouping reminiscent of Paalashtart's dedication to a mixture of Egyptian and Phoenician divinities. While modern scholars can distinguish the origins of these deities and even prescribe them an ethnicity, it is not as certain that ancient Egyptians or Phoenicians would have thought of these deities in the same terms. Rather, the evidence suggests that, as a direct result of mobility and migration and the flexibility of Mediterranean religions, both Egyptians and Phoenicians engaged in practices that were mutually comprehensible and inclusive.

In contrast, the translating of Egyptian religious language into Phoenician in the dedications cited above demonstrates that the religious practices of Phoenician immigrants were also transformed by their long-term presence in Egypt. Although such translations may have originally developed as an adaptive strategy of immigration, their appearance in Phoenician texts suggests cultural changes among the Phoenician immigrants themselves. Similar examples from the general period under investigation include two bronze statuettes of the child Horus, an Egyptian god who was called Harpokrates by the Greeks, of unknown provenance now in Madrid and in London, each bearing a Phoenician inscription that adopts Egyptian religious language (Figs. 5.3a–b and 5.4a–b).[52] Both texts begin with the phrase "May Harpokrates give life to . . . ," a phrase that on the statuette now in London is also repeated in an Egyptian text inscribed by the statuette's original Egyptian owner, who had also offered it as a votive, suggesting that the Phoenician dedicator was probably fluent enough in Egyptian religious phraseology to translate it into his Phoenician dedication.[53] This Egyptian phrase, which also occurs in the Phoenician text of Paalashtart's dedication in Memphis,

---

51. A stele with a representation of a deity with Phoenician iconographic elements, perhaps Baal Saphon, may also have been discovered from Tell Defne. The provenance of the stele is based on a verbal report by Daressy. See Aimé-Giron 1940: 447–448. The same god is mentioned in another stele from Egypt (from Ras Samra) and is also attested in Carthage and Mesopotamia: Aimé-Giron 1940: 453–457.

52. Doner and Röllig in *KAI* 52 date the one from Madrid to the fourth to the second centuries BCE. Ferron 1971: 375 and 1974: 79 dates both statues to the fifth century BCE. Vittmann 2003: 74–75 dates both to the fourth or third century BCE. The National Archaeological Museum in Madrid provides a date of mid-sixth to early fifth century BCE. The British Museum dates the production of the statue in its collection to the sixth to fourth centuries BCE.

53. The text on the statuette from London reads (Ferron 1974): ḥrpkrt ytn | ḥym l'ms bn 'šmnytn bn 'lzrmlk wḥq nn b'lbn (May Harpokrates give life to Amos, son of Eshmounyaton, son of Izrimilk. And *nn* the architect sculpted it). On p. 94, Ferron argues that the dedicator of this statuette (as that of the Madrid one: Ferron 1971: 368 and 378) was a Carthaginian who lived in Egypt, based on the onomastics on the dedication. On the translation of the Egyptian language into Phoenician, see Calabro 2015: 110–111.

(a)

(b)

FIGURE 5.3A–B Bronze statuette of Harpokrates with a Phoenician inscription (*KAI* 52)
Madrid, National Archaeological Museum, Inv. No. 2150. Photographers: (a): Pablo Linés Viñuales; (b): Raúl Fernández Ruiz.

(a)

(b)

FIGURE 5.4A–B Bronze statuette of Harpokrates with a Phoenician inscription and hieroglyphic inscription

London, British Museum 132908. © The Trustees of the British Museum.

was a common formula used in prayers to gods who were asked to give breath or life to mortals.[54] The Phoenician inscription on the Madrid statuette, in addition to adopting Egyptian divinities and Egyptian religious customs, includes both Phoenician and Egyptian names in that the names of the dedicator, his father, and grandfather are Phoenician (Abdeshmoun, Ashtartyaton, Magon) but the names of his earlier ancestors are all Egyptian. This suggests that at least some of the Phoenician immigrants who lived in Egypt intermarried with Egyptians and adopted the worship of Egyptian gods yet also retained the use of their language as a marker of a Phoenician or an immigrant identity.[55] Regardless of whether these statuettes were discovered in Egypt or in the Phoenician homeland, they demonstrate how ingrained Egyptian culture became among Phoenician immigrants.

In addition to adopting Egyptian divinities such as Harpokrates or Isis, the available evidence shows that Phoenician immigrants in Egypt also syncretized Phoenician and Egyptian divinities much as those who settled in Greek communities equated Greek divinities to their own. But rather than translating their own divinities into those of their host state, Phoenician immigrants in Egypt appear to have worshiped both the foreign divinities and their own at the same time and to have transported this mode of worship to other places in the Mediterranean. The example of the Phoenician Astarte, who was often translated into the Greek Aphrodite and the Egyptian Isis, illustrates that such syncretisms of divinities did not remain isolated among immigrant communities but over the centuries became popular and helped create a common and cosmopolitan Mediterranean culture. The stele offered by Paalashtart, which asked "the glorious goddess Isis, the goddess Astarte, and the gods" for blessings, is just one of many examples of the association of Astarte with Isis that eventually became common outside

---

54. This same phrase occurs in another text inscribed on a bronze figurine of Imhotep, the deified scribe, which was probably found in Memphis. The statuette bears both a hieroglyphic and a Phoenician inscription that together read: "Imhotep, son of Ptah, may he give life" (in Egyptian) "to Waḥipre, son of Eshmounyaton" (in Phoenician). The two texts can be read separately, with the first part identifying the statue and giving the blessing and the second part identifying to whom the statue belonged, or read together in a single message, as translated here, which would make the dedication similar to those on the two statues of Harpokrates. The strongest argument for reading the two texts together is that the Egyptian text is unidiomatic, suggesting it was composed by a non-native speaker. The Phoenician dedicator of this statuette chose to worship a specifically Egyptian deity named in Egyptian with a formulaic Egyptian request for a blessing written in unidiomatic Egyptian, even as he maintained a clearly Phoenician identity by inscribing his name and patronymic in Phoenician, a language that marked him as an immigrant. Aimé-Giron 1924: 2–11 first published this text, also discussed in Vittmann 2003: 76 and Calabro 2015: 111. The statuette is now in the Louvre (AO 2744).

55. *KAI* 52: (1) *ḥrpkrṭ ytn ḥym l*(2) *ʿbdy ʿbdʾšmn bn ʿštrtytn bn mgn bn ḥnts bn* (3) *pt bn tt bn pšmḥy* (4) *p ʿl mt [n] ṣ [d]* (May Harpokrates give life to his servant, to Abdeshmoun, son of Ashtartyaton, son of Magon, son of *ḥnts*, son of *pt*, son of *tt*, son of *pšmy*. In the year . . .).

Egypt. Further evidence of such syncretism includes a stone figurine of Isis with the child Horus inscribed with a Phoenician dedicatory text by a man called Gersaphon to Astarte, probably from Memphis, and several Phoenician amulets that depict Isis and the child Horus discovered in Sardinia, Malta, and elsewhere in the central and western Mediterranean.[56]

As Phoenicians traveled throughout the Mediterranean, some eventually began to equate Astarte, Isis, and Aphrodite, all on the same dedication, as in inscriptions on objects offered at the sanctuary at Delos. By the second century BCE, for instance, a Sidonian on Delos records the recipient of his dedication as "Isis, the mother of the gods, Astarte,"[57] and the text of another Delian offering identifies the deities to whom it was given as "Isis Soteira Astarte Aphrodite Euploia."[58] An Egyptian example is a first-century BCE hymn to Isis signed by a man named Isidoros, inscribed in Greek on the columns of the entrance to a temple at Medinet Madi in the southwestern Fayum dedicated to Isis-Thermuthis, Thermuthis being the Greek rendering of the Egyptian deity Renenutet, a deity of harvest and nourishment. This hymn praises Isis for all that she does—as founder of all life, guarantor of law and customs, grantor of a good life, of bountiful harvests, among many other things—before declaring that all Mediterranean populations have a name for her: "As many mortals live upon the infinite land, Thracians and Greeks, and as many barbarians there are, they all call in their own voices, in their own countries, your beautiful name, much honored by all. The Syrians call you Astarte Artemis Nanaia, the nations of the Lykians call you queen Leto, and Thracian men call you mother of the gods, the Greeks the great-throned Hera, sweet Aphrodite, good Hestia, and Rhea and Demeter, and the Egyptians Thioue because you alone are all the other goddesses the nations invoke."[59] Although explicitly dedicated to an Egyptian divinity, this hymn offers a great illustration of how ancient Mediterranean peoples saw their divinities in relations to others, leading to syncretistic religious practices that were common along the Mediterranean coast from West to East.

---

56. *RÉS* 535. The statuette is in the Egyptian Museum in Cairo and probably originated from Memphis. For the Egyptian or Egyptianizing iconography on Phoenician amulets throughout the Mediterranean, see López-Ruiz 2015: 63–70. Even earlier, several Egyptian products with cartouches of pharaohs of the ninth century BCE were found in Phoenician settlements in the western Mediterranean, especially in Spain. See Leclant 1991: 9 and Aubet 2001: 330–334.

57. *I.Délos* 2101.

58. *I.Délos* 2132. For dedications to double (or more) deities, see Wallensten 2014. For Isis as a maritime deity, see Bricault 2019.

59. Bernand 1969: 631–652 no. 175 (lines 14–24).

Centuries of interactions between the Phoenicians and Egyptians and their travels and permanent presence in Greek communities helped transmit their hybrid religious practices and transform the Mediterranean religions. But Phoenician texts found in Egypt also show changes in the Phoenician language spoken by Phoenician immigrants in Egypt. Strong linguistic influences from their exposure to the Egyptian language can be found, for instance, in Phoenician graffiti scratched on the building known to the ancient Greeks as the Memnonion, originally the mortuary temple of Setis I, a New Kingdom pharaoh in the early thirteenth century BCE, and where the Egyptian gods Osiris, later Serapis, and finally Bes were worshiped in Abydos. Among numerous examples of graffiti that have been found in the ancient Mediterranean is a set of Phoenician graffiti from the fifth to the third centuries BCE that was inscribed alongside graffiti left on the same building complex by Greek, Cypriot, Karian, Lykian, Aramaic, and Coptic speakers.[60] Whether the Phoenicians visiting this temple were soldiers serving as mercenaries in Egyptian armies, like those who etched their graffiti on the colossal statues at Abu Simbel several centuries earlier, or religious pilgrims, or simply passersby cannot be known with certainty, but it seems probable that they were visitors on a sacred pilgrimage to this temple.[61] Most of these graffiti (in all languages) record the name of the person who inscribed them, his genealogy, and sometimes his place of origin and his profession. Among the Phoenician graffiti, one person identified himself as a Kitian ("I am Abdeshmoun, son of Shillem the Kitian"), another as a Tyrian ("I am Paalabast, son of Sadyaton, son of Gersad the Tyrian, an inhabitant . . . in Heliopolis of Egypt, in the freedom of Abdmenqart the Heliopolitan"), and a third as a Memphite ("I am Magon, son of Bodo, son of Hafesbaal, from Memphis").[62] At least the last two of these individuals were

---

60. *KAI* 49. For the first publication of these texts and their translations see Derenbourg and Derenbourg 1885. Further discussion of these texts may be found in Kornfeld 1978 and Vittmann 2003: 62–65. Such graffiti are not dissimilar from modern street art, ranging from scratching board games on seats at the theater so that bored spectators could distract themselves, to explicit language directed at a rival or an enemy, and from drawings of religious symbols or obscene ones of genitals to the less sinister declaration that recorded someone's presence at a particular place and time, like the graffito "Kilroy was here" popularized in World War II by American soldiers.

61. Rutherford 2016: 178 discusses the possible reasons Phoenician individuals would visit this temple and the contested evidence—a papyrus in Aramaic that is most likely a forgery—that suggests they were religious pilgrims. The evidence is much stronger for the case of Aramaic, Greek, and Cypriot speakers, many of whom suggest in their graffiti that they visited on a sacred pilgrimage. The Karians who wrote their graffiti on this building complex were mercenary soldiers.

62. *KAI* 49.13, 34, and 36, respectively.

most certainly immigrants living in Egypt who were visiting the temple of Seti I at Abydos and marked their presence there.

These graffiti suggest that Phoenician pilgrims spoke in established Phoenician ways—frequently providing long genealogies of their ancestors, sometimes recording their place of origin and current residence, and writing their inscriptions in their native language rather than in Egyptian, although inflected by their familiarity with the Egyptian language. For example, most of the Phoenician graffiti on this mortuary complex begin with the personal pronoun "I am," a typical way to begin an inscription in Phoenician city-states.[63] But despite these traditional Phoenician ways of speaking and writing, several sound shifts, especially of liquid consonants, that are found on ten of the forty-nine Phoenician graffiti from the temple of Seti I at Abydos but not elsewhere in the Mediterranean suggest that such shifts occurred because of Egyptian phonetic influences. The Tyrian who lived in Heliopolis, for instance, refers to another man from the same city as Abdmenqart, shifting the "l" to an "n" in this theophoric name that would have been rendered as Abdmelqart in Phoenician or Greek contexts. Some Egyptian dialects had lost the phoneme "l" that merged with other liquid consonants, hence its possible disappearance and substitution with "n" in the graffiti from Abydos.[64] The language used to inscribe these texts has even been called "Egyptian Phoenician," denoting a Phoenician language with Egyptian influences and used by Phoenician-speaking immigrants in Egypt.

Beyond such religious and linguistic transformations, one of the most observable drastic changes among Phoenician immigrants in Egypt is how the specific migration and membership regimes they encountered in that kingdom changed their main mode of identification. Whereas Phoenician immigrants living in Carthage or Greek polities primarily identified themselves by reference to their state of origin, such as Kition or Sidon, Phoenician immigrants in Egypt did so much less, most often not stating the state from which they emigrated at all. Instead, in the thriving commercial center of Memphis, where the Egyptian authorities regulated the presence of foreigners by segregating them in different quarters according to their ethnicity (as Phoenicians, or Greeks, or Karians)

---

63. Cf. *KAI* 10; 13; 24. Several tomb inscriptions from Byblos, Sidon, and elsewhere begin in the same way.

64. Calabro 2015 and more specifically pp. 101–104. Similar shifts can be observed in Phoenician graffiti from Abu Simbel. Other linguistic influences, including the appearance of loanwords, transcription, and literal translation of Egyptian phrases occur throughout Egypt wherever Phoenician texts have been discovered (e.g., Abu Simbel, Elephantine, Memphis, Thebes). The dropping of "r" in Abdmelqat on the stele from Memphis dedicated by Paalashtart may have resulted from similar Egyptian influences. Phoenician texts from Thebes are collected in Magnanini 1973: 68–70.

regardless of which city-state they came from, with each quarter having a temple dedicated to a deity of their homeland, several texts indicate that Phoenicians, who had been present there since the seventh century BCE, started to identify themselves according to their ethnicity as Phoenicians.[65]

According to a variety of sources, the Phoenician quarter in Memphis was centered around a temple to the goddess Astarte. This evidence includes the Greek historian Herodotus' description of the different quarters in Memphis; a third-century BCE dedication in Greek to Astarte, the great ancestral goddess, by the Sidonian Abrames, which also demonstrates the continuation of the worship of gods from their homeland by immigrants; and a mid-third-century BCE letter sent from the priests of this temple to the local Egyptian authorities.[66] That letter sent by the priests to the local administrator suggests that this temple and its administrators played a similar role to that of the Phoenician trade associations in Athens and Delos, which mediated between their members and their host societies. The letter was discovered in the archive of Zenon, a mid-third-century BCE local administrator and overseer of estates in the region around Memphis and Philadelphia, who worked for a man named Apollonios—an adviser to Ptolemy II, the pharaoh of Egypt. The priests of Astarte who sent this letter, written in

---

65. As mentioned earlier, the Greek historian Herodotus suggests that Phoenician mercenaries were settled in Memphis (2.112). The cemeteries of Memphis at Saqqara have yielded ostraca (pottery shards) with Phoenician texts that may record taxes, the quality of the contents of the vessels, and to whom these belonged, all of which suggest a strong Phoenician presence in this town, perhaps involved in trade. See Segal 1983: 139–145 and pl. 35–38 and Chiera 1987, who analyzes three of the ostraca with Phoenician texts from Saqqara and suggests that they include dedications to female deities, perhaps Isis or Astarte. Similar inscriptions on vessels clearly related to trade of commodities contained in storage vessels exist from Abusir, an ancient necropolis near modern-day Cairo, dating to the sixth and fifth centuries BCE. For these texts, see Dušek and Mynářová 2013: 56–65. Other objects from Saqqara suggest the presence of Phoenicians down to the fourth century BCE. A statue of a sphinx discovered in the Serapeium in Saqqara bears two inscriptions, one in Phoenician the other in neo-Punic (*CIS* I 97), and a basin was also inscribed with both a Phoenician and a hieratic text (*RÉS* 2). See Vittmann 2003: 67–68. For Carthaginians in Egypt, see Dridi 2019c. Another stone inscription in Phoenician from Memphis is *RÉS* 917. A spearhead with a Phoenician text was also discovered here (Michailidis 1947: 65–71). Phoenician inscriptions on pottery from Memphis and Saqqara are collected in *RÉS* 1508 and Aimé Giron 1931: 1–5 nos. 1–2 and 1938: 18–27, 32. For the presence of Phoenicians in Memphis, see also Bresciani 1987: 72–75 and Thompson 2012: 81–87.

66. Herodotus 2.112 calls the goddess by her Greek analogue, Aphrodite, when he describes the ethnic quarters in Memphis. *SEG* 24 1200 records the dedication by Abrames to Astarte (θεᾶι πατρίαι μεγάληι). The papyrus *PSI* V 531 preserves the letter by the priests of Astarte. Other Phoenician gods were worshiped in Memphis during the Bronze Age, as evidenced by papyri: *P.Sallier* IV, verso 1.1–4.8 (Baalat, Qedeshet, Baal Saphon); *P.Leiden* I 343 + I 345 (Baal, Resheph, Anat, Astarte, Qedeshet, Nikkal, Shala, Ishara, Adamma, Hammarig); *P.Berlin* 8169 (Baal).

Greek, asked to be given the same price when buying oil as that granted to the Karians and Greeks in Memphis, arguing that the temple of Astarte was similar to the temples of the Karians and Greeks and therefore should be treated as such. They also identify the temple as belonging to the Phoinikoaigyptioi (Phoenico-Egyptians) in Memphis, a designation that appears for the first time in this text and suggests that the Phoenicians living there had adopted a hybrid identity marker that valued equally their immigrant origins and their current home.[67]

The Egyptian policy of segregating immigrants into quarters according to their ethnicity even when they came from different city-states likely led the Phoenician immigrants in Memphis to adopt this external (i.e., etic) perspective of their identity and make it their own (i.e., emic), based on their shared language, gods, and culture. Unlike in Athens and Delos, where professional associations helped Phoenician immigrants maintain identities centered around their home of origin, in Egypt those immigrants maintained their ancestral customs and rituals but did not necessarily differentiate which specific state these were from and adopted a broader Phoenician identity. Perhaps for this reason, Phoenician immigrants in Egypt also did not produce as many bilingual texts as those who lived in Greek polities, as far as extant sources show, and the language they spoke came to reflect their long presence in Egypt.[68] In Greek

---

67. *PSI* V 531. The letter also refers to the Karian temple in Memphis and to the temple of the Hellenomemphitai, the Greeks of Memphis, another hybrid identity that must have been adopted by the Greek community there. Other papyri in the Zenon archive suggest that trade with Tyre was common: *P.Cair.Zen.* 1, 59016; 1, 59093; 4, 59558.

68. Thompson 2009: 405 suggests that unlike the Greeks of Memphis who maintained their language during the Ptolemaic period, the Phoenicians of Memphis lost theirs, but it would have been far easier for the Greeks to continue to use Greek in a state whose official language was now Greek. While it is true that the Phoenicians of Egypt also used Greek in their official dealings with the state, there are enough texts from the fourth century BCE written in Phoenician to suggest that the abandonment of the Phoenician language was slow and that it still constituted part of Phoenician immigrant identity. By the later Hellenistic period, when Egypt was under the Greco-Macedonian rule of the Ptolemies, all but two—Abdemoun and Belistiche—of the Phoenicians who are identified as being from Ashkelon, Kition, Tyre, and Sidon have Greek names, though these are typical Greek names frequently adopted by Phoenician speakers, as discussed in the first chapter. See La'da 2002: 32 no. E253–255 (Ashkelonites: Antiochos, Aristos, Ptolemaios); 119 no. E994 (Carthaginian: Demetrios, son of Apollonios); 124 no. E1019 (Kitian: Apollonios); p. 284 no. E2417–2421 (Sidonians: Abdemoun, Antipatros, Dionysios, Sphragis; Simotera); 298 no. E2530–2537 (Tyrians: Basileides, Zenodoros, Hydoulos, Herakleitos, a son of Straton, and Belistiche). The name Belistiche occurs on a papyrus from Oxyrrhynchus from 240 BCE, where the woman with this name is identified as a Tyrian (*P. Hibeh.*, 2, 261, 4 and 262, 4), and on another from the Zenon archive (*P.Cair.Zen.* 2, 59289). On the name Belistiche and its likely Phoenician origins, see Masson 1985. On a woman named Bilistiche who was one of Ptolemy II's mistresses, see Kosmetatou 2004: 22–23 and Ogden 2008: 365–379, esp. 371–372. On Tyrians in Egypt, see Yon 2011: 53–55.

polities, Phoenician immigrants' practice of inscribing funerary and dedicatory inscriptions in both their own and their host state's language demonstrates an outward outlook that sought to claim membership and belonging in their adopted state. In Egypt, where Egyptian policies toward immigrants made such a level of integration unlikely, Phoenicians maintained the use of their ancestral script and language on monuments and private letters, worshiped Egyptian deities, and espoused a hybrid Phoenician-Egyptian identity.

Malta, Sardinia, and Sicily

Similar effects of long-term mobility and migration are visible in the three central Mediterranean islands of Malta, Sicily, and Sardinia in the second and first centuries BCE. All three islands were home to Phoenician settlements established by Phoenician city-states in the eastern Mediterranean as early as the eighth century BCE, which had been preceded by years of trade between Phoenician city-states and populations in this region.[69] These areas eventually became part of what scholars call the Punic Mediterranean following the rise of Carthage as a regional Mediterranean power after the sixth century BCE.[70] The phenomenon of tophets, the sanctuaries dedicated usually to the god Baal Hammon and filled with interred urns discussed in the earlier section on Carthage, was also present in Rabat on Malta, Sulcis on Sardinia, and Motya on Sicily, forming a group of religious sites that identified with one another and connected these city-states in a regional cultural, political, and economic network.[71] Besides the strong Phoenician presence on all three of these central Mediterranean islands, they were also home to indigenous populations, and Sicily and Sardinia were also the site of Greek city-states from the eighth century BCE.[72] The close interactions among the Phoenicians,

---

69. For recent general overviews of the Phoenician presence on Sardinia, Sicily, and Malta, see Roppa 2019; De Vincenzo 2019; and Vella and Anastasi 2019, with references. See also van Dommelen and Roppa 2014 for Sardinia, Bondì 1980 for Phoenicians in Sicily in general, the many publications of Lorenzo Nigro on the excavations on Motya in Sicily and the presence of Phoenicians there (e.g., 2004), Greco 2000 and Helas 2011 on Phoenicians in Selinous in Sicily, and Nicholas C. Vella's publications and Sagona 2002 for Phoenicians on Malta.

70. On the Punic Mediterranean, see van Dommelen and Gómez Bellard 2008; Quinn and Vella 2014; and selected essays in López-Ruiz and Doak 2019.

71. Quinn 2011 and 2013. See also McCarty 2019 on the commonalities among these tophets.

72. The presence of these groups on Sicily, Sardinia, and Malta led to the hybridization of material culture on these islands much earlier than the second century BCE. See, for instance, Tronchetti and van Dommelen 2005; van Dommelen 2006; Hayne 2010; Intrieri and Ribichini 2011; Morris 2019; and López-Ruiz 2021: 121–141.

Greeks, and indigenous populations who inhabited these islands over centuries led to the development of a more multicultural milieu than in Carthage and Egypt.[73] Although abundant sources testify to the presence of Phoenicians in these areas from the Early Iron Age, from the second century BCE onward, when epigraphic documentation becomes more abundant and can be studied side by side with material sources, it becomes difficult to identify who was a Phoenician immigrant and who was a longtime citizen or resident. As the following examples will show, bilingual and trilingual texts indicate the existence of a common culture that emerged from hybrid practices that combined local, eastern Phoenician, and other customs and transcended civic and ethnic boundaries.

A set of twin monuments discovered on Malta, famous in their own right because they were instrumental in deciphering the Phoenician language in the eighteenth century,[74] illustrate not only the strategies that immigrants adopted to become better incorporated into their host societies but how mobility and migration transformed the ancient Mediterranean region.[75] These two

---

73. Iberia and the shores of North Africa (other than Carthage) are two other regions similar to these three islands in that they were also home to Phoenician and Greek settlements, established in the eighth and sixth centuries BCE respectively, and to indigenous polities. Because written sources from the fourth to the second centuries BCE are not as numerous as they are from Malta, Sicily, and Sardinia, these regions are not included in the discussion that follows, although Phoenician immigrants there would have experienced similar processes of inclusion and integration and the creation of new hybrid identities as discussed below.

74. The abbot Jean-Jacques Barthélemy deciphered the Phoenician script. In Barthélemy 1758 he describes how he deciphered the script based on the twin monuments from Malta and coins in the Louvre's collection. See also Amadasi Guzzo and Rossignani 2007: 82 and Briquel-Chatonnet 2009: 178–184. The history of the discovery of the twin monuments, known in scholarship as "les cippes de Malte," is unclear and their provenance is unknown. Some have even disputed their findspot as Malta. For a detailed summary of their history, see Amadasi Guzzo and Rossignani 2002, and for a briefer version their 2007 entry in the exhibition catalog for an exhibit at the Institut du monde arabe, *La Méditerranée de Phéniciens: De Tyr à Carthage*.

75. An example of the creative ways in which immigrants on these islands fostered a sense of belonging in their new host state while also maintaining traditions of their homeland appears in a long, early second-century BCE Punic inscription discovered in Karaly (present-day Cagliari) that records the dedication of parts of a building offered by two priests, each of whose long genealogies included four generations of ancestors (*KAI* 65). One of these priests identified as a man from Sidon and provides the date of the dedication by referring to the name of the suffete of that year—a traditional Carthaginian and wider Punic office also found on Sardinia and used to date the year. The details of this dedication indicate that this priest, an eastern Phoenician who had emigrated to Sardinia, had retained his identity as a Sidonian while adopting the local epigraphic habits of a Punic political organization; had risen to a leadership position in the community in his role as a priest; and contributed to the religious life of the city alongside individuals who were not Sidonians, exemplifying how an immigrant could become an integrated member of a polity despite being a foreigner and perhaps a noncitizen. Evidence for the presence of Phoenicians on Sardinia is as early as the ninth-century BCE stele

monuments, which date from the second century BCE, each consist of two parts and are inscribed with the same bilingual text that records a dedication by two Tyrian brothers: a rectangular base that bears a bilingual inscription, Phoenician first and Greek below, above which sits an oval-shaped pillar with acanthus-leaf sculptures in bas relief at the pillar's base (Fig. 5.5a–b; Fig. 5.6). The text on both offerings is the same in both Greek and Phoenician, although the lines are not broken in the same way and the letter shapes look different enough that two different people probably engraved and sculpted them.[76] These texts once again exhibit the syncretisms, translations, and naming practices familiar from other examples presented in this book. The Phoenician text reads: "To our lord Melqart, lord of Tyre, your servants Abdosir and his brother Osirishamor, sons of Osirishamor, son of Abdosir, dedicated this because he heard their voices. May he bless them."[77] The two brothers' theophoric names and that of their father were Phoenicianized forms of the name of the Egyptian god Osiris, such as those observed in Egypt, Carthage, and even back in the Phoenician city-states, where the name Abdosir is recorded on several dedications and funerary inscriptions from this same period and later. Changes that originated in immigrant contexts did not remain isolated but had repercussions throughout the Mediterranean.[78]

---

from Nora inscribed in Phoenician (*KAI* 46 = *CIS* I 144). See Pilkington 2012 and Schmitz 2012: 15–31, with bibliography.

76. Amadasi Guzzo and Rossignani 2007: 81. Another Phoenician dedication was offered by two brothers to Astarte, this time from Seville in Spain, dating to some point between the eighth and the sixth centuries BCE. See Gibson 1982: 64–66 no. 16 for this text and Amadasi Guzzo 1994 for Phoenician inscriptions from Spain.

77. *KAI* 47 = *CIS* I 122bis (a): (1) *l'dnn lmlqrt b'l ṣr 'š ndr* (2) *'bdk 'bd'sr w'ḥy 'sršmr* (3) *šn bn 'sršmr bn 'bd'sr k šm'* (4) *qlm ybrkm* and (b): (1) *l'dnn lmlqrt b'l ṣr 'š ndr 'bdk* (2) *'bd'sr w'ḥy 'sršmr šn bn* (3) *'sršmr bn 'bd'sr k šm' qlm* (4) *ybrkm*. Although these twin monuments are dedicated to Melqart, a temple of the god on Malta has not been securely identified. Antiquarians of the eighteenth century presumed the provenance of the offerings was the site of Tas Silġ, in Marsaxlokk, but without any concrete evidence. As Amadasi Guzzo 1993 has shown, the sanctuary at Tas Silġ was probably dedicated to Astarte and not to Melqart, Hera, Juno, or Tanit, as previous scholars had hypothesized.

78. See Aliquot 2004: 212–213 and 213 n. 52 for the epigraphic references to the name Abdosir in Phoenician city-states. Because these monuments are dedicated by Tyrians with Egyptian-influenced names and written in the Phoenician script, scholars have argued that they were brought to Malta post antiquity (see Amadasi Guzzo and Rossignani 2002: 5–18). This is not necessary, as is demonstrated by both the example of the Kitian who brought a tombstone from Kition to Carthage and the many Phoenician-speaking immigrants in Athens, Demetrias, and Rhodes who bought and inscribed their tombstones locally but were clearly Phoenicians from the eastern Mediterranean. See also Bonnet and Bianco 2018: 40.

FIGURE 5.5A–B One of the twin monuments from Malta dedicated by two Tyrian brothers, second century BCE (*IG* XIV 600 = *KAI* 47 = *CIS* I 122bis)
Valetta, National Museum of Archaeology, Heritage Malta.

FIGURE 5.6 The second of the twin monuments from Malta dedicated by two Tyrian brothers, second century BCE (*IG* XIV 600 = *KAI* 47 = *CIS* I 122bis) Paris, Musée du Louvre AO 4818 © RMN-Grand Palais (Musée du Louvre) / Franck Raux.

These twin monuments also provide further evidence of the mutual intelligibility of ancient religions and the Mediterranean networks that enabled and strengthened religious practices across ethnic groups. In the Greek dedication, the two brothers translated their names as Dionysios and Sarapion, both appropriate translations of Osiris, who had always been identified with Dionysus and who was syncretized with the Egyptian god Apis to form the god Serapis, popular under the Ptolemies throughout the eastern Mediterranean. The two brothers also provided only their patronymic rather than a longer genealogy, as they did in the Phoenician text, mentioned their city-ethnic, and translated Melqart's name, the god to whom they had given this dedication, as Herakles: "Dionysios and Sarapion, sons of Sarapion, Tyrians, (dedicate this) to Herakles *archegetes*."[79] Whereas in the Phoenician text the brothers identify Melqart as the patron deity of Tyre, in Greek they honor Herakles *archegetes*, or Herakles the founder, a common epithet given to this god who was often equated by both ancient Greeks and Phoenicians with Melqart, a deity considered a patron god of cities and the founder of Tyre.[80] These two monuments demonstrate that the two brothers' knowledge of Greek religion was not merely passing or superficial but rather intimate and indicative of long-term and permanent interactions effected by mobility and migration.[81]

Similar evidence of religious syncretisms and a deep familiarity with the social and religious practices indigenous to various cultures is provided by a famous trilingual inscription from Sardinia written in Latin, Greek, and Punic. A bronze base of an altar, dated to either the second or first century BCE, is inscribed with a dedication first in Latin, followed by Greek, and finally by a longer and much more detailed Punic text by a man named Kleon in all three languages, who does not identify where he was from (Fig. 5.7).[82] Despite Kleon's Greek name, which is transliterated in Punic in such a way as to facilitate the pronunciation of the double consonant in the beginning, he may have spoken primarily Phoenician, given that whenever Phoenician is the longer text in all the bilingual inscriptions presented in this book, the person who had commissioned it was Phoenician.[83] Although his name appears the same in all three languages, the name of the god to whom the altar was dedicated is given as Asklepios in Greek and appropriately translated into Aesculapius in Latin and into Eshmoun in Phoenician, and the epithet used

---

79. *IG* XIV 600: (a) Διονύσιος καὶ Σαραπίων οἱ | Σαραπίωνος Τύριοι | Ἡρακλεῖ ἀρχηγέτει (now in Paris) and (b) Διονύσιος καὶ Σαραπίων οἱ | Σαραπίωνος Τύριοι Ἡρακλεῖ | ἀρχηγέτει (now in Malta). For the name translation, see Amadasi Guzzo in Amadasi Guzzo and Bonnet 1991: 6–7.

80. Malkin 2005 and 2011: 119–141; Bonnet 2009; Bonnet and Bianco 2018: 40.

81. See also Briquel-Chatonnet 2012: 626–627.

82. *CIL* 10 7856 = *IG* XIV 608 = *KAI* 66 (= *CIS* I 143). Culasso Gastaldi 2000: 20–25 first proposed a date in the first century BCE based on the social context alluded to in the inscribed text, especially the mention of suffetes. Pennacchietti 2002 dates it to the second century BCE. Marginesu 2002: 1814 identifies the suffetes as those of Karaly, which did not become a municipality until 46 BCE, the date ante quem the inscription was produced. He dates the monument to the second century BCE. Bonnet and Bianco 2018: 29 n. 25 prefer a first century BCE date, following Culasso Gastaldi.

83. Most scholars presume he is Greek based on his name. See Culasso Gastaldi 2000: 16; Marginesu 2002: 1814; Bonnet and Bianco 2018: 41. But many Phoenician speakers used only a Greek name, as many examples presented in this book have demonstrated. For the transliteration of his name, see Bonnet in Amadasi Guzzo and Bonnet 1991: 16–17.

FIGURE 5.7 Bronze altar base with a trilingual inscription in Latin, Greek, and Punic, from Sardinia, first century BCE (*CIL* 10 7856 = *IG* XIV 608 = *KAI* 66)
Turin, Museo di Antichità Inv. No. 01046. © MiC—Musei Reali, Museo di Antichità.

to describe him—Merre (Μήρρη) in Greek, Merre in Latin, and *m'ḥr* in Punic—does not appear on any other extant text and perhaps indicates a local, otherwise unknown, Sardinian god.[84]

Kleon's (or the sculptor's who inscribed the text on the altar base) facility in moving from one language and one god to another is also visible in the text in each language, which follows typical epigraphic customs of each culture represented. The Latin text identifies Kleon as a worker in the salt mines and a servant of the society (or guild) of salt miners, a typically Roman institution, who gave this gift to Aesculapius willingly and with good reason.[85] The Greek text translates the Latin word for his Roman social status as the person responsible for salt and uses a very Greek phrase, often used in dedications to Asklepios, to indicate that he dedicated the altar or base of an altar by the command of the god (κατὰ πρόσταγμα).[86] The Punic text, following Phoenico-Punic epigraphic customs, provides much more detail about the dedication itself: how much it

---

84. The translation of Eshmoun into Asklepios is evident in translations of theophoric names, as discussed in the first chapter of this book. For a discussion of the etymology of Merre, see Marginesu 2002: 1813; Pennacchietti 2002: 305 n. 14; Campus 2016: 115; Bonnet and Bianco 2018: 41. Some recent publications on this trilingual inscription that discuss the translations of names are Culasso Gastaldi 2000: 18–19; Marginesu 2002: 1813–1815; Pennacchietti 2002; Moriggi 2011: 82–86; Corbier 2012: 54–58; Campus 2016: 109–116; Bonnet and Bianco 2018: 29–31 and 41.

85. *CIL* 10 7856: *Cleon. salari(us). soc(iorum). s(ervus). Aescolapio. Merre. donum. dedit. lubens. | merito. merente*. The Latin text contains some grammatical errors, suggesting this was not the first language of the dedicant (or the scribe).

86. *IG* XIV 608: Ἀσκληπιῶι Μήρρη ἀνάθεμα βωμὸν ἔστη|σε Κλέων ὁ ἐπὶ τῶν ἁλῶν κατὰ πρόσταγμα.

weighed, that Kleon made the dedication because the god had listened to his prayers and healed him, and the year of the dedication by providing the names of the suffetes of that year, as was the Punic custom.[87] Several unique phrases in the Punic text are best read as a transcription of the Latin word *sociorum* and a translation of Kleon's status and professional affiliation with the salt workers (*'š ḥ sgm 'š b mmlḥt*), a typically Roman institutional arrangement.[88] Kleon thus exemplifies the multicultural milieu that emerged from migration and mobility: a cosmopolitan resident of a Sardinian city-state who participated in Roman culture, integrated Greek and perhaps Sardinian religious practices in his life, and followed Punic customs.

Mobility and migration in the ancient Mediterranean created a similarly complex network of transcultural associations. For instance, a second- to first-century BCE hospitality token from Lilybaion on Sicily suggests its owners belonged to the Punic, Greek, Roman, and more broadly Mediterranean cultural traditions.[89] The token, carved in ivory, represents two clasped right hands, a gesture recognizable among various Mediterranean groups, from the Persians in the East to the Iberians in the West, as a symbol of the institution of hospitality, which bound the participants into a permanent relationship (Fig. 5.8a–b).[90] The flat, reverse side of the token bears an inscription in Greek that records the establishment of hospitality, *xenia*, the Greek equivalent of Roman private *hospitium*, between Imylch, son of Imilchos, and Lyson, son of Diognetos and his descendants.[91] Although the language of this text is Greek, the format follows that of Roman

---

87. *KAI* 66 = *CIS* I 143: (1) *l'dn l'šmn m'rt mzbḥ nḥšt mšql ltrm m't 100 'š ndr 'kllyn šḥsgm 'š bmmlḥt šm[' (2) q]l' rpy' bšt šptm ḥmlkt w'bd'šmn bn ḥmlk* (To the lord Eshmoun Merre: a bronze altar of one hundred pounds in weight vowed by Kleon, a (servant) of the agents who work in the salt mines. He heard his voice; he healed him. In the year of the suffetes Himilkot and Abdeshmoun, son of Himilk). My translation is an adaptation of Pennacchietti 2002: 311; Moriggi 2011: 85; Bonnet and Bianco 2018: 41.

88. Pennacchietti 2002, esp. 306–309 and 311–312.

89. Six graffiti in Punic, Greek, and Roman have also been discovered etched on a wall of a chamber tomb in Lilibeo, each written by a different person. One of the two Punic texts and one of the three Latin probably record names. It is unclear whether these were inscribed on the wall contemporaneously or not, but they probably date from the third or second centuries BCE. These texts have not been published yet (see *SEG* 62 666), but Giglio and De Simone (2019) mention the Punic ones in their report on inscriptions from Lilibeo. I thank Maria Grazia Griffo, the director of the Marsala Museum in Lilibeo, for providing me with this information on these texts.

90. Demetriou, forthcoming b. In this article, I also argue that such tokens were used to prove the identity of their bearers as they crossed borders in the ancient Mediterranean.

91. *IG* XIV 279: Ἰμύλχ Ἰμίλχωνος | Ἰνίβαλος Χλῶρος ξενίαν | ἐπο<ι>ήσατο πρὸς Λύσων | Διογνήτου καὶ τῶν ἐγγόνων. See also Di Stefano et al. 1984: no. 153 fig. 70.

(a)

(b)

FIGURE 5.8A–B Ivory hospitality token between a Phoenician and a Greek from Lilybaion, second or first century BCE (*IG* XIV 279)
Su concessione della Regione Siciliana, Parco archeologico di Lilibeo-Marsala, 16 September 2001, Prot. No. 3301.

hospitality tokens, including the names of those involved and the declaration that the two parties had established *xenia*.[92] The names following Imylch's—Inibalos and Chlorus—are probably not his nicknames (*cognomina*) but rather a list of his ancestors, as was the custom among Phoenicians, starting with his father Imilchos, grandfather Inibalos, and great-grandfather Chlorus.[93] One can assume that Imylch was probably a Punic or Phoenician speaker, not only because his name and those of his father and grandfather (Imilchos, Inibalos) are Hellenized Punic names but also because the Greek inscription is unidiomatic,

---

92. See Demetriou, forthcoming b.

93. Crouzet 2012: 40–41.

with mistakes in the declension of Lyson's name and of the word "descendants" (both of which should be in the accusative rather than the genitive).[94] The name Chlorus suggests that Imylch also had a Roman connection, while his guest-friend Lyson and Lyson's father Diognetos both bore typical Greek names. Both the text of this inscription and the imagery of the token indicate that individuals of Greek and Punic origins, one or both of whom were living on a multiethnic island under the dominion of Rome, were bound with a handshake and this token into a private hospitality agreement. Mobility once again established an institution that transgressed ethnic boundaries and connected different communities in the Mediterranean.

Conclusion

Phoenician immigrants in Carthage, Egypt, and the central Mediterranean islands of Sicily, Sardinia, and Malta employed adaptive repertoires similar to those used in Greek polities and continued to construct their identities as immigrants primarily through the persistent use of the Phoenician language and identification with their place of origin. Yet the evidence presented here also demonstrates significant differences in the expressions of immigrant identities that developed over time and in different historical and cultural contexts. In Carthage, the immigrant identities of Tyrians became particularly salient when Carthage used its ties to its mother city of Tyre to claim kinship relations with other Punic city-states in the central Mediterranean in an attempt to create a hegemony. The overview of interactions between Phoenicians and Egyptians during approximately the fourth to the first centuries BCE captures a particular moment in time when mobility and migration throughout the Mediterranean had increased and is better documented in records produced by the immigrants themselves. But their centuries-long interactions suggest that this overview records a different moment in the process of migration than the first- or second-generation immigrants in Carthage and Greek city-states, perhaps explaining why Phoenician immigrants in Memphis espoused a hybrid Phoenician-Egyptian identity. On Sicily, Sardinia, and Malta, the centuries of coexistence of Greeks, Phoenicians, and indigenous populations gradually led to the creation of a cosmopolitan Mediterranean, in which individuals appear to have been full participants in the local, hybrid cultures. As earlier chapters have shown, the same was true of Phoenician immigrants of the same period living in Greek city-states, who in their participation in Greek civic institutions, their transition from using Phoenician on their monuments to using exclusively

---

94. Masson 1976: 93–96.

Greek, and their worship of Greek divinities gradually became indistinguishable from Greeks. By the second and first centuries BCE, Phoenician immigrants, despite being foreigners, were integral members of their host states, and usually had been so for generations, had themselves changed because of immigration, and in turn had contributed to altering their host states. As the examples presented in this chapter show, the hybridized cultural artifacts and religious practices created by immigrants and their host states did not remain locally isolated. Phoenicians helped spread them throughout the Mediterranean region as mobility and migration acted as transformative forces that connected individuals from and within different city-states, altered their identities and institutions, and changed their host societies.

Conclusion

BY THE FIRST century BCE, the effects of mobility and migration could be felt throughout the Mediterranean world. Over the course of the centuries examined by this study, societies changed from multiethnic ones, where divisions according to one's civic or ethnic origin were emphasized and significant, to cosmopolitan ones, where such divisions were bridged. Phoenician immigrants had become less invested in maintaining distinct identities and more eager to express a sense of belonging to a larger Mediterranean world. "If I am a Syrian," wrote Meleager of Gadara c. 100 BCE after living in Tyre for most of his life, "what is the marvel? One fatherland, stranger, is the Kosmos we inhabit."[1] As this book has argued, it was the movements of immigrants, particularly Phoenician immigrants, that had made this more cosmopolitan world possible.

As the previous chapters have shown, Phoenician immigrants living among Greeks, Carthaginians, and Egyptians adapted to their conditions as immigrants by employing different strategies that facilitated their lives in their host societies and enabled them to maintain links to their home states. Both these strategies and the very phenomenon of Phoenician immigration challenged their home and host societies, which responded in similarly creative ways to deal with migration. The result was that immigrants transformed Mediterranean societies.

Though these immigrants were noncitizens and without any direct political say in their host states, the evidence presented here shows that with their innovative adaptive strategies they created avenues through which they could participate in politics. Trade associations, established first in the fourth century BCE by Phoenician immigrants, not only offered a cultural locus that helped them maintain traditions of their home state but also provided them with some legal representation in their host state. As semiautonomous units whose organization

---

1. *Anthologia Palatina* 7.417.

mimicked that of a state—with assemblies, voting mechanisms, and decision-making processes—these professional associations were incorporated into their host state's political apparatus, giving immigrants the power to petition their host state and thus participate in its deliberative processes and influence its policies.

Ultimately, this symbiotic relationship between immigrants and host states also broadened what it meant to be a resident and even a citizen of a state. In a world where individuals migrated permanently or for the long term, host and home states alike were compelled to negotiate issues of taxation and manage the limits of citizenship and domicile. As presented here, the system of award giving deployed by Greek polities, which entailed granting honors and privileges to foreigners in different combinations, was one such direct consequence of states navigating the nature of their relationships with foreigners and immigrants. The processes developed by states to both promote migration and regulate the specific status of individual foreigners and migrants thereby led to the creation of a more fluid spectrum of participatory membership of a political community than previously recognized.

Beyond these fundamental changes in the political infrastructure of states, the presence of immigrants and their adaptive practices contributed to cultural changes within both the host societies and the immigrants themselves. Even as the strategies they embraced marked immigrants as different from the rest of a state's resident population and as belonging to two different worlds, those very same processes also changed the physical, linguistic, and religious landscapes of their host states. Over time, such products of migration as tombstones or religious dedications in foreign alphabets within a city's cemeteries or sanctuaries, temples dedicated to foreign gods given Greek names that equated them with Greek deities, and names of individuals that sounded Greek or Egyptian but were actually Phoenician became integrated into the social fabric of society, changed how cities looked, and altered the daily sounds of communities.

And these new amalgamations did not stay isolated in a single locale. The interconnectedness of the ancient Mediterranean world, provided mostly by people on the move, meant that innovations in religious practices, social conventions, and linguistic practices were transferable. Dedications that list Egyptian, Phoenician, and Greek deities, all equated to each other, showcase the adoption of foreign divinities across cultures, whose worship traveled far and wide in the ancient Mediterranean.

In their totality, Greek societies were profoundly altered by the contributions of Phoenician immigrants: intellectuals introduced new ideas, such as Zeno's Stoicism; traders created new institutions that became part of Greek states' political economy, and even ancient Athenian democracy; and immigrants collectively helped formed multiethnic and diverse societies that thrived throughout the Mediterranean region. While traditionally ancient Greek thought, politics, and society have been idealized and touted as the foundation of Western civilization, this book has shown that it is unlikely they would have taken the form they did without the contributions of migrants in general and of Phoenician immigrants in particular. By expanding the scholarly horizons of the field of ancient history to include the effects of migration, this book strives to provide a more comprehensive view of ancient history, one that does not privilege one ethnic group over another but studies societies in their totality. In so doing, its approach to ancient history also serves to challenge, or at least complicate, the idealization of ancient Greek culture and the presumed exceptionalism of Western culture.

Ultimately, this volume provides yet another example of the manifold ways in which *Homo migrans* have adopted and created new practices, adapted to being immigrants, and in the process created new identities. In the ancient Mediterranean, as throughout history and across the globe, mobility and migration created polities comprising a diverse population with different religions, languages, and institutions that nonetheless came together to form coherent civic bodies in which immigrants and citizens alike were integral and contributing members.

Bibliography

Abrecht, R. R. 2020. "An Immigrant Neighbourhood in Ancient Rome." *Urban History* 47: 2–22.

Abulafia, D. 2011. *The Great Sea: A Human History of the Mediterranean*. Oxford: Oxford University Press.

Adams, J. N. 2002. "Bilingualism at Delos." In *Bilingualism in Ancient Society: Language Contact and the Written Text*, edited by J. N. Adams, M. Janse, and S. Swain, 103–127. Oxford: Oxford University Press.

Aimé-Giron, N. 1924. "Glanures de mythologie syro-égyptienne." *BIAO* 23: 1–25.

Aimé-Giron, N. 1931. *Textes araméens d'Égypte*. Cairo: Institut Français d'Archéologie Orientale.

Aimé-Giron, N. 1938. "Adversaria Semitica." *BIAO* 38: 1–63.

Aimé-Giron, N. 1940. "Adversaria Semitica (III). VII. Ba'al Ṣaphon et les dieux de Taḥpanḥès dans un nouveau papyrus phénicien." *ASAE* 40: 433–460.

Akrigg, B. 2011. "Demography and Classical Athens." In *Demography and the Graeco-Roman World: New Insights and Approaches*, edited by C. Holleran and A. Pudsey, 37–59. Cambridge: Cambridge University Press.

Akrigg, B. 2019. *Population and Economy in Classical Athens*. Cambridge: Cambridge University Press.

Aliquot, J. 2004. "*Aegyptiaca* et *Isiaca* de la Phénicie et du Liban aux époques hellénistique et romaine." *Syria* 81: 201–228.

Aliquot, J. 2011. "Les Tyriens dans le monde romain, d'Auguste à Dioclétien." In *Source de l'histoire de Tyr: Textes de l'Antiquité et du Moyen Âge*, edited by P.-L. Gatier, J. Aliquot, and L. Nordiguian, 73–115. Beirut: Presses de l'Université Saint-Joseph et Presses de L'Ifpo.

Aliquot, J. and C. Bonnet, eds. 2015. *La Phénicie hellénistique: Actes du colloque international de Toulouse (18–20 février 2013)*. Lyon: Société des Amis de la Bibliothèque Salomon-Reinach.

Amadasi Guzzo, M. G. 1967. *Le iscrizione fenicie e puniche delle colonie in Occidente*. Rome: Istituto di Studi del Vicino Oriente.

Amadasi Guzzo, M. G. 1979. *Grotta Regina—II: Le iscrizioni puniche. Raporto della missione congiunta con la Soprintendenza alle Antichità della Sicilia Occidentale*. Rome: Consiglio Nazionale delle Ricerche.

Amadasi Guzzo, M. G. 1986. *Scavi a Mozia—Le iscrizioni*. Rome: Consiglio Nazionale delle Ricerche.

Amadasi Guzzo, M. G. 1988. "Dédicaces de femmes à Carthage." In *Carthago: Acta Colloquii Bruxellensis habiti diebus 2 et 3 mensis Maii anni 1986*, edited by E. Lipiński, 143–149. Studia Phoenicia 6. Leuven: Peeters.

Amadasi Guzzo, M. G. 1990. *Iscrizioni fenicie e puniche in Italia*. Rome: Libreria dello Stato.

Amadasi Guzzo, M. G. 1993. "Divinità fenicie a Tas-Silġ, Malta—I dati epigrafici." *Journal of Mediterranean Studies* 3: 205–214.

Amadasi Guzzo, M. G. 1994. "Appunti su iscrizioni fenicie in Spagna." In *El mundo púnico: Historia, sociedad y cultura*, edited by A. González Blanco, J. L. Cunchillos Ilarri, and M. Molina Martos, 193–204. Murcia: Editora Regional de Murcia.

Amadasi Guzzo, M. G. 2012. "Ancora sull'espressione 'figlio di Tiro' in fenicio." *RStudFen* 40: 107–114.

Amadasi Guzzo, M. G. 2013. "Notes sur quelques inscriptions phéniciennes provenant de l'Égée." In *Entre Carthage et l'Arabie heureuse: Mélanges offerts à François Bron*, edited by F. Briquel-Chatonnet, C. Fauveaud, and I. Gajda, 163–176. Paris: De Boccard.

Amadasi Guzzo, M. G. and C. Bonnet. 1991. "Anthroponymes phéniciens et anthroponymes grecs: Remarques sur leurs correspondances." *Studi Epigrafici e Linguistici* 8: 1–21.

Amadasi Guzzo, M. G. and M. P. Rossignani. 2002. "Le iscrizioni bilingui e gli *agyiei* di Malta." In *Da Pyrgi a Mozia: Studi sull'archeologia del Mediterraneo in memoria di Antonia Ciasca*, edited by M. G. Amadasi Guzzo, M. Liverani, and P. Matthiae, 5–27. Vicino Oriente 3. 2 vols. Rome: Università degli studi di Roma "La Sapienza."

Amadasi Guzzo, M. G. and M. P. Rossignani. 2007. "Les Cippes de Malte." In *La Méditerranée des Phéniciens: De Tyr à Carthage*, edited by É. Fontan, N. Gillmann, and H. Le Meaux, 82–83. Exhibition catalog, Institut du monde arabe, 6 November 2007–20 April 2008. Paris: Somogy.

Ameling, W. 1990. "ΚΟΙΝΟΝ ΤΩΝ ΣΙΔΩΝΙΩΝ." *ZPE* 81: 189–199.

Anthony, F. B. 2017. *Foreigners in Ancient Egypt: Theban Tomb Paintings from the Early Eighteenth Dynasty (1550–1372)*. London: Bloomsbury Academic.

Apicella, C. and F. Briquel-Chatonnet. 2015. "La transition institutionnelle dans les cités phéniciennes, des Achéménides à Rome." In *La Phénicie hellénistique: Actes du colloque international de Toulouse (18–20 février 2013)*, edited by J. Aliquot and

C. Bonnet, 9–29. Topoi Supplment 13. Lyon: Société des Amis de la Bibliothèque Salomon-Reinach.

Arnaoutoglou, I. N. 1998. "Between *Koinon* and *Idion*: Legal and Social Dimensions of Religious Associations in Ancient Athens." In *Kosmos: Essays in Order, Conflict and Community in Classical Athens*, edited by P. Cartledge, P. Millet, and S. von Reden, 68–83. Cambridge: Cambridge University Press.

Arnaoutoglou, I. N. 2003. *Thusias heneka kai Sunousias: Private Religious Associations in Hellenistic Athens*. Athens: Academy of Athens.

Aruz, J., S. B. Graff, and Y. Rakic, eds. 2014. *Assyria to Iberia at the Dawn of the Classical Age*. Exhibition catalog. New York: The Metropolitan Museum of Art.

Arvanitopoulos, A. S. 1909. Θεσσαλικὰ Μνημεῖα: Ἀθανασάκειον Μουσεῖον ἐν Βόλῳ. 2 vols. Athens: Hestia.

Arvanitopoulos, A. S. 1928. Γραπταὶ Στῆλαι Δημητριάδος-Παγασῶν. Athens: P. D. Sakellariou.

Arvanitopoulos, A. S. 1929. "Θεσσαλικαὶ επιγραφαὶ." *Polemon* 1: 27–38.

Arvanitopoulos, A. S. 1947–48. "Θεσσαλικὰ μνημεῖα: Περιγραφὴ τῶν ἐν τῷ Μουσείῳ Βόλου γραπτῶν στηλῶν Δημητριάδος-Παγασῶν." *Polemon* 3: 1–16.

Arvanitopoulos, A. S. 1949–51. "Θεσσαλικὰ μνημεῖα: Περιγραφὴ τῶν ἐν τῷ Μουσείῳ Βόλου γραπτῶν στηλῶν Δημητριάδος-Παγασῶν." *Polemon* 4: 153–168.

Arvanitopoulos, A. S. 1952–53. "Θεσσαλικὰ μνημεῖα: Περιγραφὴ τῶν ἐν τῷ Μουσείῳ Βόλου γραπτῶν στηλῶν Δημητριάδος-Παγασῶν." *Polemon* 5: 5–18.

Ascough, R. S., P. A. Harland, and J. S. Kloppenborg. 2012. *Associations in the Greco-Roman World: A Sourcebook*. Waco, TX: Baylor University Press.

Astour, M. C. 1967. *Hellenosemitica: An Ethnic and Cultural Study in West Semitic Impact on Mycenean Greece*. Leiden: Brill.

Aubet, M. E. 2001. *The Phoenicians and the West: Politics, Colonies, and Trade*. Translated by M. Turton. 2nd ed. Cambridge: Cambridge University Press.

Aubet Semmler, M. E. 2019. "Tyre and Its Colonial Expansion." In *The Oxford Handbook of the Phoenician and Punic Mediterranean*, edited by C. López-Ruiz and B. R. Doak, 75–87. Oxford: Oxford University Press.

Austin, R. P. 1944. "Athens and the Satraps' Revolt." *JHS* 64: 98–100.

Bäbler, B. 1998. *Fleissige Thrakerinnen und wehrhafte Skythen: Nichtgriechen im klassischen Athen und ihre archäologische Hinterlassenschaft*. Stuttgart: B. G. Teubner.

Badoud, N. 2010. "Une famille de bronziers originaire de Tyr." *ZPE* 172: 125–143.

Bakewell, G. W. 1999a. "εὔνους καὶ πόλει σωτήριος / μέτοικος: Metics, Tragedy, and Civic Ideology." *SyllClass* 10: 43–64.

Bakewell, G. W. 1999b. "Lysias 12 and Lysias 31: Metics and Athenian Citizenship in the Aftermath of the Thirty." *GRBS* 40: 5–22.

Bakewell, G. W. 2013. *Aeschylus' Suppliant Women: The Tragedy of Immigration*. Madison: University of Wisconsin Press.

Barbanera, M. 1992. "Ancora sulla stele funeraria di Antipatros di Ascalona: Una messa a punto." *NAC* 21: 87–103.

Baron, C. A. 2013. *Timaeus of Tauromenium and Hellenistic Historiography*. Cambridge: Cambridge University Press.

Barthélemy, J.-J., Abbé. 1758. "Réflexions sur quelques monumens phéniciens, et sur les alphabets qui en résultent." *MAI* 30: 405–427.

Baslez, M.-F. 1977. *Recherches sur les conditions de pénétration et de diffusion des religions orientales à Délos (IIe–I^e s. avant notre ère)*. Paris: École Normale Supérieure de Jeunes Filles.

Baslez, M.-F. 1986. "Cultes et dévotions des Phéniciens en Grèce: Les divinités marines." In *Religio Phoenicia*, edited by C. Bonnet, E. Lipiński, and P. Marchetti, 289–305. Studia Phoenicia 4. Leuven: Peeters.

Baslez, M.-F. 2001. "Entre traditions nationales et intégration: Les associations sémitiques du monde grec." In *La questione delle influenze vicino-orientali sulla religione greca: Stato degli studi e prospettive della ricerca. Atti del colloquio internazionale, Roma, 20–22 maggio 1999*, edited by S. Ribichini, M. Rocchi, and P. Xella, 235–247. Rome: Consiglio Nazionale delle Ricerche.

Baslez, M.-F. 2006. "Entraide et mutualisme dans les associations de cités grecques à l'époque hellénistique." In *Les regulations sociales dans l'Antiquité: Actes du colloque de Liège, 15–18 novembre 1989*, edited by M. Molin, 157–168. Rennes: Presses universitaires de Rennes.

Baslez, M.-F. 2013. "Les associations à Délos: Depuis les débuts de l'indépendance (fin du IVe siècle) à la période de la colonie athénienne (milieu du IIe siècle)." In *Groupes et associations dans les cités grecques (IIIe siècle av. J.-C–IIe siècle ap. J.-C.): Actes de la table ronde de Paris, INHA, 19–20 juin 2009*, edited by P. Fröhlich and P. Hamon, 227–249. Hautes études du monde gréco-romain 49. Geneva: Librairie Droz.

Baslez, M.-F. and F. Briquel-Chatonnet. 1991a. "De l'oral à l'écrit: Le bilinguisme des Phéniciens en Grèce." In *Phoinikeia Grammata: Lire et écrire en Méditerranée. Actes du colloque de Liège, 15–18 novembre 1989*, edited by C. Baurain, C. Bonnet, and V. Krings, 371–386. Collection d'études classiques 6. Namur: Société des Études Classiques.

Baslez, M.-F. and F. Briquel-Chatonnet. 1991b. "Un exemple d'intégration phénicienne au monde grec: Les Sidoniens au Pirée à la fin du IVe siècle." In *Atti del II Congresso Internazionale di Studi Fenici e Punici, Roma 9–14 Novembre 1987*, edited by E. Acquaro, vol. 1, 229–240. Rome: Consiglio Nazionale delle Ricerche.

Baurain, C. and C. Bonnet. 1992. *Les Phéniciens: Marins des trois continents*. Paris: A. Colin.

Becking, B. 2017. "Mercenaries or Merchants? On the Role of Phoenicians at Elephantine in the Achaemenid Period." *WO* 47: 186–197.

Belleli, V. and P. Xella, eds. 2015–16. *Le lamine di Pyrgi: Nuovi studi sulle iscrizioni in etrusco e in fenicio nel cinquantenario della scoperta*. Verona: Essedue.

Benhabib, S. 2004. *The Rights of Others: Aliens, Residents, and Citizens*. Cambridge: Cambridge University Press.

Benincampi, L. 2008. "I koinà di Rodi." PhD dissertation. Università degli studi di Trieste.

Bentz, F. L. 1972. *Personal Names in Phoenician and Punic Inscriptions: A Catalog, Grammatical Study and Glossary of Elements*. Rome: Biblical Institute Press.

Bernand, É. 1969. *Inscriptions métriques de l'Égypte gréco-romaine: Recherches sur la poésie épigrammatique des Grecs en Égypte*. Annales littéraires de l'Université de Besançon 98. Paris: Les Belles Lettres.

Bhabha, H. K. 1994. *The Location of Culture*. London: Routledge.

Bickerman, E. J. 1968. *Chronology of the Ancient World*. London: Thames and Hudson.

Bolmarcich, S. 2010. "Communal Values in Ancient Diplomacy." In *Valuing Others in Classical Antiquity*, edited by R. Rosen and I. Sluiter, 113–135. Mnemosyne Supplements 323. Leiden: Brill.

Bondì, S. F. 1980. "La penetrazione fenicio-punica e storia della civiltà punica in Sicilia: La problematica storica." In *La Sicilia antica 1.1: Indigeni, Fenici-Punici e Greci*, edited by E. Gabba and G. Vallet, 163–225. Naples: Società editrice storia di Napoli e della Sicilia.

Bondì, S. F. 1988. "The Origins in the East." In *The Phoenicians*, edited by S. Moscati, 28–37. New York: Abbeville Press.

Bonnet, C. 1988. *Melqart: Cultes et mythes de l'Héraklès tyrien en Méditerranée*. Studia Phoenicia 8. Leuven: Peeters.

Bonnet, C. 1991. "Les scribes phénico-puniques." In *Phoinikeia Grammata: Lire et écrire en Méditerranée. Actes du colloque de Liège, 15–18 novembre 1989*, edited by C. Baurain, C. Bonnet, and V. Krings, 147–171. Collection d'études classiques 6. Namur: Société des Études Classiques.

Bonnet, C. 1995. "Phénicien *šrn* = accadien *šurinnu*? À propos de l'inscription de Bodashtart *CIS* I 4." *Orientalia* 64: 214–222.

Bonnet, C. 2008. "La déesse et le roi: Nouveaux regards sur le rôle d'Astarté dans les rites d'investiture en Phénicie." *Mythos* 1: 11–23.

Bonnet, C. 2009. "L'identité religieuse des Phéniciens dans la diaspora: Le cas de Melqart, dieu ancestral des Tyriens." In *Entre lignes de partage et territoires de passage: Les identités religieuses dans les mondes grec et romain. "Paganismes," judaïsmes," "christianismes,"* edited by N. Belayche and S. C. Mimouni, 295–308. Leuven: Peeters.

Bonnet, C. 2012. "'Comme des nœds qui les unissaient tous ensemble' (Voltaire): Le processus d'*interpretatio* en Phénicie à l'époque hellénistique." *CRAI* 156: 503–515.

Bonnet, C. 2013. "The Religious Life in Hellenistic Phoenicia: 'Middle Ground' and New Agencies." In *The Individual in the Religions of the Ancient Mediterranean*, edited by J. Rüpke, 41–57. Oxford: Oxford University Press.

Bonnet, C. 2015. *Les enfants de Cadmos: Le paysage religieux de la Phénicie hellénistique*. Paris: De Boccard.

Bonnet, C. 2019. "The Hellenistic Period and Hellenization in Phoenicia." In *The Oxford Handbook of the Phoenician and Punic Mediterranean*, edited by C. López-Ruiz and B. R. Doak, 99–110. Oxford: Oxford University Press.

Bonnet, C. and M. Bianco. 2018. "S'adresser aux dieux en deux langues: Le cas des épiclèses dans les inscriptions bilingues phéniciennes et grecques." *Parcours anthropologiques* 13: 38–69.

Bonnet, C. and L. Bricault. 2016. *Quand les dieux voyagent: Cultes et mythes en movement dans l'espace méditerranéen antique*. Geneva: Labor et Fides.

Bonnet, C., É. Guillon, and F. Porzia. 2021. *Les Phéniciens: Une civilisation méditerranéenne*. Paris: Tallandier.

Bonnet, C. and V. Pirenne-Delforge. 1999. "Deux déesses en interaction: Astarté et Aphrodite dans le monde égéen." In *Les syncrétismes religieux dans le monde méditerranéen antique: Actes du Colloque international en l'honneur de Frans Cumont, à l'occasion du cinquantième anniversaire de sa mort, Rome, Academia Belgica, 25–27 septembre 1997*, edited by C. Bonnet and A. Motte, 249–273. Brussels: Academia Belgica.

Booth, C. 2005. *The Role of Foreigners in Ancient Egypt: A Study of Non-stereotypical Artistic Representations*. BAR International Series 1426. Oxford: Archaeopress.

Bordreuil, P. and A. Ferjaoui. 1988. "À propos des 'fils de Tyr' et des 'fils de Carthage'." In *Carthago: Acta Colloquii Bruxellensis habiti diebus 2 et 3 mensis Maii anni 1986*, edited by E. Lipiński, 137–142. Studia Phoenicia 6. Leuven: Peeters.

Boschloos, V. 2014. "Scarabs and Seals from the 2002–2005 Seasons at Tyre Al-Bass." In *The Phoenician Cemetery of Tyre-Al Bass II: Archaeological Seasons, 2002–2005*, vol. 1, edited by M. E. Aubet, F. J. Núñez, and L. Trellisó, 381–404. Bulletin d'Archéologie et d'Architecture Libanaises 9. Beirut: Ministère de la Culture, Direction Générale des Antiquités.

Bosma, U., G. Kessler, and L. Lucassen, eds. 2013. *Migration and Membership Regimes in Global and Historical Perspective: An Introduction*. Leiden: Brill.

Bourogiannis, G. 2012. "Introduction to the Phoenician Problematic." In *Greeks and Phoenicians at the Mediterranean Crossroads*, edited by P. Adam-Veleni and E. Stefani, 37–41. Thessaloniki: Archaeological Museum of Thessaloniki.

Bourogiannis, G. 2013. "Who Hides behind the Pots? A Reassessment of the Phoenician Presence in Early Iron Age Cos and Rhodes." *ANES* 50: 139–189.

Bourogiannis, G. 2018. "The Phoenician Presence in the Aegean during the Early Iron Age: Trade, Settlement and Cultural Interaction." *RStudFen* 46: 43–88.

Bourogiannis, G. 2020. "Φοινικικές ενδείξεις στην Κω των γεωμετρικών και αρχαϊκών χρόνων." In *Τέχνης ἐμπειρία. Τιμητικός τόμος για την Καθηγήτρια Γεωργία Κοκκορού-Αλευρά*, edited by K. Kopanias and G. Doulphis, 661–674. Athens: Institute of the Book—Kardamitsa.

Boussac, M.-F. 1982. "À propos de quelques sceaux déliens." *BCH* 106: 427–446.

Boussac, M.-F. 1992. *Le sceaux de Délos*. Vol. 1, *Sceaux publics, Apollon, Hélios, Artémis, Hécate*. Paris: École Française d'Athènes.

Boyxen, B. 2018. *Fremde in der hellenistischen Polis Rhodos: Zwischen Nähe und Distanz*. Berlin: De Gruyter.

Bresciani, E. 1987. "Fenici in Egitto." *EVO* 10: 69–78.

Bresson, A. 2016. *The Making of the Ancient Greek Economy: Institutions, Markets, and Growth in the City-States*. Translated by S. Rendall. Princeton: Princeton University Press.

Bricault, L. 2019. *Isis Pelagia: Images, Names, and Cults of a Goddess of the Seas*. Religions in the Graeco-Roman World 190. Leiden: Brill.

Briquel-Chatonnet, F. 2009. "L'abbé Barthélemy, déchiffreur du palmyrénien et du phénicien." In *Histoires de déchiffrements: Les écritures du Proche-Orient à l'Égée*, edited by B. Lion and C. Michel, 173–185. Paris: Errance.

Briquel-Chatonnet, F. 2012. "Les inscriptions phénico-grecques et le bilinguisme des Phéniciens." *CRAI* 156: 619–638.

Broodbank, C. 2013. *The Making of the Middle Sea: A History of the Mediterranean from the Beginning to the Emergence of the Classical World*. Oxford: Oxford University Press.

Brubaker, R. and F. Cooper. 2000. "Beyond 'Identity.'" *Theory and Society* 29: 1–47.

Bruneau, P. 1970. *Recherches sur les cultes de Délos à l'époque hellénistique et à l'époque impériale*. Paris: De Boccard.

Bruneau, P. 1978. "Les cultes de l'établissement des Poséidoniastes de Berytos à Délos." In *Hommages à Maarten J. Vermaseren*, edited by M. de Boer and T. A. Edridge, vol. 1, 160–190. Leiden: Brill.

Bruss, J. S. 2010. "Ecphrasis in Fits and Starts? Down to 300 B.C." In *Archaic and Classical Greek Epigram*, edited by M. Baumbach, A. Petrovic, and I. Petrovic, 385–403. Cambridge: Cambridge University Press.

Budin, S. L. 2004. "A Reconsideration of the Aphrodite-Ashtart Syncretism." *Numen* 51: 95–145.

Bull, H. 2012. *The Anarchical Society: A Study of Order in World Politics*. 4th ed. New York: Columbia University Press.

Bunnens, G. 1979. *L'expansion phénicienne en Méditerranée: Essai d'interprétation fondé sur une analyse des traditions littéraires*. Études de philologie, d'archéologie et d'histoire anciennes 17. Rome: Institut Historique Belge de Rome.

Burke, E. M. 1985. "Lycurgan Finances." *GRBS* 26: 251–264.

Burke, E. M. 1992. "The Economy of Athens in the Classical Era: Some Adjustments to the Primitivist Model." *TAPhA* 122: 199–226.

Burke, E. M. 2010. "Finances and the Operation of the Athenian Democracy in the 'Lycurgan Era.'" *AJPh* 131: 393–423.

Cabanes, P. 1976. *L'Épire de la mort de Pyrrhos à la conquête romaine (272–167 av. J.-C)*. Paris: Annales Littéraires de l'Université de Besancon.

Calabro, D. 2015. "Egyptianizing Features in Phoenician and Punic Inscriptions from Egypt." In *Semitic Languages in Contact*, edited by A. M. Butts, 97–113. Leiden: Brill.

Campus, A. 2016. "Code-switching nell'epigrafia punica." *Rationes Rerum* 7: 109–132.

Capdetrey, L. and J. Zurbach, eds. 2012. *Mobilités grecques: Mouvements, reseaux, contacts en Méditerranée, de l'époque archaïque à l'époque hellénistique*. Bordeaux: Ausonius.

Carbon, J.-M. 2016. "The Festival of the Aloulaia, and the Association of the Alouliastai: Notes concerning the New Inscription from Larisa/Marmarini." *Kernos* 29: 185–208.

Cawkwell, G. L. 1963. "Eubulus." *JHS* 83: 47–67.

Celestino, S. and C. López-Ruiz. 2016. *Tartessos and the Phoenicians in Iberia*. Oxford: Oxford University Press.

Chankowski, V. 2008. *Athènes et Délos à l'époque classique: Recherches sur l'administration du sanctuaire d'Apollon délien*. Athens: École Française d'Athènes.

Chiera, G. 1987. "Fenici e Cartaginesi a Menfi." *RStudFen* 15: 127–131.

Chiodi, S. M. 1998. "*Nergal*, un dio 'doppio': Studi Mesopotamici – 1." *RStudFen* 26: 3–30.

Cohen, E. E. 1973. *Ancient Athenian Maritime Courts*. Princeton: Princeton University Press.

Cohen, S. J. D. 1999. *The Beginnings of Jewishness: Boundaries, Varieties, Uncertainties*. Berkeley: University of California Press.

Coldstream, J. N. 1969. "The Phoenicians of Ialysos." *BICS* 16: 1–8.

Cook, J. M. 1973. *The Troad: An Archaeological and Topographical Study*. Oxford: Clarendon Press.

Cooke, G. A. 1903. *A Textbook of North-Semitic Inscriptions: Moabite, Hebrew, Phoenician, Nabataean, Palmyrene, Jewish*. Oxford: Clarendon Press.

Corbier, M. 2012. "Rileggendo le iscrizioni bilingui (votive, onorarie e funerarie): Un confronto fra testo Greco e testo latino." In *L'officina epigrafica romana in ricordo di Giancarlo Susini*, edited by A. Donati and G. Poma, 51–88. Faenza: Fratelli Lega Editori.

Corsten, T. 2019. "Name Changes of Individuals." In *Changing Names: Tradition and Innovation in Ancient Greek Onomastics*, edited by R. Parker, 138–152. Proceedings of the British Academy 222. Oxford: Oxford University Press.

Costanzi, M. 2020. "Mobility in the Ancient Greek World: Diversity of Causes, Variety of Vocabularies." In *A Companion to Greeks across the Ancient World*, edited by F. De Angelis, 13–36. Hoboken, NJ: Wiley Blackwell.

Crouzet, S. 2012. "Des étrangers dans la cité: L'onomastique révélatrice d'échanges et d'intégrations entre Grecs et Puniques?" In *L'onomastica Africana: Congresso della Société du Maghreb préhistorique, antique et medieval, Porto Conte Ricerche*

(Alghero, 28/29 settembre 2007), edited by A. Corda and A. Mastino, 39–46. Ortacesus: Sandhi.

Culasso Gastaldi, E. 2000. "L'iscrizione trilingue del Museo di Antichità di Torino (dedicante greco, ambito punico, età romana)." *Epigraphica* 62: 11–28.

Culasso Gastaldi, E. 2002. "Le prossenie ateniesi del IV secolo a.C.: Gli onorati magnogreci e siciliani." In *Συγγραφή: Materiali e appunti per lo studio della storia e della letteratura antica*, edited by D. Ambaglio, 103–123. Como: New Press.

Culasso Gastaldi, E. 2004. *Le prossenie ateniesi del IV secolo a.C.: Gli onorati asiatici*. Alessandria: Edizioni dell' Orso.

Dana, D. 2019. "Onomastic Interactions: Greek and Thracian Names." In *Changing Names: Tradition and Innovation in Ancient Greek Onomastics*, edited by R. Parker, 167–194. Proceedings of the British Academy 222. Oxford: Oxford University Press.

De Angelis, F. 2016. *Archaic and Classical Sicily: A Social and Economic History*. Oxford: Oxford University Press.

De Angelis, F., ed. 2020. *A Companion to Greeks across the Ancient World*. Hoboken, NJ: Wiley Blackwell.

De La Coste-Messelière, P. 1925. "Inscriptions de Delphes." *BCH* 49: 61–103.

De Vincenzo, S. 2019. "Sicily." In *The Oxford Handbook of the Phoenician and Punic Mediterranean*, edited by C. López-Ruiz and B. R. Doak, 537–552. Oxford: Oxford University Press.

Decourt, J.-C. and A. Tziafalias. 2007. "Cultes et divinités isiaques en Thessalie: Identité et urbanisation." In *Nile into Tiber: Egypt in the Roman World. Proceedings of the IIIrd International Conference of Isis Studies, Leiden, May 11–14 2005*, edited by L. Bricault, M. J. Versluys, and P. G. P. Meyboom, 329–363. Leiden: Brill.

Decourt, J.-C. and A. Tziafalias. 2015. "Un règlement religieux de la région de Larissa: Cultes grecs et 'orientaux.'" *Kernos* 28: 13–51.

Demetriou, D. 2010. "τῆς πάσης ναυτιλίης φύλαξ: Aphrodite and the Sea." *Kernos* 23: 67–89.

Demetriou, D. 2012. *Negotiating Identity in the Ancient Mediterranean: The Archaic and Classical Greek Multiethnic Emporia*. Cambridge: Cambridge University Press.

Demetriou, D. 2020. "Hedging Bets, Abetting Rebellions: The Role of Athens in the 4th-Century Satraps' Revolts." *Ancient West & East* 19: 97–121.

Demetriou, D. 2021. "Phoenicians." In *The Herodotus Encyclopedia*, edited by C. Baron, 1123–1124. 3 vols. Malden, MA: Wiley-Blackwell.

Demetriou, D. Forthcoming a. "Herodotus." In *Encyclopedic Dictionary of Phoenician Culture*, vol. 3.1, *The Written Sources—Greek and Roman*, edited by A. Ercolani and U. Livadiotti. Leuven: Peeters.

Demetriou, D. Forthcoming b. "Transcultural Tokens of Identity: The Mechanics of Crossing Borders in the Ancient Mediterranean." In *Identities in Antiquity*, edited by V. Manolopoulou, J. Skinner, and C. Tsouparopoulou. Rewriting Antiquity. London: Routledge.

Derenbourg J. and H. Derenbourg. 1885. "Les inscriptions phéniciennes du temple de Seti à Abydos, publiées et traduites d'après une copie inédite de M. Sayce." *Revue d'Assyriologie et d'archéologie orientale* 1: 81–101.

Di Biase-Dyson, C. 2013. *Foreigners and Egyptians in the "Late Egyptian Stories": Linguistic, Literary and Historical Perspectives.* Leiden: Brill.

Di Stefano, C. A. et al., eds. 1984. *Lilibeo: Testimonianze archeologiche dal IV sec. a.C. al V. sec. d.C.* Marsala: Chiesa del collegio.

Dietler, M. 2010. *Archaeologies of Colonialism: Consumption, Entanglement, and Violence in Ancient Mediterranean France.* Berkeley: University of California Press.

Dietler, M. and C. López-Ruiz, eds. 2009. *Colonial Encounters in Ancient Iberia: Phoenician, Greek, and Indigenous Relations.* Chicago: University of Chicago Press.

Dillery, J. 1993. "Xenophon's *Poroi* and Athenian Imperialism." *Historia* 42: 1–11.

Donnellan, L., V. Nizzo, and G.-J. Burgers, eds. 2016a. *Conceptualising Early Colonisation.* Artes 6. Brussels: Belgisch Historisch Instituut te Rome.

Donnellan, L., V. Nizzo, and G.-J. Burgers, eds. 2016b. *Contexts of Early Colonization.* Papers of the Royal Netherlands Institute in Rome 64. Rome: Palombi Editori.

Donner H. and W. Röllig. 1973–79. *Kanaanäische und aramäische Inschriften.* 3 vols. Wiesbaden: Otto Harrassowitz Verlag.

Dougherty, C. 1993. *The Poetics of Colonization: From City to Text in Archaic Greece.* Oxford: Oxford University Press.

Dougherty, C. 2001. *The Raft of Odysseus: The Ethnographic Imagination of Homer's "Odyssey."* Oxford: Oxford University Press.

Dridi, H. 2019a. "Early Carthage: From Its Foundation to the Battle of Himera (ca. 814–480 BCE)." In *The Oxford Handbook of the Phoenician and Punic Mediterranean*, edited by C. López-Ruiz and B. R. Doak, 141–154. Oxford: Oxford University Press.

Dridi, H. 2019b. "Trace archéologiques et épigraphiques carthaginoises en Égée." In *Art et archéologie du Proche-Orient hellénistique et romain: Les circulations artistiques entre Orient et Occident. Actes de la journée d'études du 29 mai 2018, Institut Catholique de Paris*, edited by C. Arnould-Béhar and V. Vassal, vol. 2, 111–121. BAR International Series 2934. Oxford: BAR Publishing.

Dridi, H. 2019c. "Trois témoignages sur l'activité de Puniques en Égypte au temps des Lagides." *Semitica et Classica* 12: 233–240.

Duncan-Jones, R. P. 1980. "Metic Numbers in Periclean Athens." *Chiron* 10: 101–109.

Dušek, J. and J. Mynářová. 2013. "Phoenician and Aramaic Inscriptions from Abusir." In *In the Shadow of Bezalel: Aramaic, Biblical, and Ancient Near Eastern Studies in Honor of Bezalel Porten*, edited by A. F. Botta, 53–69. Leiden: Brill.

Eckstein, A. M. 2006. *Mediterranean Anarchy, Interstate War, and the Rise of Rome.* Berkeley: University of California Press.

Edrey, M. 2016. "Phoenician Ethnogenesis: The Crucial Role of Landscape in the Early Shaping of Phoenician Culture." *UF* 47: 41–52.

Edrey, M. 2019. *Phoenician Identity in Context: Material Cultural* Koiné *in the Iron Age Levant*. Münster: Ugarit-Verlag.

Ehmer, J. 2011. "Quantifying Mobility in Early Modern Europe: The Challenge of Concepts and Data." *Journal of Global History* 6: 327–338.

Elayi, J. 1988. "L'inscription bilingue de Délos *CIS* I 114." *BdM* 19: 549–555.

Elayi, J. 1998. *Pénétration grecque én Phénicie sous l'empire perse*. Nancy: Presses Universitaires de Nancy.

Elayi, J. 2005. *'Abd'aštart Ier/Straton de Sidon: Un roi phénicien entre Orient et Occident*. Transeuphratène Supplement 12. Paris: Gabalda.

Elayi, J. 2006. "An Updated Chronology of the Reigns of Phoenician Kings during the Persian Period (539–333 BCE)." *Transeuphratène* 32: 11–43.

Elayi, J. 2008. "On Dating the Reigns of Phoenician Kings in the Persian Period." In *Beyond the Homeland: Markers in Phoenician Chronology*, edited by C. Sagona, 97–112. Leuven: Peeters.

Elayi, J. 2009. *Byblos, cité sacrée (8e–4e s. av. J.-C.)*. Transeuphratène Supplement 15. Paris: Gabalda.

Elayi, J. 2013. *Histoire de la Phénicie*. Paris: Perrin.

Elayi, J. 2015. "L'inscription bilingue de Délos *CIS* I 114 réexaminée." *Transeuphratène* 47: 79–84.

Elayi, J. 2018. *The History of Phoenicia*. Translated by Andrew Plummer. Atlanta: Lockwood Press.

Elayi, J. and A. G. Elayi. 2004. *Le monnayage de la cité phénicienne de Sidon à l'époque perse (Ve–IVe s. av. J.-C.)*. 2 vols. Transeuphratène Supplement 11. Paris: Gabalda.

Elayi, J. and A. G. Elayi, 2009. *The Coinage of the Phoenician City of Tyre in the Persian Period (5th–4th cent. BCE)*. Leuven: Peeters.

Elayi, J. and A. G. Elayi. 2014. *A Monetary and Political History of the Phoenician City of Byblos*. Winona Lake, IN: Eisenbrauns.

Elayi, J. and A. G. Elayi. 2015. *Arwad, cité phénicienne du nord*. Transeuphratène Supplement 19. Paris: Gabalda.

Elsner, J. and I. Rutherford. 2005. *Pilgrimage in Graeco-Roman and Early Christian Antiquity: Seeing the Gods*. Oxford: Oxford University Press.

Engen, D. T. 2010. *Honor and Profit: Athenian Trade Policy and the Economy and Society of Greece, 415–307 B.C.E.* Ann Arbor: University of Michigan Press.

Fabricius, J. 1999. *Die hellenistischen Totenmahlreliefs: Grabrepräsentation und Wertvorstellungen in ostgriechischen Städten*. Munich: F. Pfeil.

Fantuzzi, M. and R. Hunter. 2002. *Muse e modelli: La poesia ellenistica da Alessandro Magno ad Augusto*. Rome: GLF Editori Laterza.

Faraguna, M. 1992. "Atene nell'età di Alessandro: Problemi politici, economici, finanziari." *MAL* Ser. 9 Vol. 2: 165–447.

Faraguna, M. 2003. "Alexander and the Greeks." In *Brill's Companion to Alexander the Great*, edited by J. Roisman, 99–130. Leiden: Brill.

Faraguna, M. 2014. "Citizens, Non-citizens, and Slaves: Identification Methods in Classical Greece." In *Identifiers and Identification Methods in the Ancient World: Legal Documents in Ancient Societies III*, edited by M. Depauw and S. Coussement, 165–183. Leuven: Peeters.

Ferguson, W. S. 1944. "The Attic Orgeones." *HThR* 37: 61–140.

Ferguson, W. S. 1949. "Orgeonika." In *Commemorative Studies in Honor of Theodore Leslie Shear*, 130–163. Hesperia Supplement 8. Princeton: American School of Classical Studies at Athens.

Ferjaoui, A. 1992. *Recherches sur les relations entre l'Orient phénicien et Carthage*. Tunis: Fondation nationale pour la traduction, l'établissement des textes, et les études "Beït Al-Hikma-Carthage."

Ferjaoui, A. 1999. "Les femmes à Carthage à travers les documents épigraphiques." *REPPAL* 11: 77–86.

Ferjaoui, A. 2008. "Y avait-il une communauté de Tyriens à Carthage et de Carthaginois à Tyr?" In *D'Ougarit à Jérusalem: Receuil d'études épigraphiques et archéologiques offert à Pierre Bordreuil*, edited by C. Roche, 183–189. Orient & Méditerranée, 2. Paris: De Boccard.

Fermaglich, K. 2018. *A Rosenberg by Any Other Name: A History of Jewish Name Changing in America*. New York: New York University.

Ferron, J. 1971. "La inscripcion cartaginesa en el Arpocrates Madrileño." *Trabajos de Prehistoria* 28: 359–384.

Ferron, J. 1974. "La statuette d'Harpocrate du British Museum." *RStudFen* 2: 77–95.

Février, J.-G. 1951–52. "Vir Sidonius." *Semitica* 4: 13–18.

Février, J.-G. 1961. "Textes puniques et néopuniques relatifs aux testaments." *Semitica* 11: 5–8.

Finley, M. I. 1982. *Economy and Society in Ancient Greece*. New York: Viking Press.

Fisher, N. 2006. "Citizens, Foreigners and Slaves in Greek Society." In *A Companion to the Classical Greek World*, edited by K. H. Kinzl, 327–349. Malden, MA: Wiley-Blackwell.

Fontan, É, N. Gillmann, and H. Le Meaux, eds. 2007. *La Méditerranée des Phéniciens: De Tyr à Carthage*. Exhibition catalog, Institut du monde arabe, 6 novembre 2007–20 avril 2008. Paris: Somogy.

Fraser, P. M. 1970. "Greek-Phoenician Bilingual Inscriptions from Rhodes." *ABSA* 65: 31–36.

Fraser, P. M. 2009. *Greek Ethnic Terminology*. Oxford: Oxford University Press.

Gabrielsen, V. 1997. *The Naval Aristocracy of Hellenistic Rhodes*. Studies in Hellenistic Civilization 6. Aarhus: Aarhus University Press.

Gabrielsen, V. 2001. "The Rhodian Associations and Economic Activity." In *Hellenistic Economies*, edited by Z. H. Archibald et al., 163–184. London: Routledge.

Gabrielsen, V. and C. A. Thomsen, eds. 2015. *Private Associations and the Public Sphere. Proceedings of a Symposium Held at the Royal Danish Academy of Sciences and Letters, 9–11 September 2010*. Copenhagen: Royal Danish Academy of Sciences and Letters.

Garland, R. 2001. *The Piraeus: From the Fifth to the First Century B.C.* 2nd ed. London: Bloomsbury Academic.

Garland, R. 2014. *Wandering Greeks: The Ancient Greek Diaspora from the Age of Homer to the Death of Alexander the Great.* Princeton: Princeton University Press.

Garnand, B. K. 2020. "Phoenicians and Greeks as Comparable Contemporary Migrant Groups." In *A Companion to Greeks across the Ancient World*, edited by F. De Angelis, 139–171. Hoboken, NJ: Wiley Blackwell.

Gauthier, P. 1972. *Symbola: Les étrangers et la justice dans les cités grecques.* Nancy: Université de Nancy II.

Gauthier, P. 1976. *Un commentaire historique des "Poroi" de Xénophon.* Geneva: Librairie Droz.

Gibson, J. C. L. 1982. *Textbook of Syrian Semitic Inscriptions.* Vol. 3, *Phoenician Inscriptions.* Oxford: Oxford University Press.

Giglio, R. and R. De Simone. 2019. "Epigraphica Lilybetana. Tra Punici, Greci e Romani: Un decennio di ricerche (2006–2016). Note bibliografiche." In *Sprachen— Schriftkulturen—Identitäten der Antike: Beiträge des XV. Internationalen Kongresses für Griechische und Lateinische Epigraphik, Wien 28. August bis 1. September 2017*, edited by F. Beutler and T. Pantzer. Vienna: Wiener Beiträge zur Alten Geschichte online.

Ginestí Rosell, A. 2012. *Epigrafia funerària d'estrangers a Atenes (segles VI–IV aC): Die Grabinschriften der Ausländer in Athen (6. bis 4. Jh v.Chr.).* Tarragona: Institut Català d'Arqueologia Clàssica.

Giovannini, A. 1994. "Greek Cities and Greek Commonwealth." In *Images and Ideologies: Self-Definition in the Hellenistic World*, edited by A. Bulloch et al., 265–286. Berkeley: University of California Press.

Giovannini, A. 2007. *Les relations entre états dans la Grèce antique du temps d'Homère à l'intervention romaine (ca. 700–200 av. J.C.).* Stuttgart: F. Steiner Verlag.

Gomme, A. W. 1933. *The Population of Athens in the Fifth and Fourth Centuries B.C.* Oxford: B. Blackwell.

Grainger, J. D. 1992. *Hellenistic Phoenicia.* Oxford: Clarendon Press.

Gras, M., P. Rouillard, and J. Teixidor. 1989. *L'univers phénicien.* Paris: Arthaud.

Greco, C. 2000. "La necropoli punica di Solunto." In *Actas del IV congreso internacional de estudios fenicios y púnicos, Cádiz, 2–6 octubre, 1995*, edited by M. Barthélemy and M. E. Aubet, 1319–1335. Cadiz: Universidad de Cádiz.

Greenberg, M. 1997. *Ezekiel 21–37: A New Translation with Introduction and Commentary.* New York: Anchor Bible.

Greenfield, J. C. 1984. "Notes on the Phoenician Letter from Saqqara." *Orientalia* 53: 242–244.

Gruen, E. S. 1975. "Rome and Rhodes in the Second Century B.C.: A Historiographical Inquiry." *CQ* 25: 58–81.

Gruen, E. S. 2020. *Ethnicity in the Ancient World—Did It Matter?* Berlin: De Gruyter.

Gruen, E. S. 2023. "Displaced in Diaspora? Jewish Communities in the Greco-Roman World." In *Diaspora and Literary Studies*, edited by A. Naimou, 33–48. Cambridge: Cambridge University Press.

Gubel, E., ed. 1986. *Les Phéniciens et le monde méditerranéen*. Brussels: Générale de Banque.

Haake, M. 2006. "Documentary Evidence, Literary Forgery, or Manipulation of Historical Documents? Diogenes Laertius and an Athenian Honorary Decree for Zeno of Citium." *CQ* 54: 470–483.

Habicht, C. 2002. "Die Ehren der Proxenoi: Ein Vergleich." *MH* 59: 13–30.

Haegemans, K. 2000. "Elissa, the First Queen of Carthage, through Timaeus' Eyes." *AncSoc* 30: 277–291.

Hagemajer Allen, K. 2003. "Intercultural Exchanges in Fourth-Century Attic Decrees." *ClAnt* 22: 199–250.

Hall, J. M. 1997. *Ethnic Identity in Greek Antiquity*. Cambridge: Cambridge University Press.

Hall, J. M. 2002. *Hellenicity: Between Ethnicity and Culture*. Chicago: University of Chicago Press.

Hall, J. M. 2003. "'Culture' or 'Cultures'? Hellenism in the Late Sixth Century." In *The Cultures within Ancient Greek Culture: Contact, Conflict, Collaboration*, edited by C. Dougherty and L. Kurke, 23–34. Cambridge: Cambridge University Press.

Hanink, J. 2014. *Lycurgan Athens and the Making of Classical Tragedy*. Cambridge: Cambridge University Press.

Hansen, M. H. 1983. "*Rhetores* and *Strategoi* in Fourth-Century Athens." *GRBS* 24: 151–180.

Hansen, M. H. 1985. *Demography and Democracy: The Number of Athenian Citizens in the Fourth Century BC*. Herning: Systime.

Hansen, M. H. 1988. *Three Studies in Athenian Demography*. Copenhagen: Royal Danish Academy of Sciences and Letters.

Hasenohr, C. 2007. "Italiens et Phéniciens à Délos: Organisation et relations de deux groupes d'étrangers résidents (IIe–Ier siècles av. J.-C.)." In *Étrangers dans la cité romaine: "Habiter une autre patrie": Des incolae de la République aux peuples fédérés du Bas-Empire*, edited by R. Compatangelo-Soussignan and C.-G. Schwentzel, 77–90. Rennes: Presses Universitaires de Rennes.

Hasenohr, C. 2008. "Le bilinguisme dans les inscriptions de *magistri* de Délos." In *Bilinguisme gréco-latin et épigraphie: Actes du colloque, 17–19 mai 2004*, edited by F. Biville, J.-C Decourt, and G. Rougemont, 55–70. Lyon: Maison de l'Orient et de la Méditerranéen Jean Pouilloux.

Hauben, H. 1970. "The King of the Sidonians and the Persian Imperial Fleet." *AncSoc* 1: 1–8.

Hauben, H. 1987. "Philocles, King of the Sidonians and General of the Ptolemies." In *Phoenicia and the East Mediterranean in the First Millennium B.C. Proceedings of the*

Conference Held in Leuven from the 14th to the 16th of November 1985, edited by E. Lipiński, 413–427. Studia Phoenicia 5. Leuven: Peeters.

Hauben, H. 2004. "A Phoenician King in the Service of the Ptolemies: Philocles of Sidon Revisited." *AncSoc* 34: 27–44.

Hayne, J. 2010. "Entangled Identities on Iron Age Sardinia?" In *Material Connections in the Ancient Mediterranean: Mobility, Materiality and Identity*, edited by P. van Dommelen and A. B. Knapp, 147–169. London: Routledge.

Helas, S. 2011. *Selinus II: Die punische Stadt auf der Akropolis*. Wiesbaden: Reichert Verlag.

Helly, B. 1992. "Stèles funéraires de Démétrias: Recherches sur la chronologie des remparts et des nécropoles méridionales de la ville." In Διεθνές Συνέδριο για την Αρχαία Θεσσαλία στη μνήμη του Δημήτρη Ρ. Θεοχάρη, edited by E. Kypraiou, 349–365. Athens: Ταμείο Αρχαιολογικών Πόρων και Απαλλοτριώσεων.

Heltzer, M. 1985. "The Meaning of the Punic Expression from Carthago *lmy'ms 'm qrtḥdš* and the Root *'-m-s*." *OA* 24: 77–84.

Henry, A. S. 1977. *The Prescripts of Athenian Decrees*. Mnemosyne Supplements 49. Leiden: Brill.

Henry, A. S. 1982. "Polis/Acropolis, Paymasters and the Ten Talent Fund." *Chiron* 12: 91–118.

Henry, A. S. 1983. *Honours and Privileges in Athenian Decrees: The Principal Formulae of Athenian Honorary Decrees*. Hildesheim: Georg Olms.

Henry, A. S. 1989. "Provisions for the Payment of the Athenian Decrees: A Study in Formulaic Language." *ZPE* 78: 247–295.

Hermary, A. 2014. "Une petite énigme délienne: Les 'curieuses offrandes' des hiéronautes de Tyr." *RA* 2: 271–284.

Hicks, E. L. and G. F. Hill. 1901. *A Manual of Greek Historical Inscriptions*. Oxford: Clarendon University Press.

Hildebrandt, F. 2006. *Die attischen Namenstelen: Untersuchungen zu Stelen des 5. und 4. Jahrhunderts v. Chr.* Berlin: Frank & Timme.

Hodos, T. 2006. *Local Responses to Colonization in the Iron Age Mediterranean*. London: Routledge.

Hodos, T. 2020. *The Archaeology of the Mediterranean Iron Age: A Globalising World c.1000–600 BCE*. Cambridge: Cambridge University Press.

Hoerder, D. 2002. *Cultures in Contact: World Migrations in the Second Millennium*. Durham, NC: Duke University Press.

Hoerder, D. 2012. *Migrations and Belongings, 1870–1945*. Cambridge, MA: Belknap Press.

Hölscher, T. and P. von Möllendorff. 2008. "'Niemand wundere sich, sieht er dies Bild!': Bild und Text auf der Grabstele des Antipatros von Askalon." *Poetica* 40: 289–333.

Homolle, T. 1878. "Fouilles sur l'emplacement du temple d'Apollon à Délos." *BCH* 2: 9–10.

Honeyman, A. M. 1947. "Varia Punica." *AJPh* 68: 77–82.

Hopper, R. J. 1979. *Trade and Industry in Classical Greece*. London: Thames and Hudson.

Horden, P. and N. Purcell. 2000. *The Corrupting Sea: A Study of Mediterranean History*. Malden, MA: Wiley-Blackwell.

Hoyos, D. 2010. *The Carthaginians*. London: Routledge.

Huss, W. 2001. *Ägypten in hellenistischer Zeit, 332–30 v. Chr*. Munich: C. H. Beck.

Hütwohl, D. J. 2020. "Herodotus' Phoenicians: Mediators of Cultural Exchange in the Mediterranean." *RStudFen* 48: 107–120.

Ilieva, P. 2019. "Phoenicians, Cypriots and Euboeans in the Northern Aegean: A Reappraisal." *Athens University Review of Archaeology* 2: 65–102.

Intrieri, M. and S. Ribichini, eds. 2011. *Fenici e Italici, Cartagine e la Magna Grecia: Popoli a contatto, culture a confronto*. Atti del convegno internazionale, Cosenza, 27–28 maggio 2008. 2 vols. Rome: Consiglio Nazionale delle Ricerche.

Ioannou, C. 2017. "La présence phénicienne en Grèce." In *ΤΕΡΨΙΣ: Studies in Mediterranean Archaeology in Honour of Nota Kourou*, edited by V. Vlachou and A. Gadolou, 435–446. Brussels: CReA-Patrimoine.

Isager, S., and M. H. Hansen, 1975. *Aspects of Athenian Society in the Fourth Century B.C.* Translated by J. Hsiang Rosenmeier. Copenhagen: Odense University Press.

Ismard, P. 2010. *La cité de résaux: Athènes et ses associations, VIe–Ier siècle av. J.-C.* Paris: Publications de la Sorbonne.

Jansen, J. 2012. "Strangers Incorporated: Outsiders in Xenophon's *Poroi*." In *Xenophon: Ethical Principles and Historical Enquiry*, edited by C. Tuplin and F. Hobden, 725–760. Leiden: Brill.

Jigoulov, V. S. 2010. *The Social History of Achaemenid Phoenicia: Being a Phoenician, Negotiating Empires*. London: Equinox.

Johnson, A. C. 1914. "Notes on Attic Inscriptions." *CPh* 9: 417–441.

Jones, N. 1999. *The Associations of Classical Athens: The Response to Democracy*. Oxford: Oxford University Press.

Judeich, W. 1892. *Kleinasiatische Studien: Untersuchungen zur griechisch-persischen Geschichte des IV. Jahrhunderts v. Chr*. Marburg: N. G. Elwertsche.

Kaldellis, A. 2019. "Neo-Phoenician Identities in the Roman Empire." In *The Oxford Handbook of the Phoenician and Punic Mediterranean*, edited by C. López-Ruiz and B. R. Doak, 685–696. Oxford: Oxford University Press.

Kalliontzis, Y. and N. Papazarkadas. 2019. "The Contributions to the Refoundation of Thebes: A New Epigraphic and Historical Analysis." *ABSA* 114: 293–315.

Kamen, D. 2013. *Status in Classical Athens*. Princeton: Princeton University Press.

Kantzia, C. 1980. ". . . ΤΙΜΟΣ ΑΒΔΑΛΩΝΥΜΟΥ [ΣΙΔ]ΩΝΟΣ ΒΑΣΙΛΕΩΣ. Μια δίγλωσση ελληνική-φοινικική επιγραφή από τη Κω." *AD* 35: 1–16.

Karageorghis, V. 1969. "Chronique des fouilles et découvertes archéologiques à Chypre en 1968." *BCH* 93: 431–569.

Kasher, A. 1985. *The Jews in Hellenistic and Roman Egypt: The Struggle for Equal Rights*. Texte und Studien zum antiken Judentum 7. Tübingen: J. C. B. Mohr.

Kasher, A. 2008. "The Jewish *Politeuma* in Alexandria: A Pattern of Jewish Communal Life in the Greco-Roman Diaspora." In *Homelands and Diasporas: Greeks, Jews and Their Migrations*, edited by M. Rozen, 109–125. London: I. B. Tauris.

Kasimis, D. 2018. *The Perpetual Immigrant and the Limits of Athenian Democracy*. Cambridge: Cambridge University Press.

Kaufman, B. 2009. "A Citizen of Tyre in Sabratha: Colonial Identity in Punic North Africa." *MAARAV* 16: 39–148.

Kaufman, S. A. 2007. "The Phoenician Inscription of the Incirli Trilingual: A Tentative Reconstruction and Translation." *MAARAV* 14: 7–26.

Kennedy, R. F. 2014. *Immigrant Women in Athens: Gender, Ethnicity, and Citizenship in the Classical City*. New York: Routledge.

Kloppenborg J. S. and S. G. Wilson, eds. 1996. *Voluntary Associations in the Graeco-Roman World*. London: Routledge.

Knoepfler, D. 1990. "Contribution à l'épigraphie de Chalcis." *BCH* 114: 473–498.

Knoepfler, D. 1995. "Une paix des cent ans et un conflit en permanence: Étude sur les relations diplomatiques d'Athènes avec Érétrie et les autres cités de l'Eubée au IVe siècle av. J.-C." In *Les relations internationales: Actes du Colloque de Strasbourg, 15–17 juin 1993*, edited by E. Frézouls and A. Jacquemin, 309–364. Paris: De Boccard.

Knoepfler, D. 2001. *Décrets érétriens de proxénie et de citoyenneté*. Lausanne: Payot.

Kornfeld, W. 1978. "Neues über die Phönikischen und aramäischen Graffiti in den Tempeln von Abydos." *AAWW* 115: 193–204.

Kosmetatou, E. 2004. "Bilistiche and the Quasi-Institutional Status of Ptolemaic Royal Mistress." *APF* 50: 18–36.

Kourou, N. 2003. "Rhodes: The Phoenician Issue Revisited. Phoenicians at Vroulia?" In *Sea Routes ... Interconnections in the Mediterranean 16th–6th c. BC. Proceedings of the International Symposium Held at Rethymnon, Crete in September 29th–October 2nd, 2002*, edited by N. C. Stampolidis and V. Karageorghis, 249–262. Athens: Orion Press.

Kravaritou, S. 2011. "Synoecism and Religious Interface in Demetrias (Thessaly)." *Kernos* 24: 111–135.

Krings, V. ed. 1994. *La civilisation phénicienne et punique*: Manuel de recherche. Leiden: Brill.

La'da, C. A. 2002. *Foreign Ethnics in Hellenistic Egypt*. Leuven: Peeters.

LaBuff, J. B. 2016. *Polis Expansion and Elite Power in Hellenistic Karia*. Lanham, MD: Lexington Books.

LaBuff, J. B. 2023. "Prolegomena to Any Future Indigenous History of the Ancient World." *AHR* 128.

Lambert, S. D. 2002. "Fish, Low Fares and *IG* II² 283." *ZPE* 140: 73–79.

Lambert, S. D. 2006. "Athenian State Laws and Decrees, 352/1–322/1: III Decrees Honouring Foreigners. A. Citizenship, Proxeny and Euergesy." *ZPE* 158: 115–158.

Lambert, S. D. 2011. "What Was the Point of Inscribed Honorific Decrees in Classical Athens?" In *Sociable Man: Essays on Ancient Greek Social Behaviour in Honour of Nick Fisher*, edited by S. D. Lambert, 193–214. Swansea: Classical Press of Wales.

Lanfranchi, G. B. 2007. "The Luwian-Phoenician Bilinguals of Çineköy and Karatepe: An Ideological Dialogue." In *Getrennte Wege? Kommunikation, Raum und Wahrnehmung in der Alten Welt*, edited by R. Rollinger, A. Luther, and J. Wiesehöfer, 179–217. Frankfurt am Main: Verlag Antike.

Lapeyre, G.-G. 1939. "Les fouilles du Musée Lavigerie à Carthage de 1935 à 1939." *CRAI* 83: 294–304.

Leclant, J. 1991. "Prolusione: Les Phéniciens et l'Égypte." In *Atti del II Congresso internazionale di studi fenici e punici, Roma 9–14 Novembre 1987*, edited by E. Acquaro, vol. 1, 7–17. Rome: Consiglio Nazionale delle Ricerche.

Lehmann, C. M. 1994. "*Xenoi, Proxenoi*, and Early Greek Traders." *Helios* 21: 9–20.

Lemaire, A. 2003. "L'esclave." In *El hombre fenicio: Estudios y materiales*, edited by J. Á. Zamora, 219–222. Rome: Consejo Superior de Investigaciones Científicas, Escuela Española de Historia y Arqueología en Roma.

Lewis, D. M. 2011. "Near Eastern Slaves in Classical Attica and the Slave Trade with Persian Territories." *CQ* 61: 91–113.

Lewis, D. M. 2018. *Greek Slave Systems in Their Eastern Mediterranean Context*. Oxford: Oxford University Press.

Lewis, J. D. 2009. "Xenophon's *Poroi* and the Foundations of Political Economy." *Polis* 26: 370–388.

Lichtheim, M. 2006. *Ancient Egyptian Literature*. Vol. 2, *The New Kingdom*. 2nd ed. Berkeley: University of California Press.

Lidzbarski, M. 1912. *Phönizische und aramäische Krugaufschriften aus Elephantine*. Berlin: Verlag der Königliche Akademie der Wissenschaften.

Lightfoot, J. L. 2009. *Hellenistic Collection: Philitas, Alexander of Aetolia, Hermesianax, Euphorion, Parthenius*. Loeb Classical Library 508. Cambridge, MA: Harvard University Press.

Lipiński, E. 1995. *Dieux et déesses de l'univers phénicien et punique*. Studia Phoenicia 14. Leuven: Peeters.

Lipiński, E. 2004. *Itineraria Phoenicia*. Studia Phoenicia 18. Leuven: Peeters.

Lipiński, E. et al., eds. 1992. *Dictionnaire de la civilisation phénicienne et punique*. Turnhout: Brepols.

Liu, S. 2015. *Identity, Hybridity and Cultural Home: Chinese Migrants and Diaspora in Multicultural Societies*. London: Rowman & Littlefield.

López-Ruiz, C. 2015. "Near Eastern Precedents of the 'Orphic' Gold Tablets: The Phoenician Missing Link." *Journal of Ancient Near Eastern Religions* 15: 52–91.

López-Ruiz, C. 2017. "'Not That Which Can Be Found among the Greeks': Philo of Byblos and Phoenician Cultural Identity in the Roman East." *Religion in the Roman Empire* 3: 366–392.

López-Ruiz, C. 2021. *Phoenicians and the Making of the Mediterranean*. Cambridge, MA: Harvard University Press.

López-Ruiz, C. Forthcoming. "The Resilience of a 'Non-people': The Case for a Reconstructed Phoenician Identity." In *Identities in Antiquity*, edited by V. Manolopoulou, J. Skinner, and C. Tsouparopoulou. Rewriting Antiquity. London: Routledge.

López-Ruiz, C. and B. R. Doak, eds. 2019. *The Oxford Handbook of the Phoenician and Punic Mediterranean*. Oxford: Oxford University Press.

Low, P. 2007. *Interstate Relations in Classical Greece: Morality and Power*. Cambridge: Cambridge University Press.

Lucassen, J. and L. Lucassen. 2009. "The Mobility Transition Revisited, 1500–1900: What the Case of Europe Can Offer to Global History." *Journal of Global History* 4: 347–377.

Lucassen, J. and L. Lucassen. 2011. "From Mobility Transition to a Comparative Global Migration History." *Journal of Global History* 6: 299–307.

Lucassen, J., L. Lucassen, and P. Manning, eds. 2010. *Migration History in World History: Multidisciplinary Approaches*. Leiden: Brill.

Ma, J. 2003. "Peer Polity Interaction in the Hellenistic Age." *P&P* 180: 9–39.

MacDowell, D. M. 2009. *Demosthenes the Orator*. Oxford: Oxford University Press.

Machuca Prieto, F. 2019. *Una forma fenicia de ser romano: Identidad e integración de las comunidades fenicias de la Península Ibérica bajo poder de Roma*. SPAL Monografías Arqueología 29. Seville: Universidad de Sevilla.

Mack, W. 2015. *Proxeny and Polis: Institutional Networks in the Ancient Greek World*. Oxford: Oxford University Press.

Magnanini, P. 1973. *Le iscrizioni fenicie dell'Oriente: Testi, traduzioni, glossari*. Rome: Istituto di studi del Vicino oriente, Università degli studi di Roma.

Maillot, S. 2012. "La formalisation des réseaux de mobilité méditerranéens: Remarques sur les associations à l'époque hellénistique." In *Mobilités grecques: Mouvements, réseaux, contacts en Méditerranée, de l'époque archaïque à l'époque hellénistique*, edited by L. Capdetrey and J. Zurbach, 235–260. Bordeaux: Ausonius.

Maillot, S. 2015. "Foreigners' Associations and the Rhodian State." In *Private Associations and the Public Sphere: Proceedings of a Symposium Held at the Royal Danish Academy of Sciences and Letters, 9–11 September 2010*, edited by V. Gabrielsen and C. A. Thomsen, 136–182. Copenhagen: Royal Danish Academy of Sciences and Letters.

Malkin, I. 2005. "Herakles and Melqart: Greeks and Phoenicians in the Middle Ground." In *Cultural Borrowings and Ethnic Appropriations in Antiquity*, edited by E. S. Gruen, 238–257. Stuttgart: F. Steiner Verlag.

Malkin, I. 2011. *A Small Greek World: Networks in the Ancient Mediterranean*. Oxford: Oxford University Press.

Malkin, I., C. Constantakopoulou, and K. Panagopoulou, eds. 2009. *Greek and Roman Networks in the Mediterranean*. London: Routledge.

Manganaro, G. 2000. "Fenici, cartaginesi, numidi tra i greci (IV–I sec. a.C.)." *NAC* 29: 255–268.

Manning, P. 2006. "Cross-Community Migration: A Distinctive Human Pattern." *Social Evolution & History* 5: 24–54.

Manning, P. with T. Trimmer. 2020. *Migration in World History*. 3rd ed. London: Routledge.

Marcadé, J. 1953. *Receuil des signatures de sculpteurs grecs*. I. Paris: De Boccard.

Marek, C. 1977. "Der Geldumlauf der Stadt Histiaia und seine Bedeutung für die Verteilung ihrer Proxenoi." *Talanta* 8: 72–79.

Marek, C. 1984. *Die Proxenie*. Frankfurt am Main: Peter Lang.

Marek, C. 1985. "Handel und Proxenie." *MBAH* 4: 67–78.

Marginesu, G. 2002. "Le iscrizioni greche della Sardegna: Iscrizioni lapidarie e bronzee." In *L'Africa Romana. Lo spazio marittimo del Mediterraneo occidentale: Geografia, storica ed economia. Atti del XIV Convegno di Studio sull'Africa romana (Sassari, 7–10 dicembre 2000)*, edited by M. Khanoussi, P. Ruggeri, and C. Vismara, vol. 3, 1807–1825. Rome: Carocci Editore.

Markoe, G. E. 2000. *Phoenicians*. London: British Museum Press.

Martí-Aguilar, M. Á. 2019. "The Gadir-Tyre Axis." In *The Oxford Handbook of the Phoenician and Punic Mediterranean*, edited by C. López-Ruiz and B. R. Doak, 617–626. Oxford: Oxford University Press.

Martin, S. R. 2017. *The Art of Contact: Comparative Approaches to Greek and Phoenician Art*. Philadelphia: University of Pennsylvania Press.

Martin, S. R. 2018. "Eastern Mediterranean Feasts: What Do We Really Know about the Marzeah?" In *Change, Continuity, and Connectivity: North-Eastern Mediterranean at the Turn of the Bronze Age and in the Early Iron Age*, edited by Ł. Niesiołowski-Spanò and M. Węcowski, 294–307. Wiesbaden: Otto Harrassowitz Verlag.

Marzolff, P. 1994. "Développement urbanistique de Démetrias." Θεσσαλία: Δεκαπέντε χρόνια αρχαιολογικής έρευνας, 1975–1990. Αποτελέσματα και προοπτικές. Πρακτικά Διεθνούς Συνεδρίου, Λυών, 17–22 Απριλίου 1990. *La Thessalie: quinze années de recherches archéologiques, 1975–1990. Bilans et perspectives. Actes du colloque international, Lyon, 17–22 Avril 1990*, edited by E. Capon, vol. 2, 57–70. Athens: Hellenic Ministry of Culture.

Masson, O. 1969. "Recherches sur les Phéniciens dans le monde hellénistique." *BCH* 93: 679–700.

Masson, O. 1976. "Noms sémitiques dans deux inscriptions grecques." *Semitica* 26: 93–98.

Masson, O. 1979. "Le 'roi' carthaginois Iômilkos dans des inscriptions de Délos." *Semitica* 29: 53–57.

Masson, O. 1985. "Sur le nom de Bilistiché, favorite de Ptolémée II." In *Studia in Honorem IIro Kajanto*, 109–112. Arctos Supplement 2. Helsinki: Helsingfors.

Masson, O. 1994. "Nouvelles notes d'anthroponymie grecque. IV. Le nom Νεομήνιος, Νουμήνιος 'enfant de la nouvelle lune' et ses variantes." *ZPE* 102: 167–184.

Masson, O. and M. Sznycer. 1972. *Recherches sur les Phéniciens à Chypre*. Geneva: Librairie Droz.

Matić, U. 2020. *Ethnic Identities in the Land of the Pharaohs*. Cambridge: Cambridge University Press.

Matricon-Thomas, É. 2011. "Recherches sur les cultes orientaux à Athènes, du Ve siècle avant J.-C. au IVe siècle après J.-C." PhD dissertation. Université Jean Monnet–Saint-Etienne.

Matthaiou, A. P. 2016. "Συνθήκη Ἀθηναίων καὶ Σιφνίων (*Agora* XVI 50). Σημείωσις." *Γραμματεῖον* 5: 71–72.

Mazar, E. 2009–10. *The Northern Cemetery of Achziv (Tenth–Sixth Centuries BCE): The Tophet Site*. 2 vols. Barcelona: Bellaterra.

McCarty, M. M. 2019. "The Tophet and Infant Sacrifice." In *The Oxford Handbook of the Phoenician and Punic Mediterranean*, edited by C. López-Ruiz and B. R. Doak, 311–325. Oxford: Oxford University Press.

McKeown, A. 2004. "Global Migration, 1846–1940." *Journal of World History* 15: 155–189.

McKeown, A. 2011. "Different Transitions: Comparing China and Europe, 1600–1900." *Journal of Global History* 6: 309–319.

McLaughlin, J. L. 2001. *The Marzēaḥ in the Prophetic Literature: References and Allusion in Light of the Extra-biblical Evidence*. Leiden: Brill.

McLean, B. H. 1996. "The Place of Cult in Voluntary Associations and Christian Churches on Delos." In *Voluntary Associations in the Graeco-Roman World*, edited by Kloppenborg J. S. and S. G. Wilson, 186–225. London: Routledge.

Meyer, E. A. 2009. *Metics and the Athenian Phialai-Inscriptions: A Study in Athenian Epigraphy and Law*. Wiesbaden: F. Steiner Verlag.

Michailidis, G. 1947. "De la signification spéciale de certaines armes dans l'antiquité." *ASAE* 47: 47–75.

Migeotte, L. 1997. "Une souscription de femmes à Rhodes." *BCH* 117: 349–358.

Mili, M. 2015. *Religion and Society in Ancient Thessaly*. Oxford: Oxford University Press.

Millar, F. 1983. "The Phoenician Cities: A Case-Study of Hellenisation." *PCPhS* 29: 55–71.

Milojčić, V. and D. Theocharis, eds. 1976–87. *Demetrias*. 5 vols. Bonn: Rudolf Habelt.

Mitchel, F. W. 1973. "Lykurgan Athens: 338–322." In *Lectures in Memory of Louise Taft Semple, Second Series 1966–1971*, edited by C. G. Boulter et al., 163–214. University of Cincinnati Classical Studies 2. Norman: University of Oklahoma Press.

Moatti, C., ed. 2004. *La mobilité des personnes en Méditerranée de l'Antiquité à l'époque moderne: Procédures de contrôle et documents d'identification*. Rome: École Française de Rome.

Moatti, C. and W. Kaiser, eds. 2007. *Gens de passage en Méditerranée de l'Antiquité à l'époque moderne: Procédures de contrôle et d'identification*. Paris: Maisonneuve & Larose.

Moatti, C., W. Kaiser, and C. Pébarthe, eds. 2009. *Le monde d'itinérance en Méditerranée de l'Antiquité à l'époque moderne: Procédures de contrôle et d'identification*. Bordeaux: Ausonius.

Moch, L. P. 1992. *Moving Europeans: Migration in Western Europe since 1650*. Bloomington: Indiana University Press.

Moch, L. P. 2011. "From Regional to Global Repertoires of Migration." *Journal of Global History* 6: 321–325.

Moch, L. P. 2012. *The Pariahs of Yesterday: Breton Migrants in Paris*. Durham, NC: Duke University Press.

Morelli, D. 1956. "Gli stranieri in Rodi." *SCO* 5: 126–190.

Moriggi, M. 2011. "Phoenician and Punic Inscriptions in the Museo di Antichità di Torino (Turin, Italy)." *EVO* 34: 81–94.

Morris, S. P. 2019. "Close Encounters on Sicily: Molech, Meilichios, and Religious Convergence at Selinous." In *Religious Convergence in the Ancient Mediterranean*, edited by S. Blakely and B. J. Collins, 77–99. Atlanta: Lockwood Press.

Morstadt, B. 2015. *Die Phönizier: Geschichte einer rätselhaften Kulture*. Darmstadt: Philipp von Zabern.

Moscati, S. 1988a. "Stelae." In *The Phoenicians*, edited by S. Moscati, 364–379. New York: Abbeville Press.

Moscati, S., ed. 1988b. *The Phoenicians*. New York: Abbeville Press.

Mosley, D. J. 1972. "Diplomacy in Classical Greece." *AncSoc* 3: 1–16.

Moysey, R. A. 1976. "The Date of the Strato of Sidon Decree (*IG* II² 141)." *AJAH* 1: 182–189.

Mullen, A. 2013. *Southern Gaul and the Mediterranean: Multilingualism and Multiple Identies in the the Iron Age and Roman Periods*. Cambridge: Cambridge University Press.

Németh, G. 2001. "Metics in Athens." *Acta Ant. Hung.* 41: 331–348.

Nicolaou, I. 1971. *Cypriot Inscribed Stones*. Nicosia: Department of Antiquities.

Nicolaou, I. 1986. "Cypriots in the East and West. Foreigners in Cyprus (Archaic to Roman Period)." In *Acts of the International Archaeological Symposium "Cyprus between the Orient and the Occident." Nicosia, 8–14 September 1985*, edited by V. Karageorghis, 423–438. Nicosia: Department of Antiquities.

Nielsen, I. 2015. "The Architectural Context of Religious Groups on Delos." *Eretz-Israel: Archaeological, Historical and Geographical Studies* 31: 141–153.

Nigro, L., ed. 2004. *Mozia X: Quaderni di Archeologia fenicio-punica I*. Rome: Missione archeologica a Mozia.

Nijboer, A. J. 2013. "Banquet, *Marzeah*, *Symposion* and *Symposium* during the Iron Age: Disparity and Mimicry." In *Regionalism and Globalism in Antiquity: Exploring Their Limits*, edited by F. De Angelis, 95–125. Leuven: Peeters.

Niku, M. 2007. *The Official Status of the Foreign Residents in Athens, 322–120 B.C.* Helsinki: Foundation of the Finnish Institute at Athens.

Nyongesa, A. 2018. *Cultural Hybridity and Fixity: Strategies of Resistance in Migration Literatures*. Chitungwiza, Zimbabwe: Mwanaka Media and Publishing.

Oates, J. F. et al., eds. 2001. *Checklist of Editions of Greek, Latin, Demotic, and Coptic Papyri, Ostraca and Tablets*. 5th ed. Bulletin of the American Society of Papyrologists Supplement 9. Atlanta: American Society of Papyrologists.

O'Connor, D. 2003. "Egypt's View of 'Others.'" In *'Never Had the Like Occurred': Egypt's View of Its Past*, edited by J. Tait, 155–186. London: Routledge.

Ogden, D. 2008. "Bilistiche and the Prominence of Courtesans in the Ptolemaic Tradition." In *Ptolemy II Philadelphus and His World*, edited by P. McKechnie and Ph. Guillaume, 353–385. Menmosyne Supplements 300. Leiden: Brill.

Oliver, G. J. 2007. *War, Food, and Politics in Early Hellenistic Athens*. Oxford: Oxford University Press.

Oliver, G. J. 2010. "Foreign Names, Inter-marriage, and Citizenship in Hellenistic Athens." In *Onomatologos: Studies in Greek Personal Names Presented to Elaine Matthews*, edited by R. W. V. Catling and F. Marchand, 155–169. Oxford: Oxbow Books.

Osborne, M. 1981–83. *Naturalization in Athens*. 3 vols. Brussels: Paleis der Academiën.

Osborne, R. 2011. *The History Written on the Classical Greek Body*. Cambridge: Cambridge University Press.

Osborne, R. 2012. "Cultures as Languages and Languages as Cultures." In *Multilingualism in the Graeco-Roman World*, edited by A. Mullen and J. Patrick, 317–334. Cambridge: Cambridge University Press.

Paarmann, B. 2009. "L'évergétisme des étrangers à l'époque classique: Recherches sur la nature des services rendus et l'identité des bienfaiteurs." In *L'huile et l'argent: Actes du colloque tenu à Fribourg du 13 au 15 octobre 2005 publiés en l'honneur du Prof. Marcel Piérart à l'occasion de son 60ème anniversaire*, edited by O. Curty, 9–35. Paris: De Boccard.

Parker, R. 2002. "The Cult of Aphrodite Pandamos and Pontia at Cos." In *Kykeon: Studies in Honour of H. S. Versnel*, edited by H. F. J. Horstmanshoff et al., 143–160. Leiden: Brill.

Parker, R. 2017. *Greek Gods Abroad: Names, Natures, and Transformations*. Sather Classical Lectures. Oakland: University of California Press.

Parker, R., ed. 2019. *Changing Names: Tradition and Innovation in Ancient Greek Onomastics*. Proceedings of the British Academy 222. Oxford: Oxford University Press.

Parker, R. and D. Obbink. 2000. "Aus der Arbeit der 'Inscriptiones Graecae' VI: Sales of Priesthoods on Cos I." *Chiron* 30: 415–449.

Parker, R. and S. Scullion. 2016. "The Mysteries of the Goddess of Marmarini." *Kernos* 29: 209–266.

Paschidis, P. 2008. *Between City and King: Prosopographical Studies on the Intermediaries between the Cities of the Greek Mainland and the Aegean and the Royal Courts in the Hellenistic Period (322–190 BC)*. ΜΕΛΕΤΗΜΑΤΑ 59. Athens: Research Centre for Greek and Roman Antiquity; National Hellenic Research Foundation.

Patterson, C. 1981. *Pericles' Citizenship Law of 451–50 BC*. New York: Arno Press.

Paul, S. 2013. *Cultes et sanctuaires de l'île de Cos*. Kernos Supplement 28. Liège: Presses Universitaires de Liège.

Pečirka, J. 1966. *The Formula for the Grant of Enktesis in Attic Inscriptions*. Prague: Universita Karlova.

Peckham, J. B. 2014. *Phoenicia: Episodes and Anecdotes from the Ancient Mediterranean*. Winona Lake, IN: Eisenbrauns.

Pennacchietti, F. A. 2002. "Un termine latino nell'iscrizione punica *CIS* no 143? Una nuova congettura." In *La parola al testo: Scritti per Bice Mortara Garavelli*, edited by G. L. Beccaria and C. Marello, vol. 1, 303–312. Alessandria: Edizioni dell'Orso.

Perlman, S. 1958. "A Note on the Political Implications of Proxenia in the Fourth Century B.C." *CQ* 8: 185–191.

Pilkington, N. 2012. "A Note on Nora and the Nora Stone." *BASO* 365: 45–51.

Pirenne-Delforge, V. 1994. *L'Aphrodite grecque*. Kernos Supplement 4. Liège: Presses Universitaires de Liège.

Pitt, R. K. 2022. *Attic Inscriptions in UK Collections. British Museum: Funerary Monuments*. AIUK 4.6. Attic Inscriptions Online.

Pouilloux, J. 1973. "Salaminiens de Chypre à Délos." In *Études déliennes*, 399–413. BCH Supplement 1. Paris: École Françaises d'Athènes.

Pouilloux, J. 1975. "Athènes et Salamine de Chypre." *RDAC*: 111–121.

Pouilloux, J. 1976. "Chypriotes à Delphes." *RDAC*: 158–167.

Pouilloux, J. 1988. "Éntragers à Kition et Kitiens à l'étranger." *RDAC*: 95–99.

Préaux, C. 1958. "Les étrangers à l'époque hellénistique (Égypte-Délos-Rhodes)." *Recueils de la Société Jean Bodin* 9: 141–193.

Quinn, J. C. 2011. "The Cultures of the Tophet: Identification and Identity in the Phoenician Diaspora." In *Cultural Identity and the Peoples of the Ancient Mediterranean*, edited by E. S. Gruen, 388–413. Los Angeles: Getty Research Institute.

Quinn, J. C. 2013. "Tophets in the 'Punic World.'" In *The Tophet in the Phoenician Mediterranean*, edited by P. Xella, 23–48. Verona: Essedue.

Quinn, J. C. 2018. *In Search of the Phoenicians*. Princeton: Princeton University Press.

Quinn, J. C. and N. C. Vella, eds. 2014. *The Punic Mediterranean: Identities and Identification from Phoenician Settlement to Roman Rule*. Cambridge: Cambridge University Press.

Raptou, E. 2000. "La place des Chypriotes dans les villes grecques aux époques classique et hellénistique." In *Chypre et la Méditerranée orientale. Formations identitaires: perspectives historiques et enjeux contemporains. Actes du colloque tenu à Lyons, 1997, Université Lumière-Lyon 2, Université de Chypre*, edited by Y. Ioannou, F. Métral, and M. Yon, 19–31. Lyons: Maison de l'Orient et de la Méditerranée Jean Pouilloux.

Rauh, N. K. 1993. *The Sacred Bonds of Commerce: Religion, Economy, and Trade Society at Hellenistic Roman Delos, 166–87 B.C.* Amsterdam: J. C. Gieben.

Reed, C. M. 2003. *Maritime Traders in the Ancient Greek World*. Cambridge: Cambridge University Press.

Reger, G. 1994. *Regionalism and Change in the Economy of Independent Delos*. Berkeley: University of California.

Reger, G. 2003. "Aspects of the Role of Merchants in the Political Life of the Hellenistic World." In *Mercanti e politica nel monto antico*, edited by C. Zaccagnini, 165–198. Rome: "L'Erma" di Bretschneider.

Renan, E. 1880. "Inscription bilingue de Délos découverte par M. Homolle." *BCH* 4: 69–71.

Ribeiro Ferreira, J. 2004. "Próxeno e Proxenia." In *Nomos: Direito e sociedade na antiquidade clássica*, edited by D. F. Leão, L. Rossetti, and M. do Céu Fialho, 227–239. Coimbra: Imprensa da Universidade de Coimbra.

Ribichini, S. 1995. "Les Phéniciens à Rhodes face à la mythologie classique: Ruses, calembours et préeminence culturelle." In *Actes du IIIe congrès international des études phéniciennes et puniques, Tunis, 11–16 novembre 1991*, edited by M. H. Fantar and M. Ghaki, vol. 2, 341–347. Tunis: Institut National du Patrimoine.

Ribichini, S. 2009. "Eshmun-Asclepio. Divinità guaritrici in contesti fenici." In *Il culto di Asclepio nell'area mediterranea: Atti del Convegno Internazionale Agrigento 20–22 novembre 2005*, edited by E. De Miro, G. Sfameni Gasparro, and V. Calì, 201–217. Rome: Gangemi Editore.

Richey, M. 2019. "Inscriptions." In *The Oxford Handbook of the Phoenician and Punic Mediterranean*, edited by C. López-Ruiz and B. R. Doak, 223–240. Oxford: Oxford University Press.

Röllig, W. 1972. "Alte und neue phoenizische Inschriften aus dem ägäischen Raum." *Neue Ephemeris für Semitische Epigraphik* 1: 1–8.

Roppa, A. 2019. "Sardinia." In *The Oxford Handbook of the Phoenician and Punic Mediterranean*, edited by C. López-Ruiz and B. R. Doak, 521–536. Oxford: Oxford University Press.

Rovai, F. 2020. "Migration, Identity, and Multilingualism in Late Hellenistic Delos." In *Migration, Mobility and Language Contact in and around the Ancient Mediterranean*, edited by J. Clackson et al., 171–202. Cambridge: Cambridge University Press.

Rubinstein, L. 2009. "*Ateleia* Grants and Their Enforcement in the Classical and Early Hellenistic Periods." In *Greek History and Epigraphy: Essays in Honour of P.J. Rhodes*, edited by L. Mitchell and L. Rubinstein, 115–143. Swansea: Classical Press of Wales.

Ruby, P. 2006. "Peuples, fictions? Ethnicité, identité ethnique et sociétés anciennes." *REA* 108: 25–60.

Ruiz Cabrero, L. A. 2010. "La devoción de los navegantes: El culto de Astarté ericina en el Mediterráneo." In *La devozione dei naviganti: Il culto di Afrodite ericina nel Mediterraneo. Atti del convegno di Erice 27–28 novembre 2009*, edited by E. Acquaro, A. Filippi, and S. Medas, 97–135. Lugano: Athenaion.

Rutherford, I. 2013. *State Pilgrims and Sacred Observers in Ancient Greece: A Study of Theōriā and Theōroi*. Cambridge: Cambridge University Press.

Rutherford, I. 2016. "Pilgrimage in Greco-Roman Egypt: New Perspectives on Graffiti from the Memnonion at Abydos." In *Ancient Perspectives on Egypt*, edited by R. Matthews and C. Roemer, 171–189. London: Routledge.

Saba, S. 2020. *Isopoliteia in Hellenistic Times*. Leiden: Brill.

Saba, S. 2021. "Cittadinanza e archive nel Mediterraneo antico: Qualche postilla esegetica." *Historiká* 11: 83–94.

Sacco, G. 1980. "Sul alcuni etnici di stranieri in Rodi." In *RAL* 25: 517–528.

Sader, H. 1993. "Nouvelle inscription punique découverte au Liban." *Semitica* 41–42: 107–116.

Sader, H. 2019. *The History and Archaeology of Phoenicia*. Atlanta: SBL Press.

Sagona, C. 2002. *The Archaeology of Punic Malta*. Leuven: Peeters.

Sänger, P. 2013. "The *Politeuma* in the Hellenistic World (Third to First Century B.C.): A Form of Organization to Integrate Minorities." In *Migration und Integration— Wissenschaftliche Perspektiven aus Österreich*, edited by J. Dahlvik, C. Reinprecht, and W. Sievers, 51–68. Vienna: V & W unipress—Vienna University Press.

Savalli-Lestrade, I. 2012. "Collections de citoyennetés et internationalisation des élites civiques dans l'Asie Mineure hellénistique." In *Patrie d'origine et patries électives: Les citoyennetés multiples dans le monde grec d'époque romaine. Actes du colloque international de Tours, 6–7 novembre 2009*, edited by A. Heller and A.-V. Pont, 39–55. Bordeaux: Ausonius.

Schaefer, A. 1885. *Demosthenes und seine Zeit*. 2nd ed. Vol. 1. Leipzig: B. G. Teubner.

Schmitz, P. C. 2010. "The Phoenician Contingent in the Campaign of Psammetichus II against Kush." *Journal of Egyptian History* 3: 321–337.

Schmitz, P. C. 2012. *The Phoenician Diaspora: Epigraphic and Historical Studies*. Winona Lake, IN: Eisenbrauns.

Schuler, C. 2019. "Lycian, Persian, Greek, Roman: Chronological Layers and Structural Developments in the Onomastics of Lycia." In *Changing Names: Tradition and Innovation in Ancient Greek Onomastics*, edited by R. Parker, 195–216. Proceedings of the British Academy 222. Oxford: Oxford University Press.

Schweigert, E. 1940. "Greek Inscriptions." *Hesperia* 9: 309–357.

Segal, J. B. 1983. *Aramaic Texts from North Saqqâra with Some Fragments in Phoenician*. London: Egypt Exploration Society.

Shea, T. D. 2018. "Mapping Immigrant Communities through Their Tombstones in Archaic and Classical Athens." PhD Dissertation. Duke University.

Shoemaker, G. 1971. "Dionysius of Halicarnassus, *On Dinarchus*." *GRBS* 12: 393–409.

Siegelbaum, L. H. and L. P. Moch. 2014. *Broad Is My Native Land: Repertoires and Regimes of Migration in Russia's Twentieth Century*. Ithaca, NY: Cornell University Press.

Simms, R. R. 1988. "The Cult of the Thracian Goddess Bendis in Athens and Attica." *AncW* 18: 59–76.

Simms, R. R. 1989. "Isis in Classical Athens." *CJ* 84: 216–221.

Smith, S. T. 2003. *Wretched Kush: Ethnic Identities and Boundaries in Egypt's Nubian Empire*. London: Routledge.

Sommer, M. 2008. *Die Phönizier: Geschichte und Kultur*. Munich: C. H. Beck.

Sosin, J. D. 1999. "Tyrian *stationarii* at Puteoli." *Tyche* 14: 275–284.

Sosin, J. D. 2016. "A Metic Was a Metic." *Historia* 65: 2–13.

Stager, J. M. S. 2005. "'Let No One Wonder at This Image': A Phoenician Funerary Stele in Athens." *Hesperia* 74: 427–449.

Stählin, O. 1906. *Clemens Alexandrinus*. Vol 2, *Stromata Buch I–VI*. Christlichen Schriftsteller der Ersten Drei Jahrhunderte: Herausgeben von der Kirchenväter-Kommision der Königlich Preussischen Akademie der Wissenschaften. Leipzig: J. C. Hinrichs.

Stählin, F., E. Meyer, and A. Heidner. 1934. *Pagasai und Demetrias: Beschreibung der Reste und Stadtgeschichte*. Berlin: De Gruyter.

Stamatopoulou, M. 2008. "Ouaphres Horou, an Egyptian Priest of Isis from Demetrias." In *Essays in Classical Archaeology for Eleni Hatzivassiliou, 1977–2007*, edited by D. Kurtz, 249–257. Oxford: Beazley Archive and Archeopress.

Stamatopoulou, M. 2016. "The Banquet Motif on the Funerary Stelai from Demetrias." In *Dining and Death: Interdisciplinary Perspectives on the "Funerary Banquet" in Ancient Art, Burial and Belief*, edited by C. M. Draycott and M. Stamatopoulou, 405–479. Leuven: Peeters.

Stamatopoulou, M. 2018. "Demetrias: The Archaeology of a Cosmopolitan Macedonian Harbour." In Βορειοελλαδικά: *Tales from the Lands of the Ethne. Essays in Honour of Miltiades B. Hatzopoulos*, edited by M. Kalaitzi et al., 343–376. Meletemata 78. Athens: National Hellenic Research Foundation / Institute of Historical Research.

Stampolidis, N. C. 2003. "On the Phoenician Presence in the Aegean." In *Sea Routes . . . : Interconnections in the Mediterranean 16th–6th c. BC. Proceedings of the International Symposium Held at Rethymnon, Crete in September 29th–October 2nd, 2002*, edited by N. C. Stampolidis and V. Karageorghis, 217–232. Athens: Orion Press.

Stampolidis, N. C. 2019. "The Aegean." In *The Oxford Handbook of the Phoenician and Punic Mediterranean*, edited by C. López-Ruiz and B. R. Doak, 493–503. Oxford: Oxford University Press.

Stampolidis, N. C. and V. Karageorgis, eds. 2003. *Sea Routes . . . From Sidon to Huelva: Interconnections in the Mediterranean, 16th–6th Centuries BC*. Athens: Museum of Cycladic Art.

Stampolidis, N. C. and A. Kotsonas. 2006. "Phoenicians in Crete." In *Ancient Greece: From the Mycenaean Palaces to the Age of Homer*, edited by S. Deger-Jalkotzy and I. S. Lemos, 337–360. Edinburgh: Edinburgh University Press.

Starks, J. H., Jr. 1999. "*Fides Aeneia*: The Transference of Punic Stereotypes in the *Aeneid*." *CJ* 94: 255–283.

Steele, P. M. 2013. *A Linguistic History of Ancient Cyprus: The Non-Greek Languages, and their Relations with Greek, c. 1600–300 BC*. Cambridge: Cambridge University Press.

Steiner, R. C. 2011. *Early Northwest Semitic Serpent Spells in the Pyramid Texts*. Winona Lake, IN: Eisenbrauns.

Steinhauer, J. 2014. *Religious Associations in the Post-classical Polis*. Stuttgart: F. Steiner Verlag.

Steuernagel, D. 2020. "*Stationes* and Associations of Merchants at Puteoli and Delos." In *Roman Port Societies: The Evidence of Inscriptions*, edited by P. Arnaud and S. Keay, 63–84. Cambridge: Cambridge University Press.

Stucky, R. A. 1997. "Le bâtiment aux frises d'enfants du sanctuaire d'Echmoun à Sidon." *Topoi* 7: 915–927.

Stucky, R. A. 2005. *Das Eschmun-Heiligtum von Sidon: Architektur und Inschriften*. Basel: Vereinigung der Freunde Antiker Kunst.

Sznycer, M. 1975. "L' 'Assemblée du Peuple' dans les cités puniques d'après les témoignages épigraphiques." *Semitica* 25: 47–68.

Sznycer, M. 1980. "La partie phénicienne de l'inscription bilingue gréco-phénicienne de Cos." *AD* 35: 17–30.

Sznycer, M. 1999. "Retour à Cos: Nouvel examen de la partie phénicienne de la bilingue gréco-phénicienne." *Semitica* 49: 103–116.

Takács, S. A. 1995. *Isis and Sarapis in the Roman World*. Leiden: Brill.

Tang, B. 2005. *Delos, Carthage, Ampurias: The Housing of Three Mediterranean Trading Centres*. Rome: "L'Erma" di Bretschneider.

Teixidor, J. 1979. "Les fonctions de rab et de suffette en Phénicie." *Semitica* 29: 9–17.

Teixidor, J. 1980. "L'assemblée législative en Phénicie d'après les inscriptions." *Syria* 57: 453–464.

Teixidor, J. 1986. *Bulletin d'épigraphie sémitique (1964–1980)*. Paris: Librairie Orientaliste.

Tekoğlu, R. and A. Lemaire. 2000. "La bilingue royale louvito-phénicienne de Çineköy." *CRAI* 144: 961–1007.

Terpstra, T. 2013. *Trading Communities in the Roman World: A Micro-economic and Institutional Perspective*. Brill: Leiden.

Terpstra, T. 2019. *Trade in the Ancient Mediterranean: Private Order and Public Institutions*. Princeton: Princeton University Press.

Thompson, D. J. 2009. "The Multilingual Environment of Persian and Ptolemaic Egypt: Egyptian, Aramaic, and Greek Documentation." In *The Oxford Handbook of Papyrology*, edited by R. S. Bagnall, 395–417. Oxford: Oxford University Press.

Thompson, D. J. 2011. "Ethnic Minorities in Hellenistic Egypt." In *Political Culture in the Greek City after the Classical Age*, edited by O. M. van Nijf and R. Alston, 101–117. Leuven: Peeters.

Thompson, D. J. 2012. *Memphis under the Ptolemies*. 2nd ed. Princeton: Princeton University Press.

Thomsen, C. A. 2020. *The Politics of Association in Hellenistic Rhodes*. Edinburgh: Edinburgh University Press.

Tod, M. N. 1948. *A Selection of Greek Historical Inscriptions*. Vol. 2, *From 403 to 323 B.C.* Oxford: Clarendon Press.

Tréheux, J. 1992. *Inscriptions de Délos: Index*. Vol. 1, *Les étrangers à l'exclusion des Athéniens de la clérouchie et des Romains*. Paris: De Boccard.

Trevett, J. 1992. *Apollodoros the Son of Pasion*. Oxford: Clarendon Press.

Tribulato, O. 2013. "Phoenician Lions: The Funerary Stele of the Phoenician Shem/Antipatros." *Hesperia* 82: 459–486.

Tronchetti, C. and P. van Dommelen. 2005. "Entangled Objects and Hybrid Practices: Colonial Contacts and Elite Connections at Monte Prama, Sardinia." *JMA* 18: 183–209.

Trümper, M. 2002. "Das Sanktuarium des 'Établissement des Poseidoniastes de Bérytos' in Delos: Zur Baugeschichte eines griechischen Vereinsheiligtums." *BCH* 126: 265–330.

Trümper, M. 2006. "Negotiating Religious and Ethnic Identity: The Case of Clubhouses in Late Hellenistic Delos." In *Zwischen Kult und Gesellschaft: Kosmopolitische Zentren des antiken Mittelmeerraumes als Aktionsraum von Kultvereinen und Religionsgemeinschaften. Akten eines Symposiums des Archäologischen Instituts der Universität Hamburg (12.–14. Oktober 2005)*, edited by I. Nielsen, 113–140. Augsburg: Camelion.

Trümper, M. 2011. "Where the Non-Delians Met in Delos: The Meeting Places of Foreign Associations and Ethnic Communities in Late Hellenistic Delos." In *Political Culture in the Greek City after the Classical Age*, edited by O. M. van Nijf and R. Alston, 49–100. Leuven: Peeters.

Trümper, M. 2014. "The Honorific Practice of the 'Agora of the Italians' in Delos." In *Polis und Porträt: Standbilder als Medien der öffentlichen Repräsentation im hellenistischen Osten*, edited by J. Griesbach, 69–87. Wiesbaden: Reichert Verlag.

Tsetskhladze, G. R., ed. 1999. *Ancient Greeks West & East*. Mnemosyne Supplements 196. Leiden: Brill.

Tsetskhladze, G. R., ed. 2006. *Greek Colonisation: An Account of Greek Colonies and Other Settlements Overseas*. Vol. 1. Leiden: Brill.

Tsetskhladze, G. R., ed. 2008. *Greek Colonisation: An Account of Greek Colonies and Other Settlements Overseas*. Vol. 2. Leiden: Brill.

Ulbrich, A. 2008. *Kypris: Heiligtümern und Kulte weiblicher Gottheiten auf Zypern in der kyproarchaischen und kyproklassichen Epoche (Königszeit)*. Münster: Ugarit-Verlag.

Van Dijk, H. J. 1968. *Ezekiel's Prophecy on Tyre*. Biblica et Orientalia 20. Rome: Pontifical Biblical Institute.

Van Dommelen, P. 2006. "The Orientalizing Phenomenon: Hybridity and Material Culture in the Western Mediterranean." In *Debating Orientalization: Multidisciplinary Approaches to Change in the Ancient Mediterranean*, edited by C. Riva and N. C. Vella, 135–152. London: Equinox.

Van Dommelen, P. and C. Gómez Bellard. 2008. *Rural Landscapes of the Punic World*. London: Equinox.

Van Dommelen, P. and A. Roppa, eds. 2014. *Materiali e contesti dell'età del Ferro sarda. Atti della giornata di studio, 25 maggio 2012, San Vero Milis (OR)*. RStudFen 41. Rome: Fabrizio Serra Editore.

Van Gelder, M. 2013. "Favouring Foreign Traders? The Venetian Republic and the Accommodation of Netherlandish Merchants in the Late 16th and 17th Centuries." In *Migration and Membership Regimes in Global and Historical Perspective: An Introduction*, edited by U. Bosma, G. Kessler, and L. Lucassen, 141–166. Leiden: Brill.

Van Lottum, J. 2011. "Some Considerations about the Link between Economic Development and Migration." *Journal of Global History* 6: 339–344.

Van Wees, H. 2011. "Demetrius and Draco: Athens' Property Classes and Population in and before 317 BC." *JHS* 131: 95–114.

Vattioni, F. 1979. "Antroponimi fenicio-punici nell'epigrafia greca e Latina del Nordafrica." *AION(archeol)* 1: 153–191.

Vattioni, F. 1982. "I Fenici in Tessalia." *AION(filol)* 42: 71–81.

Vella, N. C. and M. Anastasi. 2019. "Malta and Gozo." In *The Oxford Handbook of the Phoenician and Punic Mediterranean*, edited by C. López-Ruiz and B. R. Doak, 553–568. Oxford: Oxford University Press.

Venticinque, P. F. 2016. *Honor among Thieves: Craftsmen, Merchants, and Associations in Roman and Late Roman Egypt*. Ann Arbor: University of Michigan Press.

Verboven, K. 2011. "Resident Aliens and Translocal Merchant *Collegia* in the Roman Empire." In *Frontiers in the Roman World: Proceedings of the Ninth Workshop of the International Network Impact of Empire (Durham, 16–19 April 2009)*, edited by T. Kaizer and O. Hekster, 335–348. Leiden: Brill.

Vestergaard, T. 2000. "Milesian Immigrants in Late Hellenistic and Roman Athens." In *The Epigraphy of Death: Studies in the History and Society of Greece and Rome*, edited by G. J. Oliver, 81–109. Liverpool: Liverpool University Press.

Vidman, L. 1970. *Isis und Sarapis bei den Griechen und Römern: Epigraphische Studie zur Verbreitung und zu den Trägern des ägyptischen Kultes*. Berlin: De Gruyter.

Vikela, E. 1994. *Die Weihreliefs aus dem athener Pankrates-Heiligtum am Ilissos: Religionsgeschichtliche Bedeutung und Typologie*. Berlin: G. Mann.

Vittmann, G. 2003. *Ägypten und die Fremden im ersten vorchristlichen Jahrtausend*. Kulturgeschichte der Antiken Welt 97. Mainz: Philipp von Zabern.

Von Bomhard, A.-S. 2012. *The Decree of Saïs: The Stelae of Thonis-Heracleion and Naukratis*. Oxford Centre for Maritime Archaeology 7. Oxford: Oxford Centre for Maritime Archaeology.

Vondeling, J. 1961. *Eranos*. Groningen: J. B. Wolters.

Walbank, M. B. 1978. *Athenian Proxenies of the Fifth Century B.C.* Toronto: Samuel Stevens.

Walbank, M. B. 1985. "Athens, Carthage and Tyre (*IG* ii² 342+)." *ZPE* 59: 107–111.

Wallace, M. B. 1970. "Early Greek *Proxenoi*." *Phoenix* 24: 189–208.

Wallensten, J. 2014. "Dedications to Double Deities: Syncretism or Simply Syntax?" *Kernos* 27: 159–176.

Walsh, J. J. 2000. "The Disorders of the 170s B.C. and Roman Intervention in the Class Struggle in Greece." *CQ* 50: 300–303.

Waltz, K. N. 1979. *Theory of International Politics*. Long Grove, IL: Waveland Press.

Warner, W. L. and P. S. Lunt. 1941. *The Social Life of a Modern Community*. New Haven: Yale University Press.

Warren, J. 2002. *Epicurus and Democritean Ethics: An Archaeology of Ataraxia*. Cambridge: Cambridge University Press.

Watson, J. 2010. "The Origin of Metic Status at Athens." *Cambridge Classical Journal* 56: 259–278.

Wendt, A. 1999. *Social Theory of International Politics*. Cambridge: Cambridge University Press.

Whitehead, D. 1977. *The Ideology of the Athenian Metic*. Cambridge: Cambridge Philological Society.

Whitehead, D. 1986. *The Demes of Attica, 508/7–ca. 250 B.C.: A Political and Social Study*. Princeton: Princeton University Press.

Whitehead, D. 2019. *Xenophon: Poroi (Revenue-Sources)*. Clarendon Ancient History Series. Oxford: Oxford University Press.

Wijma, S. M. 2014. *Embracing the Immigrant: The Participation of Metics in Athenian Polis Religion (5th–4th Century BC)*. Historia-Einzelschriften 233. Stuttgart: F. Steiner Verlag.

Wilhelm, A. 1900. "Nachlese zu griechischen Inschriften." *JÖAI* 3: 40–62.

Will, W. 1983. *Athen und Alexander: Untersuchungen zur Geschichte der Stadt von 338 bis 322 v. Chr*. Munich: C. H. Beck.

Winter, I. J. 1995. "Homer's Phoenicians: History, Ethnography, or Literary Trope? [A Perspective on Early Orientalism]." In *The Ages of Homer: A Tribute to*

Emily Townsend Vermeule, edited by J. B. Carter and S. P. Morris, 247–271. Austin: University of Texas Press.

Wolters, C. 1979. "Recherches sur les stèles funéraires hellénistiques de Thessalie." In *La Thessalie: Actes de la Table-Ronde 21–24 juillet 1975, Lyon*, edited by B. Helly, 81–110. Lyon: Maison de l'Orient et de la Méditerranée Jean Pouilloux.

Woolmer, M. 2017. *A Short History of the Phoenicians*. London: I. B. Tauris.

Xagorari-Gleisner, M. 2009. "Attische bilingue Grabreliefs des 4. Jhs. v. Chr." *AA* 2009: 113–127.

Xella, P. 2008. "I Fenici e gli 'Altri': Dinamiche di identità culturale." In *Greci e Punici in Sicilia tra V e IV secolo a.C.*, edited by M. Congiu et al., 69–79. Caltanissetta: Sciascia.

Xella, P. 2010. "Tra Cartagine e Cos (Materiali per il lessico fenicio—V)." *Semitica et Classica* 3: 85–95.

Xella, P. 2013a. "'Tophet': An Overall Interpretation." In *The Tophet in the Phoenician Mediterranean*, edited by P. Xella, 259–281. Verona: Essedue.

Xella, P., ed. 2013b. *The Tophet in the Phoenician Mediterranean*. Verona: Essedue.

Xella, P. and J. Á. Zamora. 2007. "The Phoenician Data Bank: The International Project *Corpus Inscriptionum Phoenicarum necnon Punicarum*." *UF* 39: 773–790.

Yakubovich, I. 2015. "Phoenician and Luwian in Early Iron Age Cilicia." *AS* 65: 35–53.

Yon, J.-B. 2011. "Les Tyriens dans le monde méditerranéen à l'époque hellénistique." In *Sources de l'histoire de Tyr: Textes de l'Antiquité et du Moyen Âge*, edited by P.-L. Gatier, J. Aliquot, and L. Nordiguian, 33–61. Beirut: Presses de l'Université Saint-Joseph and Presses de l'Ifpo.

Zamora, J. Á. 2007. "The Inscription from the First Year of King Bodashtart of Sidon's Reign: *CIS* I, 4." *Orientalia* 76: 100–113.

Zelnick-Abramovitz, R. 2004. "The Proxenoi of Western Greece." *ZPE* 147: 93–106.

Zernecke, A. E. 2013. "The Lady of the Titles: The Lady of Byblos and the Search for Her 'True Name.'" *WO* 43: 226–242.

Ziebarth, E. 1932–33. "Neue Beiträge zum griechischen Seehandel." *Klio* 26: 231–247.

Zuckerman, C. 1985–88. "Hellenistic *Politeumata* and the Jews. A Reconsideration." *SCI* 8–9: 171–185.

Index

For the benefit of digital users, indexed terms that span two pages (e.g., 52–53) may, on occasion, appear on only one of those pages.

Figures are indicated by *f* following the page number

Abdalonym, king of Sidon, 73–75, 83–84n.34, *See also* Diotimos, son of Abdalonymos
Abdashtart I, king of Sidon, 54–55, 70–71, 73–75, 108–11, 109*f*
Abdashtart II, king of Sidon, 77–78
Abibaal, king of Byblos, 133–34
Abu Simbel, 134–36n.48, 142–43n.64
Abydos, 43n.74, 142–43
Academy, Plato of, 1–2, 30–32
Acropolis, Athens of, 56, 92–93
Agora of the Italians, 88–90. *See also* Apolloniastai, Competaliastai, Hermaistai
Ahiram, king of Byblos, 133–34
Alexander the Great, 12–13, 75n.10, 80–82, 83–84n.34, 104–6, 120–21, 124n.10, 126n.14
Antipatros son of Aphrodisios. *See* Shem—— son of Abdashtart
Aphrodite. *See also* Astarte; Isis; Kition; trade associations: Kitian in Athens
  Ourania, 88–89
  patron deity of navigation, 73–75

  temple of on Kos, 73–77
  temple of in Peiraieus, 50, 58–59
  translation into Astarte, 24–25, 58–59, 73–77, 75n.12, 88–89, 89n.48, 140–41, 144n.66
  translation into Isis, 75n.12, 89n.48, 140–41
Apollo, 66–67, 77–78, 88–89, 101–2
Apollodoros (son of Pasion), 22n.18, 117, 118–19. *See also* Pasion; Phormio
Apolloniastai, 53n.5, 67n.38, 88–89. *See also* Agora of the Italians; Hermaistai; Competaliastai
Apollonides, son of Demetrios, 55–57, 61–62, 67–68, 104–8
Apses, 73n.7, 104–8. *See also* Hieron
Aradians
  in Athens, 44–45
  in Carthage, 126
  in Iasos, 117–18
  on Delos, 53n.5, 114n.67
  on Rhodes, 46–47, 103–4
Arados, 7–8, 17–19, 20, 41–42, 46–47, 81–82, 116
Arkeophon, 29, 94n.4

Artemis, 30–32, 47, 101–2, 141
Ashkelon, 7–8, 9, 16–19, 20, 35–36, 41–42, 59n.19, 88–90, 126–27
Ashkelonites. *See also* Shem—— son of Abdashtart
   in Athens, 44–45, 126–27
   on Delos, 88–90, 101, 113–14
   in Egypt, 145n.68
Asia Minor, 71–72, 73, 80–81, 114–16
Asklepios. *See also* Eshmoun
   temple of on Kos, 75–77, 114–16
   Merre, 151–52
   translation into Aesculapius, 151–53
   translation into Eshmoun, 25–27, 151–53
asphaleia (security), 95, 103–4, 114–16. *See also* awards; award-giving, system of
associations. *See* professional associations; religious associations; Rhodes: private associations; trade associations
Assyria, 7–8, 13–14
Assyrians, 133–34
Astarte, 24–25, 120–21, 147–48nn.76–77, *See also* Aphrodite; Isis
   in Athens, 42–44, 58–59
   on Delos, 65–66, 88–89
   in Egypt, 120–21
   on Kos, 73–77
   Palestinian, 88–89
   patron of navigation, 73–75
   on Rhodes, 42–44
   temple and priests of in Memphis, 144–45
   translation into Aphrodite, 24–25, 58–59, 73–77, 75n.12, 88–89, 89n.48, 140–41, 144n.66
   translation into Isis, 75n.12, 89n.48, 140–41
asylia (personal and property inviolability), 73, 95, 103–4, 111–12, 114–16. *See also* awards; award-giving, system of

ateleia (tax exemptions), 95, 103–4, 112–14, 117–18. *See also* awards; award-giving, system of
Athena, 46–47, 101–2
Athenians, 18n.5, 37, 44–45, 54–56, 57–58, 66, 70, 71–72, 85–86, 92–93, 96–98, 100–1, 105–6n.38, 108–11, 117
Athens. *See also* Academy, Plato of; Acropolis, Athens of; funerary art: Attic; Lykourgos; Peiraieus; professional associations; religious associations; trade associations; traders
   administrator of Delos, 52–53, 61–63, 65–67, 82–83, 113–14
   award grants to foreigners, 54–58, 70–72, 80–81, 92–95, 98–99, 102–3, 106–11, 112–13, 114–16, 117
   bilingual texts in, 11–12, 17, 25–27, 28, 30–32, 33–34, 42–44, 83–85
   citizenship laws of, 21, 96–97, 116–17
   foreign policy of, 104–11
   grain shortages in, 92–94, 104–6, 111–12
   hegemony of, 21–22, 96–97
   immigrants in, 4–6, 17–20, 30, 35–36, 39–41, 44–45, 47–48, 50, 58–60, 70, 100–1
   intermarriage, 21, 39–41, 47
   legal categories of immigration, 4–6, 21–22, 116–17
   non-Greek gods in, 42–44, 59–60
   Phoenician immigrants in, 1–2, 15–20, 30, 32–33, 37, 54–55, 70, 78–80, 85–86, 111, 126–27
   Phoenician philosophers in, 1–2, 3–4
   Phoenician trade associations in, 50–54, 60–62, 67–69, 86–87, 144–46
   state revenues of, 22–23, 57–58, 96–97
   views of foreigners and immigrants, 22–23, 97–99, 106–8, 135–36

Index

awards
  honorific (see *euergesia*; commendation; *eunoia*; proxenia)
  legal (see *ateleia*; *isoteleia*; *asphaleia*; *asylia*; *enktesis*; neutrality; *proedria*; *prodikia*; *prosodos*; *promanteia*; right to sail in and out of ports; residency; citizenship)
  monetized (*see* gold wreath; laurel wreath)
award-giving, system of, 95–96, 99–100, 101–2
  inequalities of, 118–19
  local variations, 112–14
  to promote migration, 22–23, 57–58, 95–97, 98–101, 102–16, 158
  to establish diplomatic relations, 104–6, 118–19

Baal, 83–85, 88–89. See also Poseidon
  in Athens, 42–44, 59–60, 85–86
  Berytos, patron deity of, 52–53, 63–66
  Hammon, 127–32, 131f, 146–47
  Saphon, 136–37
bankers, 9, 29n.38, 53–54, 63–64n.31, 88–90, 117. *See also* Apollodoros; Pasion; Phormio; professional associations: of bankers
Bendis, 51–52, 59–60
benefaction. See *euergesia*
benefactor. See *euergetes*
Berytians, 44–45, 65–67, 82–85. *See also* Poseidoniastai
  building of, on Delos, 63–68
Berytos, 7–8, 9, 116–17
  trade associations of, 52–53, 63–68, 82–83
Bes, 133–34, 142–43
Bible, 7–8, 130–32
bilingualism, 32–33, 126–27

bilingual texts, 9–11
  Phoenician and Egyptian, 121–22, 121f, 137–40, 145–46
  Phoenician and Greek, 16f, 17, 20, 23, 25–27, 26f, 28, 30–32, 32f, 33–34, 39f, 40f, 42–44, 52n.4, 72–75, 74f, 77–78, 78f, 83–85, 146–47, 150–52
Black Sea Region, 78–80, 94, 114–16
Boiotia, 98–99, 111–12
Boiotians, 114–16
Byblians, 8–9, 81–82
Byblos, 7–8, 9, 81–82, 130–34. See also Ahiram; Abibaal; Elibaal; Yehimilk
Byzantion, 39–41, 94

Campania, 87–88, 89–90
Canaanites, 7–8, 122
Carthage, 2–3, 7–8, 9, 11–12, 30–32, 42–44, 104–6, 122–32. *See also* Punic dialect; Punic texts; Punic Mediterranean; Punic Wars; Rome; Romans; tophet
  foundation of, 122–24
  hegemony of, 122–24, 130–32, 146–47
  immigrants in, 124–25, 127–28
  Phoenician immigrants in, 125–32, 133–34, 143–44, 150–51, 155–56, 157
  political constitution of, 80–81, 81n.26, 86–87
  sanctuary of Tanit and Baal Hammon, 127–32
  senate of, 71–72, 124–25
  slave trade, 128–29
  views of foreigners and immigrants, 71–72, 124–26
Carthaginians, 9–11, 71–72, 80–81, 114–16, 122–25, 126–27, 128–32, 157. *See also* Dido; Hannibal; Iomilchos
Chaironeia, battle of, 58n.16, 104–6
child sacrifice, 127–28
choregeia, 55–56, 111

Index

citizenship, 21, 22–23, 49, 95–96, 97–98, 111, 158. *See also* Perikles; residency; spectrum of participatory membership in a political community
   awards of, 73, 89–90, 96–97, 98–99, 107–8, 116, 117–19 (*see also* awards; award-giving, system of)
   blurring boundaries of, 4, 70–71, 95, 122
   erosion of notion of, 97–98
   fluidity of notion of, 89–90
   home state's influence over, 70–78, 82, 91, 111
   laws of, 21, 96–97
   switch, 89–90
commendation, 62–63, 107–8. *See also* awards; award-giving, system of
commercial trials, 57–58
Competaliastai, 67n.38, 88–89
cosmopolitanism, 118–19, 121–22, 125–26, 132–33, 140–41, 152–53, 155–56, 157. *See also* migration
Crete, 114–16
customs. *See also* name changing
   funerary, Phoenician, 30–32, 33–34, 35–41, 126–27
   identification with long genealogies, 30–33, 42–44, 82–83, 120–21, 126–27, 143, 150–51, 153–55
   local, adoption of, 6–7, 23, 30–33, 37–39, 41–42, 49, 63–65
   religious, maintenance of, 42–44, 51–52, 58–63, 66–67, 68–69, 82, 83–85, 124, 145–46, 157–58
Cyprus, 1–2, 7–8, 11n.30, 29, 32–33, 42–44, 94, 104–6, 126–27, 130–33. *See also* Kitians; Kition; Salamis

Delians, 101–2

Delos, 11–12, 44–45, 53–54, 87–88, 98–99, 108–11. *See also* Agora of the Italians; Apolloniastai; bankers; Berytians; Competaliastai; Herakleistai; Hermaistai; Poseidoniastai; professional associations; trade associations; traders
   bilingual texts from, 77–78, 78*f*
   free port of, 52–53, 61–62, 65–66, 113–14
   granting awards, 101–3, 107–8, 112–14
   patron god of, 66–67
   Phoenician dedications on, 77–78, 80–82, 88–90, 101–2, 141
   Phoenician trade associations on, 50–54, 56n.12, 59n.19, 61–65, 66–69, 82–87, 144–45
   temple inventories of, 80–82
Delphi, 47–48, 98–99, 101, 102–3, 112–14
Demetrias, 11–12, 23, 37–38, 41–42, 49, 126–27. *See also* funerary stelae
   bilingual texts in, 17, 25–27, 30–32
   foundation of, 19–20, 80–81
   intermarriage in, 47, 80–81
   Phoenicians in, 17–19, 28, 30
   Phoenician gods in, 42–44
Demetrios Poliorketes, 19–20, 80–81, 107–8
Demosthenes, 97–98, 102–3
Dido, 122–24
dikai emporikai. *See* commercial trials
Dionysus, 51–52, 150–51
Diotimos, son of Abdalonymos, 73–77
diplomacy, 2, 57–58, 62–63, 68–69, 70–71, 72–73, 77–78, 80–81, 94, 122–24
   award-giving system as tool of, 95, 98–99, 101–4, 108–11, 118–19
   through religious acts, 77–80, 81–82, 91

Domseleh son of Domhano, 24–25, 33–34, 35–36

Egypt, 2–3, 7–8, 38–39, 43n.74, 43–44n.75, 61–62, 80–81, 120–21, 132–48, 155–56. *See also* Isis; Harpokrates; Horus; Memphis; Osiris; Serapis
   art of, 133–34, 135–36
   bilingual texts in, 9–11, 120–22, 137–40, 145–46
   language of, 143
   Phoenician gods in, 136–37
   Phoenician immigrants in, 8–9, 30–32, 121–22, 132–46
   Phoenician texts in, 9–12, 134–35, 142–43
   views of foreigners and immigrants, 135–36, 144–46
Egyptians, 43–44nn.74–75, 132–33, 134–37, 142–43, 155–56, 157
   in Carthage, 128–29
   in Greek communities, 17–20, 50, 60n.23
Eirene of Byzantion, 39–41, 39*f*
eisphora (capital taxes), 54–55, 70, 94, 95, 111–12
Elephantine, 134–35
Elibaal, king of Byblos, 133–34
enktesis (the right to own property), 56, 57–58, 73, 94, 95, 96–97, 101, 103–6, 111–12, 113–14. *See also* awards; award-giving, system of
   to build sanctuaries, 33, 50, 58–60, 61–62, 63–65
enslaved persons, 2, 9, 21–22n.16, 68n.41, 95–96n.7, 97–98, 117, 128–29. *See also* slavery
ephebeia, 44–45
epidamia, 116–17

epidamoi, 21–22
eranoi, 51–52
Eshmoun, 25–27, 33–34, 65n.33, 73–77. *See also* Asklepios
   translation into Asklepios, 25–27, 75–77, 152–53
Eshmounazor II, king of Sidon, 133–34
ethnicity, 8–9n.26, 41–42, 44–45, 52–53, 122, 125–26, 135–37, 143–44. *See also* identity
   Phoenician, 3–4, 8–9, 12–13, 28–29, 144–46
euergesia (benefaction), 45–46, 62–63, 70, 72–73, 75–77, 82–86, 88–89, 91, 95, 96–97, 100–2, 103–6, 112n.58, 116, 117–18. *See also* awards; award-giving, system of
euergetes (benefactor), 45–46, 47, 56, 66, 82–85, 94, 96–97, 99–100, 101–2, 107–8, 117–18
eunoia, 99–100. *See also* awards; award-giving, system of
Euxitheus, 97–98

funerary art. *See also* customs: funerary; funerary stelae
   Attic, 15, 37–39, 126–27
   Phoenician, 37–39, 41–42, 126–27, 133–34
funerary stelae. *See also* funerary art; customs: funerary
   bilingual (Phoenician and Greek), 16*f*, 17, 20, 23, 25–27, 26*f*, 28, 30–32, 32*f*, 34, 35*f*, 39*f*, 40*f*, 42–44, 130–32, 145–46
   naiskos, 37–41
   painted stelae, 19–20, 37–38, 41–42
   reuse of, 33
   shaft stelae, 37–38, 126–27

gods, foreign
  adoption of by Phoenicians, 66, 120–21, 128–29, 133–34, 136–41, 158
  worship of in Athens, 42–44, 59–60
  worship of in Demetrias, 42–44
  worship of in Egypt, 136–37
gold wreath, 3–4, 56, 57–58, 62–63, 71–72, 80–81, 85–86, 94, 95, 99–103, 104–6, 107–8
grain shortages, 56–58, 92–93, 104–6, 111–12

Hannibal, 124–25
Harpokrates, 137–41, 138*f*, 139*f*
Heliopolis, 142–43
Hellenization, 12–13, 81n.26
Herakleides of Salamis, 26n.29, 92–97, 93*f*, 98–101, 104–6, 107–8, 114–16
Herakleistai, 52–53, 61–63, 66–68, 85–87
Herakles, 37, 47, 52n.3, 61–63, 86–87. See also Melqart
  translation into Melqart, 25–27, 61–62, 150–51
Hermaistai, 53n.5, 67n.38, 88–89. See also Agora of the Italians; Apolloniastai; Competaliastai; professional associations; trade associations
Herodotus, 134–36, 144–45
hiera naus (sacred ship), 35–36, 78–80
Hieron, 73n.7, 104–6, 107–8. See also Apses
hieronautai, 77–80, 78*f*
Horus, 120–21, 137–41
hospitium, 153–55

Iasos, 116, 117–18
Iberia, 7–8, 11n.30, 13–14, 147n.73
identity, 8–9, 8–9n.26, 28, 38–39, 49, 82, 88–89, 157. See also ethnicity
  civic, 3–4, 8–9, 33–34, 44–45, 47–48, 58–59, 61–62, 68–69, 78–80, 82, 83–85, 91, 126, 145–46
  hybrid, 30, 37–38, 121–22, 126, 144–46, 155–56
  immigrant, 2–3, 33–34, 49, 126–27, 130–32, 137–40, 155–56, 159
  linguistic, 17, 39–41, 140–41
intermarriage, 21, 39–42, 44–46, 47, 137–40
inviolability. See *asylia*
Iomilchos, king of Carthage, 80–81. See also Carthage; Carthaginians; Philokles, king of Sidon
Isis, 43–44n.75, 78–80, 120–22, 128–29, 136–37, 140–41, 144n.65, See also Aphrodite; Astarte
  Athens in, 50, 59–60
  hymn to, 141
  translation into Aphrodite and Astarte, 75n.12, 89n.48, 140–41
isoteleia (equality in taxation), 95, 96–97, 103–4, 111–12. See also awards; award-giving, system of
Israel, 7–8, 16–17
Italy, 87–88, 89–90, 104–6

Jews, 9
  name changing in modern periods, 24
  politeumata of, 61–62

Kadmos, 3–4
Karians, 142–45
Keos, 117–18
Kitians, 11n.30, See also Zeno, Kition of
  in Athens, 25–27, 32–33, 37–38, 44–45
  in Carthage, 126–27, 130–32
  demos of, 61–62, 67–68
  in Egypt, 142–43
  on Rhodes, 32–33
  trade association of, 50, 51*f*, 58–63, 67–68
Kition, 1–2, 3–4, 7–8, 9, 17–19, 20, 25–27, 28, 30–32, 42–43n.72, 50, 127–28, 130–32, 143–44. See also professional associations; trade associations

Astarte/Aphrodite in, 58–59
bilingualism, 32–33, 58–59, 126–27
koinon, 67–68, 78–80, 83–85, 84f, 86–87
Kos, 11–12, 57–58n.14, 73–77, 104–6, 114–16
Krates, 1–2, 3–4

Laodikeia, 7–8. *See also* Berytos; Berytians
Laodikeians, 45–46. *See also* Berytos; Berytians
laurel wreath, 80–81, 101–2, 113–14
Lebanon, 7–8, 16–17
Leto, 101–2, 141
Libyans, 122–24, 128–29
Lindos, 46–48, 103–4
Livy, 71–72, 124–25
Lykians, 141, 142–43
Lykourgos, 20n.12, 57–58, 97n.12

Macedon, 19–20, 58n.16, 80–81, 104–6
Macedonians, 7–8, 104–6. *See also* Alexander the Great, Demetrios Poliorketes
Malta, 2–3, 7–8, 11–12, 122, 127–28, 133–34, 140–41, 146–51, 155–56
marzeaḥ, 41–42, 83–85
material culture, bicultural, 6–7, 9–11, 35–36, 38–42, 85–86, 121–22. *See also* funerary art; funerary stelae
matroxenoi, 5n.15, 21–22
Meleager (of Gadara), 157
Melqart, 25–27, 53–54, 60n.22, *See also* Herakles
  patron deity and founder of Tyre, 61–62, 124, 150–51
  translation into Herakles, 25–27, 61–62, 150–51
Memnonion, 142–43
Memphis, 120–21, 135–41, 142–43, 145–46, 155–56. *See also* Egypt; Naukratis
  ethnic quarters of, 134–35, 143–45
mercenaries, 9, 124–25, 134–36, 142–43

metics, 4–6, 17–19, 21–22, 95–98, 111–12, 116–17. *See also metoikion*
  introduction of, 21–22
  limitations of, 21–22, 44–45
  obligations of, 21–22, 111
metoikion, 4–6, 21–22, 54–55, 70, 111, 116–17
migrants. *See also* customs; metics; migration
  attitudes towards, 11–12, 21, 44–45 (*see also* Athens; Carthage; Egypt; stereotypes)
  exclusion of by host state, 6–7, 44–45, 145–46
  inclusion of by host state, 6–7, 23, 44–45, 49, 96–97, 111–12, 116, 118–19, 127–28
  influences of on host states, 2, 4, 14, 42–44, 45–46, 49, 50, 56, 68–69, 136–37, 155–56, 157–58
  integration into host society initiated by migrants, 4, 9–11, 14, 23, 24–25, 30, 37, 44–45, 53–54, 65–66, 89–90, 147–48, 158
  participation in political community of host society, 44–47, 49, 61–62, 68–69, 157–58
  repertoires and adaptive strategies of, 2–3, 4, 6–7, 9–11, 23, 24–25, 29, 33, 44–45, 49, 53–54, 62–63, 68–69, 120–22, 136–40, 147–48, 155–56, 157–58
  sense of belonging in host-society, 2–3, 9–11, 16–17, 23, 29, 44–45, 89–90, 111–12, 116, 145–46, 147–48n.75, 153–55, 157, 158
migration. *See also* migrants
  effects on religious practices, 25–27, 73–75, 136–37, 147–51, 155–56
  Greek terminology of, 5–6n.17
  leading to cosmopolitanism, 118–19, 121–22, 125–26, 132–33, 140–41, 146–47, 152–55, 157, 159

migration (*cont.*)
  and membership regimes, 2–3, 6–7, 14, 21–23, 44–45, 53–54, 95, 98–99, 102–3, 118–19, 121–22, 125–26, 143–44
  promotion by migrants, 68–69
  promotion by home state, 81–82
  promotion by host state, 57–58, 95, 96–99, 100–1, 102–16, 158
  regulation by home state, 14, 71–72, 73, 91
  regulation by host state, 54–55, 95–99, 135–36, 158
military service, 94, 95, 96–97
Mithridates, 19–20
Moscati, Sabatino, 13–14
Mysia, 71–72

name changing, 6–7, 23, 24–44, 85–86, 120–22, 136–37
  adoption of Greek names, 24–25, 27–28, 45
  common Greek names of Phoenicians, 25–28, 56, 82–83, 88–89, 101n.21
  Hellenization of Phoenician names, 3n.5, 24–25, 28, 30–32, 33–34, 46–47, 53n.5, 73–75, 73n.7, 80n.23, 82–83, 114–16, 153–55
  in modern periods, 24
  translation of Phoenician names, 27–28, 30–33, 82–86, 150–51
Naples, 87–88, 89–90
Naukratis, 54n.8, 135–36
Neaira, 97–98
Neapolis. *See* Naples
Nergal, 33–34, 42–44, 59–60
neutrality, 114–16. *See also* awards; award-giving, system of
Nile, 120–21, 134–36
North Africa, 7–8, 130–32

Old Oligarch, 97–98

orgeones, 51–52, 60n.23
Orontes, 71–72
Oropos, 98–99, 102–3, 111–12
Osiris, 120–22, 142–43, 150–51

Paalashtart, 120–22, 121*f*, 136–41, 143n.64
Pasion, 29n.38, 117, 118–19. *See also* Apollodoros; Phormio
Peiraieus, 1–2, 17, 39–41, 42–44, 50, 83–85, 117
Peloponnesian War, 17–19, 21, 117
Perikles, 21
Persian king, 54–55, 70, 108–11
Persians, 9, 153–55
philotimia, 92–93, 99–100
Philokles, king of Sidon, 80–82, 83–84n.34, 101–3, 107–8
Phoenician language, 12–13, 17, 23, 29, 142–43, 145n.68, 147–48, 155–56. *See also* identity
Phoenician priests, 33–34, 42–44, 144–45, 147–48n.75
Phoenician script, 9–11, 23, 29, 120–21, 145–46, 147n.74
phoenix, 124
Phoinikoaigyptioi, 144–45
Phormio, 29n.38, *See also* Apollodoros; Pasion
pilgrimage, 124, 142–43. See also *theoria*
pilgrims, 78–80, 142–43. See also *theoroi*
politeuma, 61–62. *See also* Jews
Polybius, 124–25
Poseidon, 60n.22, 63–66, 67–68, 82–83, 88–89
Poseidoniastai, 52–53, 63–68, 64*f*, 82–83, 86–87, 88–89. *See also* Berytians; Berytos
private associations. *See* professional associations; religious associations; Rhodes; trade associations
prodikia, 113–14. *See also* awards; award-giving, system of

proedria, 95, 96–97, 101, 113–14, 117–18. See also awards; award-giving, system of
professional associations, 50, 51–52, 53–56, 57–58, 59–60, 62–65, 67–69, 78–80, 82, 91, 145–46, 157–58. See also Rhodes; trade associations; traders
of bankers, 53–54
of Italians on Delos, 89–90
of sailors, 53–54
of Sidonians in Athens, 83–87, 84f
of traders and shipowners, 55–57
of wine and olive oil merchants of, 53–54
promanteia, 113–14. See also awards; award-giving, system of
prosodos, 101, 113–14. See also awards; award-giving, system of
prostates, 21–22, 116. See also metics
proxenia, 54–55, 56, 70, 95, 101, 102–3, 104–6, 108–11. See also awards; award-giving, system of
award granted to promote migration, 103–4, 106
in combination with other awards, 111–16, 117–18
proxenos, 46–47, 56, 57–58, 94, 99–100, 103–6, 116–18
Prytaneion, 70, 108–11
Psammetichos I, pharaoh of Egypt, 134–35
Ptolemaic dynasty, 61–62, 80–81, 144–45, 145n.68, 150–51
Punic dialect, 124n.11, 126, 151–52
Punic Mediterranean, 12–13, 146–47
Punic texts, 85–86, 146–47, 152–53
Punic Wars, 122–25
Puteoli, 87–88

Rameses II, pharaoh of Egypt, 134–35, 135–36n.48

refugees, 2, 9, 125–26
religious associations, 51–52, 60n.23, 78–80. See also Bendis
residency (award), 98–99, 111, 113–14, 116–19. See also awards; award-giving, system of
Rhodes, 20, 23, 37–38, 47–48, 49, 116
bilingual texts in, 25–27, 32–33
foreigners in, 20
legal categories of immigrants, 116–17
migration and membership regime of, 21–22
Phoenician gods worshiped in, 42–44
Phoenician immigrants in, 11–12, 17–19, 20, 30, 32–33, 45–47, 126–27
private associations of, 45–46, 47, 68–69, 103–4
public associations of, 68–69
Rhodians, 45–48
Rhodos, 47–48, 116–17
right to sail in and out of ports, 114–16, 117–18. See also awards; award-giving, system of
Roma, 65–66
Romans, 11–12, 13, 87–88, 124–25. See also Carthage; Punic Wars
on Delos, 53n.5, 66–67
recipients of awards in Athens, 98–99n.16
rivalry with Carthage, 7–8, 12–13, 122–24
stoicism, 1–2
Rome, 71–72, 87–88, 153–55. See also Carthage; Punic Wars
conquest of Greece by, 44–45
control of Delos by, 52–53, 61–62, 65–67, 82–83
rivalry with Carthage, 122–25
senate of, 113–14, 124–25

Sakon, 42–44, 59–60
Salamis (Cyprus), 29, 94, 104–6

Samos, 114–16, 117
Saqqara, 136–37
Sardinia, 2–3, 7–8, 11–12, 37–38, 122, 127–28, 140–41, 146–47, 147–48n.75, 151–52, 155–56
Serapis, 142–43, 150–51
Setis I, pharaoh of Egypt, 142–43
settlers, 2, 5–6n.17, 7–8, 9–11
Shem—— son of Abdashtart, 15–17, 16*f*, 24–25, 30–32, 33–38, 35*f*, 78–80, 126–27
Sicily, 2–3, 7–8, 104–6, 122, 127–28, 146–47, 153–56
Sidon, 7–8, 9, 17–19, 20, 41–44, 57–58, 70–71, 73, 116, 143–44.
   Eshmoun, 25–27, 73–77
   joint dedication with Tyre, 77–80, 78*f*, 81–82
   kings of, 54–55, 70, 73–80, 101–2, 107–11, 133–34
   koinon of in Athens, 50, 83–87, 84*f*
Sidonians, 8–9, 27–28, *See also* Abdashtart I; Abdashtart II; Abdalonym; Apollonides, son of Demetrios; Diotimos, son of Abdalonymos; Domseleh son of Domhano; Philokles, king of Sidon
   in Athens, 17–19, 33–34, 37–38, 44–45, 54–56, 59–60, 67–68, 70–71, 83–87, 99–100, 104–6, 108–12
   in Carthage, 128–29, 143–44
   on Delos, 77–82, 113–14, 141
   at Delphi, 112–13
   in Demetrias, 41–44
   in Egypt, 144–45
   on Keos, 117–18
   on Kos, 75–77
   on Miletos, 117–18
   on Rhodes, 20, 45, 46–47
   on Samos, 114–16
   on Sardinia, 147–48n.75

Skythians, 9, 17–19
slavery, 95–96, 122–24. *See also* enslaved persons
social mobility, 4, 24, 29, 46–47, 68–69, 113–14, 117–19
Socrates, 1–2, 95–96. *See also* Xenophon; Zeno, Kition of
Spartans, 117, 124–25
Spartokids, 107–8
spectrum of participatory membership in a political community, 4–6, 95–96, 106, 111, 116–19, 158. *See also* citizenship; metics; migrants
   blurring boundaries, 4, 70–71, 97–98, 122
stereotypes, 3–4, 29n.38
   of Carthaginians, 122–24
   of Phoenicians, 29, 122–24, 132–33
Stoa Poikile (Painted Stoa), 1–2
Stoicism, 1–2, 29, 158–59. *See also* Zeno, Kition, of
Straton. *See* Abdashtart I
subscriptions, 45–46, 111–12
suffete, 80–81, 86–87, 152–53
syncretism (translations of gods), 6–7, 25–27, 42–44, 52–53, 58–59, 63–66, 75–77, 85–86, 88–89, 121–22, 140–41, 150–52
synodos (synod), 62–63, 67–68, 86–87
Syria, 7–8, 80–81
Syrians, 19–20, 141, 157

Tabnit, king of Sidon, 133–34
Tale of Wenamun, 132–33
Tanit, 30–32, 130–32
Tanit and Baal Hamon, sanctuary of, 127–29, 130–32, 131*f*, *See also* tophet
taxation. *See ateleia*; *eisphora*; *isoteleia*
Teos, 73
Thebes (Boiotia), 1–2, 80–81, 114–16
Thebes (Egypt), 132–33, 143n.64

theoria, 79n.21, 110n.54
theoroi, 78–80, 124
Thessaly, 17, 19–20, 43–44n.75, 111–12
thiasoi, 51–52, 67–68, 86–87
Thonis-Herakleion, 135–36
Thrace, 114–16
Thracians, 9, 17–19, 98–99, 141
tophet, 127–28, 146–47
trade associations. *See also* Berytians; Berytos; Delos; Herakleistai; Poseidoniastai; professional associations; traders
  adoption of host state's political structures, 62–63, 66–68
  benefactions to, 82–83, 85–86, 88–90
  Berytians on Delos, 63–67, 82–83, 86–87
  civic identity of, 58–59, 82–83, 145–46
  Delos on, 52–53, 54, 61–67, 86–87, 144–45
  incorporation of into host state's political infrastructure, 57–58, 61–62, 68–69, 157–58
  Kitian in Athens, 50–52, 51*f*, 58–61, 67–68
  as maintaining religious traditions, 51–52, 58–59, 66–67, 68–69, 82, 157–58
  as mediators with the host state, 50–52, 54, 55–57, 60–61, 63–65, 66–69, 99–100
  political infrastructures of, 61–63, 67–68, 82–83, 157–58
  as providing a link with home state, 4, 39–41, 42–44, 51–52, 58–59, 60–61, 66–67, 68–69, 80–81, 83–85, 124
  quasi-state character of, 51–52, 54, 56–57, 67–68, 157–58
  Sidonian in Athens, 54–55, 70, 104–6
  Tyrian in Puteoli, 87–88
  Tyrian on Delos, 61–63, 66–68, 86–87

traders, 2, 9, 13–14, 53–57, 77–78, 107–8, 114–16, 125–26, 158–59.
  See also Apollonides, son of Demetrios; Apses; Herakleides of Salamis; Hieron
  associations of (*see* professional association; trade associations)
  Berytian on Delos, 63–65, 82–83
  in Egypt, 132–33, 134–36
  Egyptian in Athens, 60n.23
  Kitian in Athens, 50, 58–60, 61–62, 67–68
  as recipients of awards, 57–58, 68–69, 94, 104–6, 111–12, 113–16
  Sidonian in Athens, 54–55, 70–71, 111, 112–13
  Tyrian in Puteoli, 87–88
  Tyrian on Delos, 61–62
trilingual inscriptions, 10n.27, 146–47, 151–52, 152*f*
Tyre, 7–8, 9, 17–19, 20, 41–42, 73, 87–88, 104–6, 116, 124–25, 150–51, 157. *See also* Carthage; Herakles; Melqart; Herakleistai
  and Carthage, 71–72, 122–26, 130–32, 155–56
  constitutional changes in, 81–82
  control over trade association in Puteoli, 87–88
  joint dedication with Sidon, 77–80
  patron deity (founder) of, 52–53, 61–62, 150–51
  trade associations of, 52–53, 61–62, 66–68, 85–87
Tyrians, 8–9, 113–16. *See also hieronautai*; Herakleistai
  in Athens, 2n.4, 17–19, 45–46
  in Carthage, 71–72, 122–25, 128–29, 130–32, 155–56
  on Delos, 61–68, 77–80, 85–86
  in Egypt, 134–36, 142–43

Tyrians (*cont.*)
   in Malta, 150–51
   in Puteoli, 87–88
   on Rhodes, 20, 47–48
   in Teos, 73

xenia, 95, 96–97, 153–55

Xenophon, 1–2, 96–98, 106, 107–8

Yehimilk, king of Byblos, 133–34

Zeno, Kition of, 1–2, 3–4, 7–8, 29, 158–59
Zenon, archive of, 144–45
Zeus, 46–47, 83–85, 101–2